Comedy in Music

William Hogarth, *Laughing Audience*. Metropolitan Museum of Art, Dick Fund, 1917.
(See *The Encyclopedia of Art* [New York: Golden Press, 1961].)

Comedy in Music

A Historical Bibliographical Resource Guide

Enrique Alberto Arias

GREENWOOD PRESS
Westport, Connecticut • London

Library of Congress Cataloging-in-Publication Data

Arias, Enrique Alberto.
    Comedy in music : a historical bibliographical resource guide / Enrique Alberto Arias.
      p. cm.
    Includes bibliographical references (p.) and index.
    ISBN 0-313-29980-3 (alk. paper)
    1. Humor in music—Bibliography. 2. Humor in music. I. Title.
ML128.H75A75 2001
781.5′9—dc21   99–046020

British Library Cataloguing in Publication Data is available.

Library of Congress Catalog Card Number: 99–046020
ISBN: 0-313-29980-3

First published in 2001

Greenwood Press, 88 Post Road West, Westport, CT 06881
An imprint of Greenwood Publishing Group, Inc.
www.greenwood.com

Printed in the United States of America

The paper used in this book complies with the
Permanent Paper Standard issued by the National
Information Standards Organization (Z39.48–1984).

10 9 8 7 6 5 4 3 2 1

Contents

Preface

This book results from courses I have taught on its subject. At that time I realized that no general source related to comedy in music and that bibliography was only available on particular aspects or periods of comic expression in music. It was this lack that inspired the present study.

The chapters have been designated according to the conventional musical periods. They are organized by genres and related musical works. Throughout well-known compositions are related to those that are more obscure. I have also included several works from the Hispanic tradition as well as that of Eastern Europe to show the vitality of these areas. The bibliography on this topic has turned out to be immense; thus, I have principally included those items that support the repertory discussed.

Chapter 1

Introduction

"Man is only man when he plays."
Schiller

"Serious" music predominates in academic presentations of the history of music. The present book, however, examines a wide variety of comic music from the Middle Ages to the present. Many examples considered will be familiar to the average concert listener, but others are more obscure. At times, connections are drawn between famous comic works and those—now forgotten—that influenced them.

Comic music is often considered superficial and simple—less intricate than is worthy of great art. This book demonstrates that this view is incorrect. Such composers as Haydn and Beethoven composed comic music or included comic passages or movements to offer contrast in some of their most important compositions.

For many listeners comic music means musical comedy. Although musical comedy is considered, many other genres that express humor and comedy are examined; thus the book presents a historical and stylistic overview from the Middle Ages to the present.

Instrumental music became a medium for expressing comedy and humor by the 18th century. Partly influenced by such thinkers as Johnson and Kant, composers and critics applied comedy and humor to symphony, sonata, and quartet. Haydn soon was considered the era's principal "humorous" composer because of his elegantly witty instrumental music.

Humor had an increasing impact on the music of the 19th and 20th centuries. Schumann, for example, not only wrote about comedy in music (B762), but made comedy and humor integral features of his style. Later artistic revolutions as Surrealism and Dada were partly influenced by a re-examination of the implications of comic absurdity.

DEFINITIONS OF IMPORTANT TERMS

Comedy in the broadest sense is the antithesis of tragedy. The term comes from the Greek word *komos*, a procession in honor of the god Dionysus held during his spring festivals. Comedy suggests the playful aspects and vital rhythms of life. According to Susanne K. Langer: "Comedy is an art form that arises naturally whenever people are gathered to celebrate life, in spring festivals, triumphs, birthdays, weddings, or initiations. For it expresses the elementary strains and resolutions of animate nature" (B141, 331).

Comedy takes many forms, including ritual, and can involve caricature, burlesque, farce, and slapstick. Caricature isolates and exaggerates traits; parody mocks style. Travesty and burlesque likewise ridicule compositional procedures, but perhaps to an even greater degree. Caricature, as we will see, often parodies musical conventions within the context of a genre.

Humor is a general category. The term comes from the Middle English word *humour*, or fluid from a plant or animal. According to the *Encyclopedia of Philosophy* (B375, v. 4, 90), humor involves a breach of the usual order of events by breaking the rules of convention. What belongs to one situation is introduced into another, or given elements of masquerade. It is characterized by wordplay, nonsense, small misfortunes, or veiled insults. The article goes on to say that "most theories find the essence of humor in one or another of the following: superiority, incongruity, and relief from restraint." Typically, incongruity occurs when the exalted is juxtaposed with the trivial or disreputable. Arthur Koestler finds that humor, like scientific discovery, fuses disparate ideas (B135, 59).

Wit, on the other hand, involves intellectual play. Although comedy is sometimes physical, wit is more cerebral. Gilbert Highet discovered that the word *satire* comes from the Latin word *satura*, which originally meant a medley or confection (B109, 303). Satire is the concrete manifestation of wit in the form of a poem, a play, or, in the present context, a musical composition.

Freud (B79), Bergson (B17), and Pirandello (B186) examined the philosophical and psychological implications of humor. Jan Huizinga's *Homo Ludens* demonstrated that play is intrinsic to all humans—even art and religious forms result from it. Huizinga writes: "In play there is something 'at play' which transcends the immediate needs of life and imparts meaning to the action. All play means something" (B117, 1).

PRINCIPAL TECHNIQUES OF COMIC MUSIC

The following outline cites some of the principal compositional techniques used by composers to achieve comic effects:

1. *Through the use of a comic text.* Comic texts make an immediate impact, and even a mediocre setting of funny words is certain of some success. Although comic texts are found as early as 13th-century motets, it is 18th-century *opera buffa* that first explores all the facets of verbal comedy. Accordingly, Mozart's *Le nozze di Figaro* (1786)(W369) achieved a perfect union of comic text and action. The use of comic text is the principal means of conveying humor until the later 18th century, when instrumental genres also participated in comedy.

2. *Through musical parody.* The composer pokes fun at a style or even a particular work. Mozart's *Ein musikalischer Spass* (1787)(W384), for instance, ridicules common 18th-century practices. In this particular example, Mozart satirized the general instrumental style of his time as practiced by an inept composer. Hans Joachim Moser mentions a set of variations by the obscure composer Siegfried Ochs (1858-1929) on "Kommt ein Vogel geflogen," in which each variation is modeled on the style of a particular composer (B164, 96).

3. *Through unexpected juxtapositions of syntactical elements.* Changing phrase lengths, unexpected turns of melody or dynamics, and unusual contrasts of texture are employed by many composers to achieve musical wit. An example occurs in the minuet from Haydn's Symphony No. 104 (1796)(W344), where the normal flow of the music is interrupted by rests followed by a crescendo roll on the timpani. These rests disturb the phraseology and are followed by an equally unexpected change to a piano dynamic.

4. *Through the use of musical description.* The bird calls in Beethoven's *Pastoral Symphony* (1808)(W431) and the bleating of the sheep in Strauss's *Don Quixote* (1897)(W963), for example, require clear musical responses. But often the descriptive techniques are more subtle. For example, Medieval Italian *caccie* (W8) employ texts that include nonsense or onomatopoetic syllables to illustrate hunting or market scenes. Particular types of description, such as battle pieces, bird pieces, or parodies of how one learns music, attract composers over the centuries (B164, 24ff.).

5. *Through references to particular styles.* Techniques associated with folk or popular music can give a passage or movement a humorous twist. Thus the drone and clumsy folklike dance that are featured in the last movement of Haydn's Symphony No. 82 (1786), known as *The Bear* (W337), are responsible for the symphony's nickname. Hindemith uses the Shimmy, which had just come into vogue, in the *Suite 1922* for Piano (W797).

6. *Through the use of incongruency.* Haydn's Symphony No. 60 (*Il Distratto*) (1774)(W335) contrasts many styles and ideas with parodistic intent.
7. *Through unusual orchestral devices.* Such examples as the tuning of the violins in the last movement of Haydn's Symphony No. 60 (1774)(W335) or the *col legno* effects in the last movement of Berlioz's *Symphonie fantastique* (1830)(W449) create unexpected orchestral colors.
8. *Through allusions to a famous comic character.* Such works as Elgar's symphonic poem on Falstaff (1913)(W762) and Strauss's depiction of the celebrated rogue Till Eulenspiegel (1895)(W965) are descriptive but also inspired by a given character.
9. *Through unusual effects of texture, dynamics, rhythm, and melodic design.* 18th-century *opera buffa* often highlights the comic features of the bass voice through exaggeratedly large intervals. In Mozart's *Der Schauspieldirektor* (1785)(W370), the two sopranos sing in a high register to show off.
10. *Through strange keys and distant modulations.* Renaissance madrigals and motets or Baroque cantatas occasionally set off text through dissonance or distant harmonic movements. The humor consists in the subtle implications of these musical devices.
11. *Through reference to past styles.* In the 20th century, such Neoclassic composers as Stravinsky and Hindemith employ 18th-century forms and instrumentation but within new contexts. The composer here plays on the listener's awareness of the style of Vivaldi, Bach, and others of this period.
12. *Through the quotations of various musical materials.* In the Renaissance, as we shall see, the quodlibet was a genre created by blending many musical quotations in vertical and horizontal orders. C. Höpfner's operetta for men's voices *Das Gastspiel der Lucca* (1875)(B164, 95) is exclusively composed of quotations from the works of Mozart and Weber. Often comic operatic overtures of the Romantic were essentially medleys of the principal melodies of the given opera. Charles Ives often used this technique in such a work as his *Holidays* (1912-13)(W807).
13. *Through movement titles.* The Italian term scherzo or "joke" is often used in the works of Haydn and Beethoven. By the 19th century, the third movement of a symphony or string quartet is commonly a scherzo. The designation scherzo almost always implies a movement with a lighter and playful character. The scherzo from Tchaikovsky's Symphony No. 4 (1878)(W629), for example, contrasts with the rest of this gloomy symphony by reason of its pizzicati and quick figurations.
14. *Through tempo modifications.* From the late 18th century on, composers frequently modify tempi with such words as *vivo*, *vivace*, or *scherzando*. The increasingly precise tempo designations of Haydn and Beethoven not only indicate pace but also imply mood and style. Many finales of Haydn symphonies (late 18th century)(Ww330-44), for example, reflect their character through tempo designations.

15. *Through visually curious notation.* The complicated polyphony of the late 14th century, puzzle canons of the Renaissance and the Baroque, and aleatoric music of the 20th century employ curious musical notations. Baude Cordier's "Belle bonne" (late 14th century)(W2), for example, is notated in the shape of a heart.

16. *Through genre designations.* The phrase *opera buffa* designates an intrinsically comic genre. Less obvious but equally suggestive are such terms as *canzonetta, chansonetta*, and *operetta*. The diminutives imply vocal types that are shorter and lighter than madrigal, chanson, and opera, respectively. *Humoresque* is used by Schumann and composers thereafter to designate a "humorous" work for piano solo or chamber group. Schumann's own *Humoreske* (1838)(W603), for example, is one of the Romantic period's most original works.

17. *Through performance styles.* Performance styles can also be humorous. Victor Borge (Bb28–29, Dd42–46) poked fun at the pompous mores of classical music through caricaturing well-known pieces of music. Likewise, Anna Russell satirized Wagner (Dd2–4).

18. *Through texting of instrumental works.* Vocal arrangements with satiric texts are occasionally made of instrumental works. Hans Joachim Moser mentions an anonymous 19th-century arrangement of Mozart's overture to *Die Zauberflöte* (W371) for men's quartet that begins, "Vivat Carl Maria Weber" (B164, 96).

19. *Through the use of chance.* During the 18th century, *ars combinatoria*, or the chance combining of phrases was a discussed by theorists and composers. Aleatoric music comes to be an important movement in the 20th century inspired by the works of John Cage (W713).

20. *Through the use of* soggetto cavato. The Renaissance chapter concludes with a consideration of *soggetto cavato*, or the substitution of solmization syllables for letters. Thus, as we will see later in the book, Schumann plays with the associations of the letters *ASCH* and *SCHA* in *Carnaval* (1835) (W600).

MAJOR STUDIES OF COMIC MUSIC

Richard Hohenemser's "Über Komik und Humor in der Musik" (B576) was a pioneering study. This article cites a number of 19th-century aestheticians who question whether music can express comedy. Hohenemser cites several comic passages from Beethoven's bagatelles and selected works by Schumann. Luigi Cherubini's opera *Le Crescendo* (1810)(W483) is mentioned for its scene in which a bass tries to sing in the soprano range.

Henry F. Gilbert's "Humor in Music" was one of the first articles on the subject in English (B537). Although relatively short and now dated, it has several interesting insights. Gilbert demonstrates a close connection between tragedy and comedy, since they are both extremes. He then goes on to discuss some very well-known examples of comic effects, such as the sudden forte chord in the Andante of Haydn's Symphony No. 94 (*The Surprise*) (1791)(W341), or Debussy's parodying of a dance style in his prelude *General Lavine-eccentric* (1912–13)(W750).

Zofia Lissa's paper "Die Kategorie des Komischen in der Musik" (B647) is a central study. After considering many questions regarding the psychology of humorous composition, Lissa notes the importance of the composer's intentions. Furthermore, Lissa highlights three types of comic expression:

1. The reproduction of sonorous or visual effects, such as Rameau's *La Poule* (circa 1728)(W266), with its imitation of a cackling hen. Special instances of this category involve unusual speech effects, as in the stuttering aria from Cavalli's *Giasone* (1649)(W182).
2. At times, a well-known style is parodied, such as Pepusch and Gay's *The Beggar's Opera* (1728)(W210), which uses *opera seria* as its point of departure.
3. Lissa includes the use of background music in comic films, where absolute synchronization occurs between the music and action. This differs from opera in that the "actors" move without reference to music and at the speed of natural action.

Other studies explore particular genres or composers. Alfred Einstein's article "Die Parodie in der Villanelle" (B504) and Nino Pirrotta's "*Commedia Dell' Arte* and Opera" (B716) offer penetrating studies of comic techniques in a particular repertory. Rudhyar D. Chenneviere's "Erik Satie and the Music of Irony" (B464) was the first of many studies of this composer.

Manfred Bukofzer's "Allegory in Baroque Music" (B451) unfortunately appears in a journal that is no longer readily available. This study, which notes that programmatic music can address the sense of sight through allegory, has important implications for the study of comic music as a whole. According to Bukofzer, there are two types of program music: that which depends on a precise imitation (such as the sound of a trumpet or of a bird) and that which is allegorical. The programmatic effect of the latter results from an intellectual relationship established between the listener and the given music event. Bukofzer compares signs, allegories, and symbols and notes that allegory depends on musical procedures that are significant only through context and reference.

Hans Joachim Moser's *Corydon: Geschichte des Mehrstimmigen General-bassliedes und des Quodlibets im Deutschen Barock* (B164) has generally been overlooked in studies on comic music. This is partly because its title implies that it is exclusively a study of the quodlibet and song in the Baroque period. However, this now very rare book and anthology of examples thoroughly examines many comic types. Moser studies such comic vocal genres as the description of fairs, contests between cuckoos and nightingales, and parodies of professions. The index of this source provides an important overview of its contents (B164, 100).

Unusual works and examples are highlighted. For example, Moser cites a 16th-century source from Basle in which the notes are shaped like fruits (B164, 39). Another instance is the date of composition of Joseph Gregor Werner's *Musikalisher Instrumental-Calender* (W409); 1748 is indicated through the sizes of the intervals at one point in the bass part (B164, 43).

Orlande Lassus is considered the principal humorous late Renaissance composer, with many of his works discussed (B164, 27). Various compositions that are based on the sounds of animals, in particular cats, are also briefly described (B164, 27), as are vocal works that parody the learning of solmization (B164, 48). In addition, many examples are that use repeated syllables and other verbal distortions are mentioned (B164, 34–5).

Gretchen A. Wheelock's *Haydn's Ingenious Jesting with Art: Contexts of Musical Wit and Humor* (B249) has analytic implications for the study of comic music of all sorts. Laurie-Jeanne Lister's *Humor as a Concept in Music: A Theoretical Study of Expression in Music, the Concept of Humor and Humor in Music with an Analytical Example-W.A. Mozart, Ein musikalischer Spass, KV 522* (B147) likewise draws upon a wide range of philosophic and musicological literature.

Glen Watkins's *Pyramids at the Louvre: Music, Culture, and Collage from Stravinsky to the Postmodernists* (B245) contains important insights into musical collage, and analyzes the impact of film music on major composers and the ongoing awareness of *commedia dell' arte*. Minimalism, popular culture, and Postmodernism all receive careful and illuminating attention. Watkins shows that absurdity influences many revolutions in contemporary culture. Thus, like Moser's *Corydon* (B164), this book presents a more comprehensive understanding of musical humor.

The increasing number of dissertations on comic topics in music suggests the fertility of this field. David Weintraub's "Humor in Song" (B358), for example, considers comedy in vocal music through the analysis of many specific examples as well as citations of bibliography not found in other sources.

Comedy and humor in music have been debated for their Postmodernist implications. Rossanna Dalmonte's "Towards a Semiology of Humour in Music" (B483) was inspired by the work of Jean Jacques Nattiez and builds on Zofia Lissa's categories. Kendall L. Walton's "Understanding Humor and Understanding Music" (B802) explores the connections between analysis and understanding a piece of music. His views are expanded and refined in Marian A. Guck's "Taking Notice: A Response to Kendall Walton" (B555).

ORGANIZATION AND BIBLIOGRAPHIC FEATURES

The book is organized into short chapters based on the conventional periods of music history. These are followed by a works' list and bibliographies. The following bibliographic features enhance the text:

1. Each work is given a numeric designation W1, W2. This designation refers to an entry for the composition. An entry consists of the following: Composer (last name, first name), title of the work cited, and publication information. References to readily available anthologies, thematic catalogues, relevant bibliography (using the abbreviation system B1), and closely related works are provided. A list of abbreviations is found at the beginning of the bibliography.
2. A bibliography on comedy and humor in music is presented after the works list. This section is organized into standard categories: books, dissertations, reference sources, and articles. Each item is given a numeric designation: B1, B2. When a specific reference is made to an item of bibliography during the course of the discussion, these abbreviations are also cited, followed by a page number.
3. A discography of humorous recordings is presented after the bibliographies. Although the content of these recordings may draw upon scores, these recordings (such as those designated "Hoffnung Festival") have a striking autonomy. These are given the designations D1, D2.
4. Further anthologies are given for reference. These are given the designations R1, R2.
5. The index at the end of the book is organized according to names and genres together with the references to relevant works.

I would like to thank Bonnie Tipton Long, Mary O'Dowd, and Dr. Susan Filler for their help and suggestions regarding this book. In addition, Mr. Andrew Schultze, artistic director of Ars Musica Chicago, has brought both appropriate bibliography and repertory to my attention.

Chapter 2

The Medieval Period

THE POETIC TRADITION

Goliards, the "beatniks" of the Middle Ages, were wandering scholar-poets who flourished in England, France, and Germany in the 12th and 13th centuries. These dropouts from society, known for their excess, were educated and frequently studied for the priesthood. Many of their poems reflect their reputation for gluttony and amorous achievement.

The *Carmina Burana* is the principal source for this poetry (W12). Well known to listeners through Carl Orff's effective 20th-century settings of selected texts (W862), the *Carmina Burana* originally was a manuscript collection of sacred and secular monodies from the 12th and 13th centuries. Probably of Austrian origin, the *Carmina Burana* included a wide range of German and Latin texts as well as a Passion play and a parody of the Mass for the Feast of Fools.

Many songs from this collection are delightfully comic. For example, "Procurans odium," which parodies a love song, states that "hate can be used to one's advantage." "Bache, bene venies," a drinking song, employs a conductus from *The Play of Daniel* (W18) while praising the god Bacchus. "Exiit diliculo" is about a farmer's daughter who sees a student in the fields and asks him to "play," and "Alte clamat Epicurus" notes that a full stomach is like a god. "Michi confer venditor"—a parody of a dialogue between Mary Magdalene and a perfume merchant from a Passion play—ends with the moral: "The world is full of joy when women are pleasing to men."

THE FRENCH SECULAR TRADITION

The term *jeu-parti* was used for a debate, often about love, occasioning opportunities for dialogue. This repertory often explores the various possibilities of the term *jeu*, or play, through word games or clever allusions.

Le jeu de Robin et Marion (W1) was composed in 1280 by Adam de la Halle as an entertainment for the court of Naples. This allegorical tale about the love between Robin and Marion employs a series of dialogues and seventeen short intervening monodies (probably not by de la Halle), which outline the encounters between these two shepherds.

Marcabru's "L'autrier jost'una sebissa," a *pastorela* from the 12th century (W5), narrates a knight's encounter with a young maid in the fields and his attempts to make love—a common theme in this literature. A complex dialogue evolves sung to a simple melody.

Dance songs, termed in the sources either *balada* or *dansa*, were rhythmically energetic. Refrains invited the audience to participate, creating a structure that alternated solo and choral sections. Such words as *hey* or *come* suggest this participation.

Richard H. Hoppin notes that parody is found in the trouvère repertory: "On the frivolous side, jeux partis debated amorous dilemmas, and *sottes chansons* (foolish songs) imitated the serious chanson in parodies that were ribald when they were not obscene" (B113, 303).

The inclusion of such *sottes chansons* is found in one of the principal sources of the 14th century: the *Roman de Fauvel* (W19), the title of a poem in two parts by Gervais de Bus. This medieval satire on corruption is symbolized by a horse named Fauvel, each letter of whose name stands for a vice (flattery, avarice, and so on). The second half of this long allegorical poem was completed in 1314; in 1316 Chaillou de Pestain added isorhythmic motets and monodies that complement the narrative. Twelve brief quotations of parodies of secular French song highlight this oddly amusing story.

The *sottie* was a satirical revue reinforced with songs and obscenities (B232, 79). Much of this repertory was part of an oral tradition, known to us through illustrations or condemnations by ecclesiastical authorities.

THE GERMAN SECULAR TRADITION

The Minnesingers, active in Germany in the later 13th and earlier 14th centuries, were influenced by French secular poetry. Many Minnesinger poems highlight amorous pursuits or the joys of spring. Neidhart von Reunenthal's "Maienzit" (early 13th century)(W7) sounds the common theme of May as a time for amorous pleasure.

The Meistersingers, active in Germany in the 14th through 16th centuries, continued the traditions of the Minnesingers. Many melodic types they used were clearly comic: *Kurze Affenweiss* (brief monkey melody), *Vielfrassweiss* (gluttony melody), *Spitzige Pfeilweiss* (pointed arrow melody). The Meistersingers' pedantry and lack of creativity are the principal themes of Wagner's opera, *Die Meistersinger von Nürnberg* (1868)(W637).

PARODIES OF RITUAL AND LITURGICAL DRAMA

The Feast of Fools, held on or around January 1 and particularly popular in France, offered an occasion for satire and ridicule of liturgical institutions and personages. A mock pope or bishop was elected, ecclesiastical ritual parodied, and low and high church officials allowed to change place. Specific parodies of liturgical rituals also were common, resulting in the satire of established practice. David Weintraub notes such types as the *Missa de potatoribus* (Drinkers' Mass), *Officium Lusorum* (Office of Players), and *Officium Ribaldorum* (Office of the Licentious) lambasted liturgical functions (B358, 107).

In Germany and Austria, as George A. Test points out, the Fastnacht festival involved plays that satirized all social classes. These included the singing of hymns to vulgar tunes (B232, 82). Similarly, "On the Death of the Duke of Suffolk" puts phrases from the Requiem Mass into the mouths of the Suffolk dead (B232, 171).

Liturgical drama combined stories for the most important religious feasts with short monodies. Increasingly comedy created diversion in the form of self-sufficient episodes. *The Play of Daniel* (late 12th century)(W18), is the most elaborate and musically unified liturgical drama. *Le Fils de Gédron* (late 12th century)(W14) concerns the miraculous return of a son through the intervention of St. Nicholas. Writing of the development of liturgical drama after 1300, Hoppin notes: "Freed from the restrictions of the Church, the vernacular plays treated their Biblical or legendary subject matter with great freedom and a lively sense of humor. Scenes with the devil in hell seem to have been particularly popular" (B113, 186).

The famous monophonic conductus "Orientis partibus" or "Song of the Ass" (W17) illustrates the syllabic style found in songs for these plays. Featured in a liturgical play at Beauvais from around the 13th century, this song was sung while the Virgin Mary rode into the cathedral on an ass. Each line thus ends with the refrain "Hez, Sir Asne, hez."

COMIC POLYPHONY

Polyphony presented opportunities for comic expression because of its inherent potential for dialogue or implied questions and answers. "Summer is Icumen In" (W22), a rota or canon for four voices with two supporting parts, was written in England about 1250. This famous composition is marked by a rhythmic energy and harmonic richness caused by the alternation of two triads.

Although the 13th century motet had begun as a sacred type, it quickly took on erotic and occasionally playful implications. In addition, the motet practice of setting several texts simultaneously prompted wordplay and symbolic references between the voices. "On parole-A Paris-Frèses nouvele" (mid-13th century)(W16) features a street call in the tenor, while the other voices use a quick syllabic style.

Liturgical motets occasionally were changed into comic works by substituting texts. "Hare, hare-Balaam-Balaam" (W15) expands a two-voice motet based on an Epiphany sequence for the Sarum rite. The two top voices describe brewers and drinking in the transformed version of this work.

Many motets employ the pastoral tradition of Robin and Marion, thus forming a special group (W19). Erotic references and playful allusions are part of the texts, which relate these works to Adam de la Halle's *Le jeu de Robin et Marion* (W1).

The *caccia* dominated Italian secular writing of the 14th century. The term *caccia* is derived from the Italian word for chase, although it is unclear whether its etymology stems from the voices' "chasing" each other or from the frequent text references to hunting scenes. Nicolò da Perrugia's *caccia* "Dappoi che'l sole" (W8) tells the story of a fire, with such questions as "Where is it?" and responses "It's up here." charmingly highlighted. "Se je chant" (W21), a French canon from the same time, has the rhythmic verve, use of nonsense syllables, and strict replication of voices associated with the Italian *caccia*.

Oswald von Wolkenstein's polyphonic songs from the 14th century mirror German 13th-century monody; thus his compositions are satiric or subtly erotic. "Der May" (W9) depicts the call of the cuckoo with a descending third and the sounds of other birds through quick syllabic writing.

RHYTHMIC COMPLEXITY AND EXPRESSIVE TEXT SETTING

Rhythmic complexity, sophisticated notations, and complicated visual patterns dominated late 14th-century French secular music. Many composers who worked in this style were associated with the papal court at Avignon—a center of intense cultural and intellectual activity. Composers of the *Ars Subtilior* notated their works in curious ways; thus Baude Cordier's chanson "Belle bonne" (W2) takes the form of a heart—probably because of the composer's name.

Solage, active in the late 14th century and involved in the notational complexity of the *Ars Subtilior*, wrote a well-known rondeau, "Fumeux fume" (W10). The low range, the odd melodic shapes caused by accidentals, and the expressive treatment of the text are striking. The humor of the text results from the play on the word *fumeux*, related to an "Order of Smokers" that promoted literature.

Other 14th-century compositions likewise reflect the meanings of their texts. Lorenzo Massini's little-known madrigal "Dolgomi a voi" (W6) employs parallel fifths to illustrate "those who make a fuss about all our notes." Grimace's "Alarme, alarme" (W3) anticipates the Renaissance genre of the battle piece by highlighting the key word of the title through repetition.

Guillaume de Machaut's rondeau, "Ma fin est mon commencement" (W4), presents the same melody as the tenor voice, but backward; the contratenor moves backward from the last pitch to the first during the latter half of the composition. These techniques echo the text, which begins, "My end is my beginning and my beginning my end."

DEPICTIONS OF INSTRUMENTAL MUSIC

As early as the Patristic period, instrumentalists were viewed with suspicion by ecclesiastical authorities. Asked whether *joculatores* (or players) had hope of salvation, the 12th-century ecclesiastic Honorius of Autun responded with a re-sounding "They have no hope, for they are in every way the ministers of Satan" (B99, 50).

Often instruments or instrumentalists were thought to symbolize the devil. Vices were often depicted as dancing, and musicians shown as opposites of such heavenly musicians as David. Reinhold Hammerstein noted that dancers in ludi-crous poses often stood for Salome or *luxuria*, thus implying lust and avarice (B99, 59).

Dances constituted a major instrumental type. Included among these are *sal-tarelli*, or "jumping" dances, so named because of their acrobatic movements. *Saltarelli* from the 14th century are notable for their strong rhythms and clear-cut phrases, often with the key motives repeated (R1).

The *danse macabre* tradition dominated the later Middle Ages (W13)(B100 and B160). Many manuscripts of the period depict death, often holding a musical instrument, dancing with those who are about to die. The dancelike song "Ad mortem festinamus" (W11), from the 14th-century Spanish source known as *Llibre   Vermell*,   illustrates   this   fascination   with   death.

Chapter 3

The Renaissance Period

Music during the Renaissance was viewed as a form of pleasure intimately related to the theory of the four humors. Modes and styles, accordingly, were associated with the sanguine humor, or the humor of jollity. Furthermore, Gioseffo Zarlino, the late 16th-century theorist, demonstrated that the major third expressed happiness (B259, 31f). Philosophic discussions of Aristotle's theories about comedy as well as the performance of classical comedies also focused awareness on comedy's musical potential.

THE FRENCH CHANSON

Although chansons of the 15th century prefer serious texts, several chansons by Guillaume Du Fay and Gilles Binchois are comic. Binchois's "Files à marier" (W31), an admonition to girls against marrying, is notable for its rhythmic vitality and dialogue between the voices. Du Fay's "Ce jour le doibt" (W51) is an example of a May song. The rondeau "Donnez l'assault" (W52), a mock battle piece, imitates the shots of cannons. "Bon jour, bon mois" (W49) and "Ce jour de l'an" (W50) are good-humored New Year's songs. At the end of the 15th century, Jacob Obrecht composed some chansons based on playful Dutch folk songs. "Tsaat een meskin" (W110) and "T'Andernaken" (W109) are examples.

Josquin Desprez's chansons manifest a striking variety of forms and text moods. Often, however, chansons employ recondite techniques of canon and musical derivation, blending wit and intellectuality. One of the best known, "Faute d'argent" (W79), combines a popular melody in canon with three other motivically derived voices. The text laments the lack of money, suggesting, however, that even a sleeping woman will wake up for cash. "Basiez-moy" (W78) is likewise canonic. Here a young man entreats his girlfriend to kiss him. "Une musque de Biscaye" (W81) and "Petite Camusette" (W82) also use canon.

Some chansons are based on several melodies that retain their texts and rhythmic profiles. Antoine Busnois's "Amours nous traitte" (W35) is an example. Dialogues enliven this chanson, whose humor results from the short phrases of the popular melody's text.

Popular melodies known as *chansons rustiques* often appeared in chansons of this time. These monophonic songs usually employed an ABA form and texts that avoided literary sophistication. Two books of French popular songs were commissioned by the court of Louis XII, suggesting their wide popularity. These monodic tunes are simple and catchy, and such chansons as "Faute d'argent" are based on them. Rabelais refers to some of these favorite melodies in Book II, chapter 16, and Book IV, chapter 35, of *Gargantua and Pantagruel* (B191).

Influenced by an improved printing technology and the wider audience it reached, a new type of chanson evolved in the 1520s and 1530s. Commonly described as "Parisian," this style remained popular through midcentury and was disseminated by Pierre Attaingnant, the important French music publisher. Clearly articulated sections, sharply etched rhythms, and light homophony are characteristic. Texts often pun and highlight nonsense syllables. Pierre Passereau's lively "Il est bel et bon" (W114) sings of a good husband who does not beat his wife while she takes her pleasures. Orlande Lassus's popular "Bon jour, mon coeur" (W86) is typically lighthearted and articulates each phrase of text.

The program or descriptive chanson also gained wide popularity in the 1530s and 1540s as a result of Attaingnant's publications. They are like the chansons just described in style but are on a larger scale. Clément Janequin wrote chansons in which battles, talking birds, and other lively events are described through repeated chords, dialogue textures, and parlando treatment of text.

Probably the most famous example, "La bataille: Escoutez tous gentilz" (W73), celebrates the French victory at Marignano in 1515. The sounds of cannons and the running of horses are here imitated. Other descriptive chansons by Janequin include "Le chantes oiseaux" (W75) and "L'alouette" (W72)—both bird concerts; "Les cris de Paris" (W76) (with calls of Parisian vendors); and "Le caquet des femmes" (which describes women's gossip) (W74).

OTHER CHANSON TYPES

Some Renaissance chansons combine the quotations of popular tunes and texts. The French word *fricassée* describes these sometimes witty, sometimes obscene mixtures of musical materials. An anonymous *fricassée*, published by Attaingnant in 1536, combines snippets of twenty-nine chansons by thirteen composers, including such notables as Josquin, Willaert, and Sermisy (W151).

The *air de cour* became popular by the end of the 16th century. Le Roy and Ballard's *Livre d'Airs de Cour miz sur le Luth* (1571) was the first collection of these simple songs with lute accompaniment. Gabriel Bataille's "Qui veut chasse une migraine" (W27) sings of how to escape the woes of a migraine headache.

The *vaudeville* was related to the *air de cour* by reason of its simplicity and strophic structure. A single melody often served for many texts with the same metric structure—texts that were usually satiric and alluded to contemporary events. Nicolas de la Grotte's "Quand ce beau printemps" (W84) is typical in its simple syllabic style and straightforward accompaniment.

MASSES

Although the Mass was viewed as the most serious of all genres, a number of 16th-century Masses used the polyphonic materials of secular works and participated in the energy of their models. Thus Lassus's *Missa Doulce memoire* (1577)(W90) is based on Sandrin's chanson by that title, and the *Missa Entre vous filles* (1581)(W91) transforms a popular chanson by Clemens non Papa. The vivacious style of the original chansons is evident in both these Masses. Several Renaissance Masses also are derived from the materials of Janequin's battle chanson, including Tomás Luis de Victoria's celebrated polychoral *Missa pro Victoria* (1600)(W135).

Masses sometimes use other comic techniques as well. For example, Heinrich Isaak's *Missa Carminum* (early 16th century)(W70), written not for liturgical but for private use, quotes a number of German lieder in a texture that is light and melodious. Johannes Cornago's *Missa Mappa Mundi* (late 15th century)(W40), on the other hand, employs a light Italian song for its cantus firmus, which praises Sicily as the best place in the world. Indeed, many Masses by such masters as Josquin, Mouton, and Lassus show a clear connection to secular writing.

LIGHTER ITALIAN SECULAR TYPES

The *frottola* dominated secular writing of the early 16th century. Steady rhythms, a limited harmonic vocabulary, and simple melodic lines are typical *frottola* traits. Clearly marked sections derived from the structures of the poetry as well as homophony confer a quasi-popular and improvisatory quality.

Between 1504 and 1514, the Venetian printer Ottaviano Petrucci published eleven books of *frottole* representing various musical structures and text themes. Gustave Reese (B195, 159) cites a Latin *frottola*, "Rusticus ut asinum" (W156), which includes a passage in black notation to imply mock sorrow on the words "oyme, oyme, cur moreris, asine?" ("oh, oh, why are you delaying, donkey?").

Although Bartolomeo Tromboncino and Marchetto Cara dominated the writing of *frottole*, Netherlandish composers working in Italy also created examples. For instance, Josquin wrote the *frottola* "Scaramella" (W83) inspired by a stock figure known for daring and bravado. Josquin's "El grillo è buon cantore" (W80), one of the most popular of his works, imitates the sound of a cricket.

16th-Century *villanesche*, *villanelle*, and *canzonette* emphasized liveliness, contrast of duple and triple pulsations, and a restricted harmonic-melodic vocabulary. Dialect and bawdy texts prevailed in the *villanesca*—a type associated with Naples. Composers sometimes composed parallel fifths to convey a deliberately crude musical outlook. Lassus's "Matona mia cara" (W88) includes subtle obscenity in this song about German soldiers in Italy.

Lassus's many *villanesche* are striking for their variety. The 1581 book features a number of *moresche* in Neapolitan dialect representing Negro slaves of southern Italy. Some of these *villanesche* highlight the ribald characters of Gorgia, Lucia, and others derived from *commedia dell' arte*. *Zanni* are *villanesche* that refer to comic servants from the *commedia dell' arte* tradition; *giustiniani* usually represent three old, but still lustful, men who stutter. On the other hand, the *greghesca*, to words by Antonio Molino, mixed Greek and Venetian dialects. In addition to dialect, obscenity and street language played an important role in *villanelle*.

Related to the *frottola*, the *villotta* (associated with Venice) is based on a folk or folklike tune, either in the refrain section or as a cantus firmus in the tenor. Later, the *villotta* mixed melodies in a musically untutored style. Filippo Azzaiolo, active in Bologna in the middle 16th century, wrote many examples that combine nonsense syllables and references to popular melodies (W23).

The carnival, held at Florence just before Lent, inspired outrageous, satiric *canti carnascialesci*. Even the celebrated Lorenzo de'Medici wrote *canzoni a ballo* for one of these carnivals. "Orsu car' Signori" (W152), a well-known carnival song, has a text that refers to the then-common practice of selling papal bulls, or pronouncements.

The *balletto* is a dance song type, popular in the late 16th century. Giovanni Gastoldi's first collection, *Balletti a cinque voci* (1591), includes descriptive titles that the individual texts elaborated. Typically in two or more sections, each ending with a fa-la-la refrain, the *balletto* used a symmetric structure with internal repetitions. Gastoldi's "L'Ardito" (1591)(W60) is about taking up arms against love; "Viver lieto voglio" (W61) sings of the joys of a happy life.

The *canzonetta*, as the term implies, is a light song for few voices and, like the *balletto*, included internal repetitions. Orazio Vecchi's "Fa una Canzona senza note nere" (W132) is about a song "without black notes," implying "without sorrow." Giuseppe Caimo's "Mentre il Cuculo" (W36) presents a play on double meanings associated with the word *cucu*.

THE ITALIAN MADRIGAL

Although most madrigals were serious, some sounded comic themes. Claudio Monteverdi's "Io mi son giovinetta" (W245) creates a minidrama between a shepherd and his lover. Dialogues between the three upper and three lower voices simulate questions and answers, and brilliant melismas highlight the text's humorous charm. Other madrigals likewise used echo technique to clever effect. Luca Marenzio's "O tu che fra le selve" (W97) highlights the puns of Tasso's text; Orlande Lassus's popular "O la, o che bon eccho" (W89) has a double chorus in eight voices, with the second chorus echoing the phrases of the first.

Occasionally madrigals employ what the Germans refer to as *augenmusik*, or the musical representation of a visual image. For example, Marenzio's "Cedan l'antiche tue chiare vittorie" (W94), an apostrophe to Rome, represents Roman arches by ascending and descending lines in several of the voices. In the same composer's "Già torna" (W95) the waves of the sea are likewise set graphically. "Mi fa lasso languire" (W96) employs the solmization syllables *mi, fa, la,* suggested by the text.

Madrigals usually appeared in collections whose titles imply a controlling theme. *Il Trionfo di Dori* (1592)(R17) concludes each madrigal with the refrain "Viva la bella Dori." This collection influenced *The Triumphes of Oriana* (1601)(R18), dedicated to Elizabeth I of England. Here the refrain "Long live fair Oriana" appears at the end of each madrigal.

ENGLISH SECULAR MUSIC

The part-songs of Henry VIII and his contemporaries grew out of the intensely social atmosphere of the English court. Henry VIII's "Pastyme with Good Company" (W66) sets the tone for much subsequent English secular music through its homophony and clear articulation of text.

The English interest in Italian music climaxed with the publication in 1588 of the *Musica Transalpina* (R16), a collection of Italian madrigals with the substitution of English texts by Nicholas Yonge. *Musica Transalpina* became immensely popular and inspired native composers, such as Thomas Morley, to employ Italian characteristics.

English madrigals emphasized wordplay, assonance, or alliteration. Composers highlight these features through repetition, contrast of texture, or an arresting harmonic-contrapuntal device. Thomas Morley's "Phillis I Fain Would Die Now" (W102) employs a typically clever text. Included are the lines: "I love thee! But plain to make it, Ask what thou wilt and take it."

Morley's contemporaries also emphasized text expression. Thomas Bateson's "Those Sweet Delightful Lilies" (W28) strikes the lightly ironic tone typical of the genre. Thomas Weelkes's "Thule, the Period of Cosmography" (W141) is a virtuoso madrigal with many geographical references. Thomas Vautour's "Shepherds and Nymphs" (W130), a playful pastoral, underlines the words "trooping, whooping, drooping" through contrasting musical pacing.

John Wilbye's "Thus Saith My Cloris Bright" (W142) is based on a poem attributed to Giovanni Guarini and used by Marenzio for "Dice la mia bellissima Licori" Wilbye highlights the implied eroticism and irony of the pastoral text through alternating textures. Chromaticism is found in John Ward's "Hope of

My Heart" (W136), where it occurs on the word *pain* and contrasts with the dotted figure on "still thunder forth."

Thomas Weelkes's "As Vesta Was from Latmos Hill Descending" (W138), a fine example of word painting, is included in *The Triumphes of Oriana* (R18). On the passage "First two by two, then three by three together, Leaving their goddess all alone," Weelkes has written a short duet, then a trio, followed by a single voice "all alone."

Morley's "Now Is the Month of Maying" (W101) and "Sing We and Chant It" (W104)—both from his 1595 book of balletts—are modeled on *balletti* by Gastoldi. Other balletts are strangely ironic in that the fa-la-la refrain follows a deeply serious text, as illustrated by Weelkes's "O Care, Thou Wilt Despatch Me" (W139).

Morley's *Booke of Ayres, or Little Short Songs* (1600) was written for solo voice and lute. Included in this collection is Shakespeare's "It was a lover and his lass" (W100). Thomas Campion, also a fine poet, composed many lighter epigrammatic songs (W37).

John Dowland was the master of the genre. "Fine Knacks for Ladies" (W46) illustrates Dowland's wit. "Say, Love, If Ever Thou Didst Find" (W47) highlights the word *she* through sequence and repetition; "Up, Merry Mates!" details adventures at sea (W48).

THE ENGLISH CATCH

The catch thrived in the 17th and 18th centuries, but English examples of the late 16th century already use canon and humorous texts. Christopher Simpson's *A Compendium of Practical Musick* (1667)(R12) describes the catch or round as a simple canon in three or four parts in which the voices begin at the same pitch. Richard Deering wrote a catch based on street cries from London (W44). Such phrases as "New oysters, new walfleet oysters" are highlighted. Deering also wrote "Country Cries" (W43), which incorporates the popular melody "Harvest Home."

SPANISH SECULAR MUSIC

By the late 15th century, the bold secular spirit of the Italian Renaissance was felt in Spain. The *Cancionero de Palacio* (R13), or songbook for the palace, mirrored the tastes of the court of Ferdinand and Isabella. Some *Cancionero* songs are humorous, but a few are frankly obscene. "Rodrigo Martínez" (W155) is about a handsome hero who mistakes geese for cows. "Dale si le das" (W148) has a quick syllabic section that pauses before the ends of words to suggest erotic connotations.

On the other hand, "Riu riu chiu" (W154), from a slightly later time, is a popular Christmas song about protecting the Christ child from a wolf. Juan

Ponce's "Ave, color vini clari" (W115), one of many Renaissance drinking songs, parodies the "Ave Maria" text and sacred motet style of the time. Juan Vásquez was influenced by Italian practices. "¿De Dónde Venis?" (W129) uses contrapuntal imitation to highlight the key phrase of text: "Where do you come from, my love? I well know where you have been."

The *ensalada*, the Spanish word for salad, originally implied a poem of free form and mixed content. It came, however, to designate a satiric vocal work that combined contrasting styles and musical materials. The *ensalada* achieved popularity in the extended, often quasi-dramatic, works by Mateo Flecha, the elder. "La Bomba" (W57), for example, tells the story of sailors who encounter a storm at sea and who need a pump, or "bomba," to bail out the water.

THE *VILLANCICO* IN LATIN AMERICA

The *villancico* evolves in the Hispanic world—thus including the Western Hemisphere—to include dialect, references to Africa, and many comic innuendoes. *Guineos* or *Negritos* were composed for African *cofradías*, or brotherhoods devoted to some particular form of charity. Juan Gutiérrez de Padilla's "A la Xacara" (W112) invites the participants to dance the *Xacara*, a rhythmic dance, in celebration of Christmas; Gaspar Fernández's *Guineo*, "Tantarrantan, a la Guerra van" (W56), spoofs vainglorious soldiers.

GERMAN SECULAR MUSIC

The *Glogauer* (R14) and *Lochamer* (R15) songbooks are the principal sources of later 15th-century German repertory. A lied from the *Glogauer* with the title "Es ist ein Schloss in Österreich" (W150) describes a castle in Austria made of cinnamon and cloves.

Ludwig Senfl, a German composer of the 16th century, wrote many humorous songs. Senfl employed popular melodies in his lieder, incorporated into the general texture through imitation. In "Ein Maidlein zu den Brunnen ging" (W121) a young man tells a maiden to be off if she will not love him since there are many others available.

An anonymous 16th-century song, "Es gingen drei Baur'n" (W149), tells the story of three peasants who look for a bear but regret their quest at meeting one. Senfl's "Oho! So Geb' Der Mann In'n Pfenning" (W122) is based on a lied published by Wolfgang Schmeltzel in 1544. The text begins, "Oh! If the man would give us a penny, then we could have wine."

The *villanesca*, *canzonetta*, and *balletto* influenced German composers of the 16th century, particularly Hans Leo Hassler, who spent time in Italy. For example, "Tanzen und springen" (W65) is similar in style and structure to Gastoldi's *balletti*.

QUODLIBET

The term *quodlibet* was originally applied to university debates examining a wide range of subjects; *quodlibet* (a Latin word meaning "whatever you wish") also designated a musical type, like the French *fricassée*, which incorporated several melodies and texts. The *Glogauer* collection (R14) has a fascinating quodlibet on the chanson "O Rosa Bella" (R14), used as a top line over fragments from famous German melodies and texts.

Isaak's "Donna di dentro" (W69), perhaps the most famous example, incorporates several popular melodies, including "Fortuna d'un gran tempo." Matthias Greiter combined four German tunes and texts in "Eselein" (W64). The texts are retained in each of the four parts, resulting in a verbal cacophony. Isaak's *Missa Carminum* (W70) is an example of a sacred quodlibet that combines many folklike melodies.

COMIC THEATER IN THE RENAISSANCE

Greek and Roman comedies were studied and translated, inspiring contemporary writers. For example, *Eoidicus* by Plautus was staged at Rome in 1468 and the *Andria* by Terence was seen in Florence in 1472. In addition, the *Menaechmi* by Plautus was heard in an Italian translation in Ferrara in 1486.

Music, dancing, pantomimes, and tableaux were added to performances of Roman comedy and their imitations (B106, 61). In Iacopo Sannazaro's *Il Trionfo di Fama* (1492)(W118), written in celebration of the Spanish capture of Granada, Fame enters to the music of a viol, bagpipe, flute, and rebec. Instrumental music sometimes was heard between the scenes or acts of such productions. Pastoral drama, such as Giovanni Guarini's celebrated *Il Pastor Fido* (1590), often suggested the inclusion of contrasting madrigals. Such madrigal composers as Marenzio, Wert, and Monteverdi selected text excerpts from this drama for madrigal settings.

Instrumental pieces, chansons, or quotations therefrom often were also important in French secular theater of the 16th century. Often characters appeared on stage singing a fragment of a chanson that reflected his or her personality. Mary Springfels writes: "While for the most part actors were called upon to sing only snatches of things, occasionally the action was built around the performance of a chanson. In the cruel farce *Le Savetier Marguet*, the wife-beating husband sings the bawdy ballad 'J'ay ung billard'; Marguet is forced to reply with 'J'ay un connin vestu de soye.' In a few plays, like Marguerite of Naverre's *Mont de Mersan*, an entire role will consist of chanson fragments" (B776, D47).

Occasionally vocal works fulfilled a specific function in particular comedies. Thus Philippe Verdelot's "O dolce notte" (W133) was intended for Machiavelli's comedy *Mandragola* (1526), and the same composer's "Quanto sia liet d'giorno" was heard in Machiavelli's *Clizia* (c. 1524)(W134). Juan del Encina, a Spanish composer working at Naples in the later 15th century, wrote short pieces meant to be performed in his own plays. These pieces, called *cuatro de empezar* (beginning pieces for four voices), are often humorous and functioned, as the term implies, as opening choruses (W54).

Music was heard in both Shakespeare's tragedies and comedies in the form of songs—often well known—alarums for trumpets, and other types of incidental instrumental music. Set off from the plays by their shorter lines and verse structures, these songs were often performed as separate pieces. Individual actors sometimes performed music. Gustave Reese writes: "Shakespeare's fellow actor, Will Kemp, was famous for his end-piece 'jigs' which were part dance, part pantomime, part song—rude, slapstick affairs, accompanied by pipe and tabor" (B195, 881).

COMMEDIA DELL' ARTE

Commedia dell' arte originated in 1550 in Italy as improvised theater, although the term is from the 18th century. It continued as an active theatrical form until the 19th century. Dancing and music were integral to performances, with the actors playing such stereotypes as Pantalone, Zanni, and Pulcinello. The actors wore masks and costumes that related to the traits of the characters they were playing. Speeches were performed extempore. Demonstrating the importance of music, contemporary prints often depicted characters holding lutes and other musical instruments.

THE MADRIGAL CYCLE

The madrigal cycle, which enjoyed a brief popularity at the end of the 16th century, is directly linked to *commedia dell' arte*. This type consists of a group of madrigals loosely related by their common theme and *commedia dell' arte* stereotypes. The inherently dramatic potential of the madrigal was highlighted by featuring questions and answers, dialogue between different characters, and juxtaposing, sometimes abruptly, contrasting textures.

Orazio Vecchi's *L'Amfiparnaso* (1597)(W131) is the best-known instance. The title refers to its mixture of comic and serious styles, or the two sides of Mt. Parnassus, the Greek mythical mountain of poetic accomplishment. *L'Amfiparnaso* consists of 15 pieces grouped into a prologue and three acts. Most madrigals emphasize the texts through homophony; the dialect portions are reminiscent of the more earthy *villotta-villanesca* tradition. A musical satire of Cipriano de Rore's famous "Anchor che col partire" occurs at the beginning of Act III in Dr. Gratiano's song. The original top part is retained, and the lower voices are new. The first line, which means "Again since I have to leave you," is transformed into "Anchor ch'al parturire," or "Again since I give birth."

Adriano Banchieri, a major theorist and composer of sacred music, wrote *La Pazzia senile* (1598)(W25), modeled on *L'Amfiparnaso*. Such stock characters as Pantalone and Dr. Gratiano are included in this takeoff on senility. A parody of Palestrina's celebrated madrigal "Vestiva i colli" highlights the work. Banchieri's *Festino nella sera del giovedi grasso* (1608)(W24) contains a *contrappunto bestiale*, in which learned contrapuntal practice is lambasted through the braying of an ass and the sounds of other animals. Giovanni Croce's *Triaca Musicale* (1590)(W42) depicts a contest between a cuckoo and a nightingale.

RENAISSANCE INSTRUMENTAL MUSIC

Renaissance dances employed elaborate choreography with dramatic implications. Whereas the pavane and galliarde were courtly and sedate, the chaconne and sarabande, imported from colonial Mexico, were frequently condemned by ecclesiastics as lascivious. Vocal chaconnes of the period often end with the refrain "Vamonos á Chacona" or "Let us go to Chaconne." At this time the word *chaconne* implied a place of perfect happiness.

Dance titles often refer to their origins or styles. Thus the *Glogauer Liederbuch* (1455–60) includes a dance curiously entitled *The Rat's Dance* (W153). The title probably refers to a well-known song of the time incorporated into this vigorous instrumental work. Humorous titles continue in the dance repertory of the early 16th century. Hans Weck's *Hopper dancz* (W137) is, as the title implies, a jumping dance, and Hans Neusiedler's *Hoftanz* (W107) concludes with a second part marked "Der Hupf auff," suggesting that the dancers likewise "jump up." *Ein Judentanz* (W108) is marked by short repeated phrases and a formula-like melody. Bernhard the Elder wrote a dance with the humorous title *A Good Dance which can lead one to Marriage* (W30).

Many dances from the 16th-century publications of Susato and Attaingnant carry the names of the chansons used as their source material. The *bergerette* "Dont Vient Cela" (W123) by Claudin de Sermisy is turned into a basse dance in a Susato publication of 1531. The harmonic-melodic outlines of the chanson are followed, and the dance is extended into several repeated sections.

Sometimes a chanson's popularity results in multiple transformations. Thus the anonymous chanson "C'est Grand Plaisir" (W147) is found as a keyboard transcription in an Attaingnant publication of 1531 and becomes a *Tourdion* in the same publisher's publication of 1547. Diego Ortiz's treatise *Trattado de Glosas* (1553)(B176) includes many arrangements of popular chansons and madrigals. The variety of his arrangements demonstrates the increasing interest in virtuosity for its own sake. Michael Praetorius's *Terpsichore* (1612)(W116) is the most famous of all Renaissance collections of dances. Its dances reflect the French style of the high Renaissance and are often formed into short suites, as in the case of the *Ballet du Roy pour sonner après*.

Variations often used popular or folk melodies with humorous texts. The Spanish melody "Guárdame las Vacas," whose text speaks of guarding the cows, spawned variations by Luys de Narváez and Enriquez de Valderrábano (W106 and W128). English composers of the late Renaissance wrote particularly brilliant sets for keyboard on such melodies as "The Carman's Whistle" (W146) and "Callino Casturarme" (W144).

The light chanson style also influenced the instrumental canzona of the later 16th century. Some Renaissance theorists refer to the *Canzona Allegre* (W145), implying the vivacious nature of these pieces. Many canzonas are simply instrumental arrangements of popular chansons, such as Andrea Gabrieli's use of Thomas Crecquillon's "Ung gay bergier" (W59) for one of his *canzoni francesi*.

Instrumental battle pieces formed an important genre in the late Renaissance. Matthias Werrecore's *Battaglia taliana* (W98) vividly imitates the sounds of horses running and cannons firing. Isaak's *A la battaglia* (W71) was used for a scene in Lorenzo de Medici's *Rappresentazione di San Giovanni e Paolo* (1471). Janequin's "La bataille" (W73), mentioned earlier, becomes a principal model for many instrumental works. Andrea Gabrieli, for example, wrote *Aria battaglia per sonar d'instrumenti da fiato* (W58), which expands this chanson's musical contents.

DESCRIPTIVE TITLES

Many English keyboard works found in the *Fitzwilliam Virginal Book* (collected 1606–19) are elaborately descriptive. For example, John Bull's *The King's Hunt* (W34) emphasizes a simple chord progression, repeated with increasingly energetic figurations. As the piece comes to a conclusion, the scurrying sixteenth notes suggest that the king's party is nearing their prey. Bull's *Les Buffons* (W33) is a set of variations on a French theme that highlights "twirling" figurations.

Ensemble pieces also participated in this descriptive tendency. Morley's *Il Grillo* (W105) imitates the sounds of a cricket through quickly repeated notes. Descriptive instrumental techniques are also found in Tobias Hume's *Poeticall Musicke* (1607) (W68). Titles often employ clever plays on words. For instance, Christopher Tye, active during the middle 16th century, composed *In Nomines* for ensembles of instruments with such peculiar designations as *In Nomine Crye* (W127).

Shorter dancelike pieces were sometimes called "toys." Bull, Orlando Gibbons, and Thomas Tomkins wrote a number of delightful instances for lute or keyboard. For example, Tomkins's *A Toy: Made at Poole Court* (W126) parodies scholastic practice by contrasting simple with extremely complex contrapuntal sections. Giles Farnaby's *His Humor* (W55) also spoofs academic procedures.

BALLET

Balthasar de Beaujoyeux's *Balet comique de la royne* (1581)(W29) combines music from various sources with mythological ideas. As the title suggests, this was a court entertainment, but its popularity resulted in arrangements for solo lute by Robert Ballard.

MUSIC AND PLEASURE

Many titles for secular collections include *deliciae*, the Latin word for delights. For example, Christoph Demantius's collection for lute is entitled *Conviviorum Deliciae* (1608)(W45), and the Dutch composer Joachim van den Hove called his lute book *Delitiae Musicae* (1612)(W67). Such collections reflect the growth of groups, particularly in Germany, devoted to the pleasures of music.

References to music's relationship to courtly amusement appear in the writings of many philsophers and theorists. Baldassare Castiglione's *Il Libro del Cortegiano* (1528)(B43) covers all aspects of etiquette but also refers to music's power to charm. Morley's *Plaine and Easie Introduction* (1597)(B163) not only discusses music theory, but also considers lighter songs.

As suggested previously, music plays a major role in Rabelais's *Gargantua and Pantagruel* (1532 and 1534)(B191). The young Gargantua is taught to dance and play various instruments, evidencing the author's considerable knowledge of music. Rabelais lists composers, including Josquin, Obrecht, and Brumel, who, at one point in the novel, sing a bawdy song about Tibault (probably referring to Tubal, the mythical inventor of music).

CANONS AND OTHER SYMBOLIC GAMES

Renaissance composers and theorists delighted in sophisticated verbal and visual games. The Flemish theorist Johannes Tinctoris described a canon in his musical dictionary, *Terminorum musicae diffinitorium* (1475)(B234), as "a rule showing the purpose of a composer behind a certain obscurity." Later, the Spanish theorist Ramos de Pareia devotes much of the *Musica Practica* (1482) to intricate canons, including various examples of verbal puzzles (B192).

Du Fay's *Missa L'homme armé* (late 15th century)(W53), for example, has a canon at the Agnus Dei indicated "cancer eat plenus et redeat medius." This means "Let the crab go fully and return halfway," requiring the tenor voice to proceed in full values backward and go forward in half values. Since crabs were thought to walk backward, retrograde canons were referred to as "crab" canons.

Canons occasionally were represented visually. For example, a chapter of Morley's *Plaine and Easie Introduction* (1597)(B163) includes a canon in the form of a cross. Pietro Cerone ends *El Melopeo y Maestro* (1613)(B44 and B406) with a chapter on enigmatic canons. These take such bizarre shapes as elephants, keys, chessboards, and balances. *Soggetto cavato* was a common procedure in which vowels in a name or phrase were substituted by the appropriate solfège syllables to create a musical idea. Cara's *frottola* "A la absentia" (W143) has the phrase "So la fe che mia signora." This is translated into sol la fa re mi, or the note pattern GAFDE. Josquin and his contemporaries often used *soggetto cavato* to honor a patron or symbolize a sacred idea (B7, 282–83).

Willem Elders demonstrated that subtle number symbolism is often found in Renaissance sacred music (B70). Individual words, such as *error*, *sin*, or *repentance*, may trigger changes of mode or introduction of unexpected accidentals. Caspar Othmayr, a Protestant composer of the early 16th century, used these devices in *Symbola* (1547), which, as Gustave Reese notes, is "a collection of motets whose texts feature the heraldric mottoes, or *symbola*, of thirty-four illustrious men of the day" (B195, 682). Othmayr's "Octo sunt passiones" (W111), for instance, relates the eight passions to the eight Renaissance modes. *Gematria* is number symbolism in which each letter of the alphabet receives a numeric value. This "game," according to Allan W. Atlas, is sometimes applied to note values   to   determine   structures   and   phrase   lengths   (B7,   59).

Chapter 4

The Baroque Period

ITALIAN COMIC OPERA

Claudio Monteverdi's lost *La finta pazza Licori* (1627) seems to have been the first comic opera. It apparently was about a young girl whose love causes her to go mad and was written in an experimental style. The 1637 opening of San Cassiano in Venice as a public opera house created the need for more diverse libretti. Pastoral mythology, which had characterized the earliest operas, gave way to history or romance. By the 1640s, comic episodes became increasingly common—undoubtedly because of their popular appeal.

Some early operas already include comic episodes, such as Stefano Landi's *La morte d'Orfeo* (1619)(W225), with its drinking song for Caronte. Landi's *Il Sant'Alessio* (1632)(W226), written in Rome, was one of the first to feature comic scenes. An energetic duet for the servants using patter song—a device typical of much later comic opera—is found. Francesco Cavalli's *Giasone* (1649)(W182), one of the most successful of all 17th-century Venetian operas, includes a funny confrontation between Orestes and Demo, the stammering dwarf from Aegeus's court. Demo's stuttering offers Cavalli many opportunities for buffo effects. Partly because of the extraordinary success of *Giasone*, other operas by Cavalli and his contemporaries highlighted comic scenes for servants, advisers, and older women in love with young men.

Comic arias were set off by their clear strophic structure, syllabic style, and limited musical range. Some typical devices included are exaggerated text painting, extended melismas, and quick syllabic writing. Comic characters often addressed themselves directly to the audience, frequently adopting an ironically moralistic tone (B202, 301). A self-conscious attitude of satirizing opera conventions is sometimes found. For example, Antonio Sartorio's *Seleuco*

(1666)(W273) contains a scene in which the court singer tries to find the proper song for the love-sick Antonio.

A taste for comedy was also, as we have seen, present in Rome. Giulio Rospigliosi, later Pope Clement IX, wrote the text for the earliest purely comic opera that survives, Virgilio Mazzocchi and Marco Marazzoli's *Chi soffre speri* (1639)(W240). Donald J. Grout (B93, 73) notes that this opera includes dialogue in a style that anticipates secco recitative. *Dal male il bene* (1653), with music by Marco Marazzoli (W238) and Antonio Maria Abbatini, is musically more sophisticated. The libretto for this work, again by Rospigliosi, shows the influence of the adventure plays of Calderón de la Barca. Alessandro Scarlatti, usually credited with the crystallization of the Neapolitan *opera seria*, also wrote operas with many comic scenes *La caduta dei decemviri* (1697)(W275), *Il prigionero fortunato* (1698)(W278), and *Eraclea* (1700)(W276). *Il Trionfo dell'onore* (1718)(W279) is Scarlatti's most forwardlooking comic opera because of its *galant* style and charmingly farcical elements.

Influenced by developments in Italy, Georg Philipp Telemann wrote a number of comic operas that anticipate the style of later *opera buffa* in their symmetric melodies and clearly defined accompaniments. *Pimpinone* (1725)(W281), an *intermezzo*, and a full-scale opera *Der geduldige Socrates* (1721)(W280) are chief among these. *Pimpinone* anticipates Pergolesi's *La Serva Padrona* (1733)(W399)—to be discussed in the next chapter—and *Der geduldige Socrates* highlights Socrates's domestic difficulties and contains slapstick elements.

FRENCH *COMÉDIE-BALLET* AND *OPÉRA-BALLET*

French opera crystallized by the 17th century. Jean-Baptiste Lully, a Florentine turned Frenchman, blended Italian and French characteristics in the *comédie-ballet*. Lully was influenced by his working relationship, although rather short-lived, with the great French comic playwright Molière (Jean-Baptiste Poquelin). The *comédie-ballet* paralleled the English masque in its diversity of theme and irregular structures. Lully was a comedian and dancer as well as a composer, and often participated in his own works. He composed the ballets for the Italian play *Amore malato* (1657)(W232) by Francesco Buti in which he played the role of Scaramouche. His later ballets regularly featured comic scenes. *Ballet de la Raillerie* (1659)(W235) includes an amusing dialogue between French and Italian music, while the *Ballet de L'Impatience* (1661)(W234) "contains a grotesque *récit* of the 'snuff takers' for a three-part choral ensemble in canzonetta style" (B37, 153). In 1664, Lully and Molière began their collaboration. Lully wrote music for such famous Molière plays as *L'amour médecin* (1665)(W233), *Les amants magnifiques* (1670)(W231), and *Le bourgeois gentilhomme* (1670)(W236). The music for this play about a would-be gentleman is descriptive, especially in the hilarious "Turkish" ceremony at the end. Lully's operas include comic interludes, probably influenced by contemporary Venetian practice. *Alceste* (1674)(W230) features a satiric scene for Caron, the oarsman to the underworld. Such a scene pokes fun at classical mythology, beginning a French tradition that would continue into the works of Offenbach and Poulenc.

Marc-Antoine Charpentier also composed incidental music, most notably for Molière's *Le Màlade imaginaire* (1673)(W186), a clever play about a hypochondriac. The induction of the protagonist into the medical profession that occurs at the end employs a funny takeoff on Latin jargon. Charpentier added an *Intermède* to Molière's *Le Marriage Forcé* (1671)(W187), which parodies Italian music. The first part contains strange chromaticism on the phrase "O la belle harmonie"; the second, entitled *Les grotesques*, employs exaggerated melismas to imitate the sounds of dogs, cats, and birds.

Opéra-ballet grew out of *comédie-ballet*. It flourished in the early to mid 18th century and consisted of a prologue followed by three or four acts. Reflecting the requirements of the Académie Royale de Musique, the *opéra-ballet* featured a separate subject or theme in each of its acts. Exotic topics and colorful costumes, often modeled on dress from different parts of the world, enlivened these works, which clearly were intended for enjoyment. André Campra's *L'Europe galante* (1697)(W180), the first example, reflects the passion for world exploration and colonization. Jean-Philippe Rameau's *Les Indes galantes* (1735)(W262) features brilliant *divertissements* and elegant vocal passages. Exoticism is evident in this work's evocation of colonial Peru and juxtaposition of musical styles. *Les fêtes d'Hébé* (1739)(W261) further exhibits the typical allegorical cast of this genre with its section devoted to poetry, music, and dance. *Comédie-ballet* was affected by changing public tastes. Luigi Cherubini's *Anacréon* (1803)(W482), which emphasizes pantomime and powerful symphonic characterization, is the last example.

Le Sage's *Télémaque* (1715)(W228) satirizes serious operatic conventions and thus falls within the context of operatic parodies that were so popular at the time. Hardly a serious opera was composed that did not receive parody treatment. Jean-Philippe Rameau's *Platée* (1745)(W263), his only comic opera and the most important French comic opera of the time, mocks Italian *opera seria*. Of special importance is an *air de danse* for "Sad Madmen," which juxtaposes comic and sentimental styles within a few measures. *Platée* also satirizes favorite French operatic conventions, thus relating it to the controversy between French and Italian styles that was then raging. For example, a chaconne is heard in the middle of the opera rather than at the end.

THE MASQUE AND RELATED FORMS

The English masque, a 17th-century dramatic type inspired by later Renaissance Italian practices, combined speech and song on allegorical themes. Extravagant scenery, rich costumes, and brilliant stage effects enriched a genre that praised and amused the English monarchy. *The Masque of Lord Hayes* (1607)(W179) has music by Thomas Campion. The surviving two lute songs and three dances suggest the general style of the genre. With the appearance of Ben Jonson's *Masque of Queens* (1609), comic and burlesque antimasques appear. Typically, the antimasque was performed by professionals and preceded the main masque, with the participants grotesquely dressed.

Masquelike compositions are occasionally found outside England, frequently continuing the *intermezzo* practices of the previous century. The Neapolitan *Festa a Ballo "Delizie di Posilipo Boscaresce, a Maritime"* (1620)(W221), a *pasticcio* of works by Camillo Lambardi, Giovanni Maria Trabaci, and Pietro Antonio Giramo, combines dances, songs, and choral numbers in both Italian and Spanish. Antonio Draghi, associated with the Hapsburg court, wrote a *Mascha "Trionfa Il Carneval"* (W207) during the Turkish siege of Vienna of 1683 as a comic antidote to the grim situation.

MUSIC FOR PLAYS

After the severity of the Puritan Commonwealth, with its interdiction of all public entertainment, the Restoration of the monarchy in 1660 marked the return of plays. Bawdy situations and risqué humor prevail in the works of Congreve, Dryden, and their contemporaries. These plays often included songs and incidental music. Henry Purcell wrote music for "semioperas," as these plays were then called. The principal examples are *Dioclesian* (1690)(W252), *King Arthur* (1691)(W254), *The Fairy-Queen* (1692) (W253), and *The Tempest* (c. 1695)(W255). *The Fairy-Queen* typifies Restoration practice by adapting Shakespeare's *A Midsummer Night's Dream*, but with additional material. The original version included four masques, but a fifth was added for the 1693 revival. The first masque, for example, contains a scene for a drunken poet not found in the original Shakespeare play.

Spanish theater reached its height in the 17th century with the plays of Lope de Vega and Calderón de la Barca. Although most of these plays were serious, many included comic episodes—a practice that, as we have seen, impacted Italian *opera seria* of the time. The principal composer for Calderón's plays was Juan Hidalgo, whose songs reveal irony and complex allusions to mythology (W216).

BALLAD OPERA

Ballad opera dominated the English stage in the next generation, partly as a reaction against the rigid conventions of *opera seria*. *The Beggar's Opera* (1728)(W210) by John Gay, with music by Christopher Pepusch, was the first example, but also the most important because of its popularity and impact on this short-lived genre. This disarming work, with its undertone of satire and social commentary, employs many popular melodies. Kurt Weill transformed *The Beggar's Opera* as *Die Dreigroschenoper* (1928)(W1009).

Although ballad opera lasted only a short time, later English operas were influenced by its simplicity. Thomas Arne's *Comus* (1738)(W292) and particularly *Thomas and Sally* (1760)(W293) have the homely quality associated with *The Beggar's Opera*.

The Beggar's Opera was enormously popular in America during the 18th century and inspired similar works (B219). Andrew Barton's *The Disappointment: Or, the Force of Credulity* (1767)(W172) was the first ballad opera published in America. Pantomimes and arrangements from operas were also common. Oscar G. Sonneck cites a program of 19 January 1787 at Philadelphia with a diversity of contents: "The Ouverture to Rosina, to which will be added, a Pantomime called 'Harlequin's Frolic,' in which will be introduced a Musical Entertainment, called 'The Reapers,' with the original music" (B219, 74). Scenery, dancing, and mixed combinations of songs were emphasized. Often serious operas, such as André-Ernest-Modeste Grétry's *Richard Coeur-de-lion* (1784)(W313), served as the basis for such entertainments.

ENGLISH BURLESQUES AND COMIC OPERAS

Pantomimes and burlesques are frequently found by the mid-18th century. Such actors as David Garrick employed songs and outlandish costumes in their performances, imitating *commedia dell' arte*. English composers took well-known models for burlesque, the term at this time implying a satirical parody of a stage work. John Fredrick Lampe's *The Dragon of Wantley* (1737)(W222) persiflages the Handelian style, as does its sequel, *Margery; or, A Worse Plague Than the Dragon* (1738)(W223). Lampe's mock opera after Shakespeare's *A Midsummer Night's Dream*, *Pyramus and Thisbe* (1745)(W224), includes an aria for the lion. The score indicates the sections to be "roared" with a wavy line.

Handel sometimes experimented with the combination of genres. *Acis and Galatea* (1718, 1732)(W214), on a text by John Gay and others, combines the traditions of pastoral opera and masque. Elements of parody occur, especially in the part for the giant Polyphemus and in the mock-pastoral text. Although *Semele* (1744)(W215) is frequently considered an oratorio, it is actually an English comic opera in which the chorus plays a major role. Here classical mythology is satirized through strong sexual overtones.

CANONS, CATCHES, GLEES, AND DRINKING SONGS

A catch was an entertaining canon or round for male voices written as one musical line. Each voice was required to "catch" its beginning at the right time. A glee, on the other hand, was a simple harmonized song for three or more male voices, typically consisting of alto, tenor, and bass. The term is derived from the

Anglo-Saxon *gligge*, a word that means music. Early 17th-century glees often concerned eating and drinking.

Thomas Ravenscroft's *Pammelia* (1609)(R24), the first English printed collection of rounds and catches, was enormously popular. Inspired by Ravenscroft's collection, John Hilton's *Catch That Catch Can* (1652)(R23) includes both sacred and secular canons. Two canons from this collection illustrate its frequently convivial theme: No. 34 "Come Let Us Cast the Dice Who Shall Drink" and No. 42 "Dainty Fine Aniseed Water Fine." In 1761, the first catch club was formed; in 1783 a glee club was founded at the home of Robert Smith in St. Paul's Churchyard for the purpose of singing glees, catches, and canons. In 1790, Samuel Webbe composed "Glorious Apollo" (W288), which thereafter was always sung at these meetings. During the later 18th and early 19th centuries, numerous glee clubs were founded in Britain and the United States, often at colleges and universities.

After 1660, simple homophonic drinking songs for two or three parts also became popular in France. Some of the major composers of the period, such as Marc-Antoine Charpentier (W185), contributed to the genre. These songs often protest against the established order through subtle references.

SOLO SONGS

Elizabeth Rogers Hir Virginall Booke (1656)(R25) is an anthology of keyboard and vocal pieces from the later 16th and earlier 17th centuries. Several songs from the collection feature a playful style appropriate to domestic surroundings. Kaiser Leopold I was a gifted composer of the later 17th century. His "Amor Care," an amusing parody of the lament, is about the woes Cupid causes, with key words such as *ouch* and *miserere* highlighted (W227).

Henry Purcell's songs, many of which were written for plays, were collected and published in *Orpheus Britannicus* (1706). "Man Is for the Woman Made" (W258) from *The Mock Marriage* contrasts the changing ideas of the text through repetition and short phrases. "I'll Sail Upon the Dog Star" (W257) from *A Fool's Preferment* is more melismatic and features large leaps. "Nymphs and Shepherds" (W259) continues the playful pastoral tradition of the late 16th century; "Hence with Your Trifling deity!" (W256) for *Timon of Athens* is a vigorous drinking song.

A work for three solo voices and basso continuo, ascribed to Giacomo Carissimi in a 17th-century source at the Paris Conservatory, has the peculiar Latin title "Venerabilis barba Capucinorum" (W181). This text, which means "the venerable beard of the Capuchin monks," is separated into individual letters and syllables, creating a verbal game.

COMIC MADRIGALS AND CANTATAS

The continuo madrigal and, later, the cantata were perfect comic media because of their flexibility and intimacy. Tarquinio Merula's set of continuo madrigals, "Nominativo Hic Haec Hoc" and "Nominativo Quis vel qui" (1623)(W241), parody how to learn Latin declensions. These witty pieces were published many times during the 17th century and falsely ascribed to various composers under the title *Rudimenta grammaticae*. Latin cases are sung to ever-reduced note values and with increasing confusion. This type of spoof of academic procedures is found again in Telemann's *Der Schulmeister* (early 18th century)(W282), discussed later.

Monteverdi's *Scherzi Musicali* (1607, 1632)(W246) are masterpieces of comic art, as the title of the collection implies. Many traits of the *frottola*, such as energetic rhythms and light textures, are continued in these charming works for three voices, which include instrumental interludes. His *Il Ballo delle Ingrate* (1608)(W243) is on a larger scale and includes elements of the grotesque. High and low art are contrasted through an emphasis on the ambiguity of the "ungrateful women." Such *balli* as this continue the Renaissance *intermedio* in their heterogeneous combinations of song and dance.

The late Baroque secular cantata crystallized into a series of arias and secco recitatives, with serious or Arcadian subjects prevailing. However, a number of cantatas are comic—some even satirizing the cantata tradition itself. Mario Savioni wrote a cantata on the death of Dido (before 1641)(W274), which "is essentially a comic parody of the heroine's death, set to a text by Francesco Melesio" (B719, 109). The text plays with alliteration, such as the final line illustrating Dido's death with the sound "din-don."

Charpentier's *Ad Beatam Virginem Canticum* (late 17th century)(W183) ends with a passage that has dots over the notes "to express shakiness of old age suggested by the text" (B45, 250). Charpentier also composed a half serious, half comic cantata, *Epitaphium Carpentarii* (late 17th century)(W184). This outrageous satire of the cantata-oratorio tradition also includes a passage for three angels, which parodies Catholic liturgy. Giovanni Bassani wrote a charming cantata, *Il Musico Svogliato* (W173), about a singer reluctant to sing because he has a cold. Benedetto Marcello's cantata *Stravaganze d'Amore* (early 18th century)(W239) includes an aria, "Amor tu sei," which expresses the extremes of love through 5/4 meter; the voice part and the basso continuo alternate enharmonic equivalents. Antonio Caldara's *Il Giuoco del Quadriglio* (W177) was commissioned by the Empress Elisabeth Christine for the Viennese imperial court in the early 18th century. In the original performance, the four sopranos were shown seated around a table playing the popular card game of quadrille. This cantata is thus like a short comic opera.

COMIC CANTATAS AND QUODLIBETS BY GERMAN COMPOSERS

Johann Melchior Gletle's *Vorlesung über die Gesundheit* (1684)(W213), a cantata written in a mixture of Latin and German, is a health recipe. It begins with a parody of a Gregorian intonation formula and continues with detailed prescriptions on diet and ways to increase strength. Valentin Rathgeber's *Die Bettelzech* (1737)(W268) is a complete dramatic scene about various beggars. Telemann's *Der Schulmeister* (early 18th century)(W282) parodies dry academic traditions. Here a pompous schoolmaster teaches recalcitrant pupils solfège. The centerpiece of the work is a fugue with deliberate harmonic clashes.

Johann Sebastian Bach composed over twenty secular cantatas, many of which are, in effect, small comic operas. Most of these were composed for the Collegium Musicum at Leipzig, which were regularly staged performances with boys singing the female roles. The best known humorous cantatas are the *Wedding Cantata* (1723)(W160), the *Hunting Cantata* (1730)(W162), the *Coffee Cantata* (c. 1735)(W163), *Aeolus Appeased* (1725)(W161), *Phoebus and Pan* (1729)(W159), and the *Peasant Cantata* (1742)(W164). The nicknames are derived from the particular theme of each work. The *Coffee Cantata* includes large-scale da capo arias, including one in praise of drinking coffee. Bach composed a virtual miniature opera about the heroine Lieschen's addiction to coffee. *Phoebus and Pan*, mentioned in the opening section of the book, features a singing contest between these mythological characters. The *Peasant Cantata*, written in a mixture of Plattdeutsch and Hochdeutsch, details the daily concerns of peasants. This cantata begins with a quodlibet on German folk melodies.

Quodlibets and humorous songs abound in the German Baroque. Valentin Rathgeber composed many that are structurally akin to the form of a cantata (Ww269–71). One instance is a duet between "Melancholico Lamente" and "Gioviale Consolante" (1733)(W269), which contrasts happiness and sorrow.

COMIC DESCRIPTIVE INSTRUMENTAL MUSIC

The love of description and virtuoso display inspired a large body of instrumental programmatic music. For example, *Elizabeth Rogers Hir Virginall Booke* (1656)(R25) includes short keyboard pieces with such beguiling titles as *The Fairest Nymphs the Valleys or Mountains Ever Bred* and *What If the King Should Come to the City*. The instrumental capriccio also invited special, "capricious" effects. Carlo Farina's *Capriccio Stravagante* (1636)(W208), for example, is a veritable zoo with its imitations of dogs, cats, and other animals. Johann Jacob Walther's *Scherzi da violino solo* (1676)(W287), influenced by Farina, employs many advanced violin techniques. Notable is the early use of the word *scherzo*, the Italian word for joke.

Girolamo Frescobaldi wrote *Capriccio on the Call of a Cuckoo* (1624)(W209). Johann Kaspar Kerll's *Capriccio Cücu* (W218) continues this "bird" tradition, as does the final fugal movement of Bach's keyboard sonata in

D (1704)(W171). The subject of the fugue bears the indication "Thema all'Imitatio Gallina Cuccu" and employs the falling interval of a third. Alessandro Poglietti's *Capriccio über das Hennergeschrey* (late 17th century)(W250) portrays the cackling of a hen through quickly repeated notes leading to dissonant seconds, and *Rossignolo* (late 17th century)(W251) imitates the song of a nightingale.

The best known capriccio of the period, Bach's *Capriccio on the Departure of a Brother* (1704)(W168), was written when Bach's brother was leaving for Sweden. Bach's capriccio narrates the brother's departure, the sorrow felt by those left behind, and concludes with a fugue based on the sound of the horn announcing the brother's return. Continuing the Renaissance tradition, Baroque composers wrote battle pieces. Johann Kaspar Kerll's *Battaglia* (late 17th century)(W217), Clamor Heinrich Abel's *Sonata-Bataillen* (1676)(W157), and Heinrich Biber's *La Battaglia* (late 17th century)(W175) are among many examples.

Telemann's orchestral *Burlesque de Quixotte* (early 18th century)(W283), based on the celebrated novel by Miguel de Cervantes, includes a description of the Don's fanciful confrontation with the windmills. *Musique de table* (early 18th century)(W284), a series of quartets, features lighthearted dialogues among the instruments, thus anticipating the Classic style. Marin Marais's Sonata for viola da gamba and basso continuo (late 17th century)(W237) describes a gallstone operation. Louis-Antoine Dornel called his solo sonatas of 1711 after famous composers: *La Marais, La Couperin*, and so on (Ww204–205). According to William S. Newman, he also employed such designations as "Fugue gay" and "Allemande comique," implying even serious styles could be transformed (B171, 371).

Diversion and elegance are implied in titles for many Baroque collections. Nicolas Chédeville, for example, termed one group of sonatas *Les Galanteries amusantes, Sonates a deux musettes* (1739)(W188). This set also includes descriptive pieces as well as imitations of drone instruments, fashionable during this period of mock-pastoral pursuits. François Couperin's *Soeur Monique* (1717)(W199) employs Rococoesque ornamentation as does *Le Gaillard-boiteux* (1717)(W196). Couperin's rondeaux are often descriptive, as exemplified by *Les baricades mistérieuses* (1717)(W193) and *La distrait* (1717)(W194), the latter a description of confusion. Often instruments are imitated, as in *La harpée* (1730)(W197) or *Le bandoline* (1713)(W192). The 18th-century fascination with clock effects is found in *Le tic-toc-choc, ou les maillotins* (1717)(W200).

Anticipating Erik Satie, Couperin sometimes used amusing titles, such as *Les fastes de la grande et ancienne Mxnxstrxndxs* (1717)(W195), which describes a feast of the old musician's guild called Menestrandes (each vowel of the name substituted by an *x* to heighten the mystery). Couperin honored his great contemporaries Corelli and Lully with trio sonatas entitled *L'apothéose de Corelli* (1724)(W190) and *L'apothéose de Lully* (1725)(W191), respectively.

These celebrate the combination of French and Italian styles. Each movement is given a programmatic description, with both composers finally reaching the heights of Parnassus.

Rameau used descriptive titles less often than Couperin. However, *La Poule* from the Suite in G minor (c. 1728)(W266) captures the clucking of the hen with an upward moving arpeggio. Ottorino Respighi's suite for orchestra, *Gli Uccelli* (1927)(W906), includes this piece as well as other "bird" pieces from the period. Rameau's *Le rappel des oiseaux* from the Suite in E minor (1724)(W267) features repeated patterns between the hands. François Dagincourt and Claude Daquin also composed charming descriptive pieces for the clavecin. (Ww.201–203).

Like Couperin, Rameau occasionally employs enigmatic titles, such as *Les Cyclops* (1724)(W264); *L'egiptienne* (1728)(W265) reflects the kind of exoticism prevalent in his *Les Indes galantes* (W262), discussed earlier in this chapter. Jacques Aubert's Sonata No. 10 of Book 3 has a "Carillon" (early 18th century), or a charming depiction of bells (W158). According to William S. Newman, Michel-Gabriel Besson's ten Sonatas for violin and basso continuo (1720)(W174) feature fanfare and musette effects, thus increasing their appeal to amateur audiences (B171, 375). In a similar effort to capture the public's interest, Jean-Jacques Naudot, flutist of the later 18th century, wrote light, diverting music for vielle, hurdy-gurdy, and musette (W247).

Instrumental compositions bearing the title *burlesque* also appeared during the Baroque. The term is from the Italian word *burlare*, which means to make fun of. Bach wrote a *Burlesca* movement striking for its large leaps in the harpsichord, Partita No. 2 in A minor (1727)(W170). Couperin's *Le Gaillard-boiteux* (1722)(W194) and *Les Satires chavre-pieds* (1730)(W198) are called "dans la goût burlesque." All these burlesques are distinguished by sprightly rhythms and sometimes unusual harmonic progressions.

BACH'S *GOLDBERG VARIATIONS*

Bach's *Goldberg Variations* (1741–42)(W169) alternate humorous with the canonic variations; thus there are variations that contrast with the serious canonic variations by featuring rapidly alternating chords and the crossing of hands. In addition, the quodlibet that appears just before the return of the theme features the songs "Ich bin so lang nicht bei dir g'west" and "Kraut und Rüben."

CONCERTOS AND RELATED ORCHESTRAL FORMS

Programmatic concerti often explored unusual instrumental effects. Vivaldi's *Four Seasons* (c. 1725)(W285)—the first four concertos of his Op. 8—cover a wide spectrum of styles, but often refer to rustic music through the imitation of drones and dances. The descriptive sonnets, probably by Vivaldi himself, guide the listener through these wonderful concerti. In addition, Vivaldi composed many other descriptive concertos with such topics as night or the sounds of birds. The concerto Op. 8 No. 5 (c. 1725)(W286), entitled *La Tempesta di mare*, reflects the waves of the sea through sixteenth-note scales in the outer movements.

Bach's *Brandenburg Concerto* No. 1 (1721)(W165) ends with a minuet featuring trios with raucous horn passages. The *Brandenburg Concerto* No. 2 (1721)(W166), famous for its stratospheric trumpet passages, includes an ebullient finale, with each instrument taking solo turns. The *Brandenburg Concerto* No. 5 (1721)(W167) concludes with a giguelike movement. Francesco Geminiani's *The Inchanted Forrest* (1754)(W211) was intended for a Parisian stage production of scenes from Torquato Tasso's *Gerusalemme liberata* (mid-1570s). Although not a concerto in the strict sense, it has imaginative orchestration and contrasting movements that relate it to other works just cited.

CONTROVERSIES, SATIRES, AND TREATISES

French satire often takes the form of novels. Nicolas Boileau's *Le Lutrin* (1667)(B25), for example, presents two clerics who argue about where to put a musical lectern. The enormous success of a 1752 Parisian performance of *La Serva Padrona* (W399) sparked the "Guerre des Bouffons," or the battle between performers of comic opera. Surprisingly, the Italians were defended by some of the leading French intellectuals of the time, including Jean-Jacques Rousseau whose *Le devin du village* (1752)(W272) was written in response to this dispute. Denis Diderot, on the other hand, conceived the satire *Le Neveu de Rameau* (c. 1761)(B63) as a defense of the French style.

Wolfgang Caspar Printz (B189) and Athanasius Kircher (B128) wrote complex treatises with sometimes curious sections. Other theorists, inspired by the satiric novels of John Fielding and Jonathan Swift, preferred a narrative form. Friedrich Melchior Grimm's *Le petit prophète de Boehmischbroda* (1753)(B92), a biblical parody, consists of twenty-one chapters of musical prophecy by "Gabriel Joannes Nepomucenus Franciscus de Paula Waldstorch, called Waldstoerchel, native of Boehmischbroda in Bohemia."

Johann Kuhnau, a prolific composer, wrote several satires, including *Musicalische Quack-salber* (1701)(B139) about a badly trained musician named Carassa who goes to Italy to study the latest musical outlooks. In a similar vein, Friedrich Erhardt Niedt's *Musikalische Handleitung* (1700, 1706, 1717)(B173) narrates the education of a music student named Tacitus (Latin for the "silent one"). Benedetto Marcello's *Il teatro alla moda* (1720)(B154), the most famous musical satire of the period, mocks the conventions of serious operas. Marcello's many specific references provide an invaluable source of information about how *opere serie* were actually composed.

Chapter 5

The Classic Period

Opera buffa, brilliant instrumental genres, and lighter entertainment music prevail in the later 18th century. Haydn and Mozart delighted in syntactical sophistication and the parody of musical genres, paralleling literary practices of the time. Juxtaposition of contrasting ideas, witty and unexpected turns of thought, and optimism pervade the music of the later 18th century.

Leonard Ratner (B194, 21f.) lists major features of late 18th-century comic practice. These are mimicry, wit, parody ("placing a serious topic in a more or less ridiculous light"), and artful imitation of musical bungling. Other stylistic features are references to the bizarre, the "Turkish" style, battle scenes, and magic. Also typical are references to clocks and related mechanical devices, as found in the second movement of Haydn's Symphony No. 101 (1793–94)(W343).

In addition, the period distinguished between high and low styles. Thus the symphony is complex, and the divertimento, as the term implies, is more popular. However, increasingly works by Haydn and Mozart in the high style refer to traits of the low style. Even the first movement of Mozart's magnificent *Jupiter* Symphony (1788)(W382), for example, includes comic elements. Cyclic works in the high style—principally the symphony—can include comic touches at any point but the minuet and finale more strongly feature humor. In general, cyclic works moved from the serious to the comic, reflecting the period's emphasis on optimism.

INTERMEZZI AND OPERA BUFFA

Opera buffa achieved a perfect balance of structure, wit, imagination, and drama. The roots of this genre are in the *intermezzo* as well as in the many smaller vocal and instrumental forms of the early 18th century. By 1700, comic scenes had been banished from serious operas, thus suggesting to composers the possibility of writing separate comic works. *Intermezzi*, written for two or three singers and small orchestra, often employed stock types from *commedia dell' arte*. The two acts of the *intermezzo* were performed between the three acts of a serious opera. In the early period, the *intermezzo* occasionally referred directly to the serious opera it accompanied. Eventually, the *intermezzo* was given an autonomous plot, usually featuring a servant girl, patter songs, and Neapolitan dialect.

Giovanni Pergolesi's *La Serva Padrona* (1733)(W399) caused a sensation. *La Serva* includes a cast of three characters, one of them a mute. The story about a serving maid who becomes a dominating mistress is reflected in countless subsequent *opere buffe*. Notable is the appearance of the *basso buffo* as a distinguishing trait of Italian comic opera, with large skips one of the principal features. Serpina in *La Serva* is an example of a *soubrette*, or pert servant girl who always has the answers. This type is found in later operas, such as the role of Despina in Mozart's *Così fan tutte* (1790)(W365).

Opera buffa developed many of the stylistic-structural features of the *intermezzo*, but eventually on a larger scale. The plots, also based on *commedia dell' arte*, employed a limited number of clearly defined story lines and simple stock characters. Aria structures were varied, as larger arias employed instrumental forms. Secco recitative served as linkage between arias and allowed the drama to move forward at the pace of speech. The dynamic harmonic-motivic language found in later 18th-century symphonies and string quartets allowed composers to capture the characters' variegated moods.

Ratner lists eleven characteristics of *opera buffa* (B194, 394). These are a spectrum of affects and topics, prominence of the bass voice, short phrases and repetition of figures, quick changes of affect, many ensembles, patter songs, transparent scoring, a stock of familiar clichés, relatively short forms, pinpoint word-painting, coloratura for extravagant or parodistic effect. In addition, realistic plots, unisons, doubling between voice and orchestra, short introductions, and the dramatic importance of the concerted finale were typical.

Much of the action in *opera buffa* occurs in the first two acts and in the concerted finales. The conclusion of these finales was referred to as the *imbroglio* (or "confusion") because of the complexity of its action and music. Often the final act seemed almost an afterthought to the main action. By the 1790s, the third act was phased out; thus, for example, Mozart's last comic opera, *Così fan tutte* (1790)(W365), has only two acts.

In the 1740s, the Italian playwright Carlo Goldoni grouped the characters of his comedies into serious, comic, and "mezzi." Influenced by Goldoni, *opere buffe* of the later 18th century employed more serious characters—usually a serious pair of lovers—and more complex plots. This emotional variety is reflected in the title page designations. Thus, for example, Mozart's *Don Giovanni* (1787)(W366) is called a *dramma giocoso*, whereas Haydn's somewhat earlier *Orlando paladino* (1782)(W319) is termed a *dramma eroicomico*. The following operas, for example, employ Goldoni texts:

Baldassare Galuppi, *Il filosofo di campagna* (1754)(W310)

Niccolò Piccini, *La buona figliuola* (1760)(W401)

Mozart, *La finta semplice* (1768)(W368)

Haydn, *Lo speziale* (1768)(W320)

Florian Gassmann *La contessa* (1770)(W311)

Haydn, *Il mondo della luna* (1777)(W318)

Mozart's *Le nozze di Figaro* (1786)(W369) is the quintessential *opera buffa*. Emotional complexity and the sustained musical designs are striking, particularly in the finales. *Le nozze* is based on a libretto by Lorenzo Da Ponte, also the librettist for two of Mozart's later *opere buffe*: *Don Giovanni* (1787)(W366) and *Così fan tutte* (1790)(W365). Da Ponte used Pierre Beaumarchais's play *Le Marriage de Figaro* as his source. This play was part of a trilogy about the adventures of a barber from Seville named Figaro. As we will see in the next chapter, Rossini's *Il Barbiere di Siviglia* (W563) introduces the central character; Mozart's opera concerns his subsequent adventures. Both *Don Giovanni* and *Così fan tutte* have occasioned wide critical commentary. Their ironic tone and ambivalence toward sexuality make them strikingly modern. Intricate musical designs, particularly evident in the ensembles, allow subtle interplay among the characters.

Haydn's major contributions to comic opera have increasingly attracted attention. *Il mondo della luna* (1777)(W318) contains, as suggested by its title, a charming depiction of the world of the moon, replete with moonmen; *La vera costanza* (1779)(W321) prefigures *Le nozze di Figaro* in its juxtaposition of classes. *L'incontro improvviso* (1775)(W317), on the other hand, an example of a Turkish opera anticipates Mozart's *Die Entführung aus dem Serail*. This Haydn opera, in turn, uses Gluck's *La recontre imprévue* (1764)(W312) as its model. Haydn's *Orlando paladino* (1782)(W319) combines serious, comic, and fantastic elements and thus parallels *Don Giovanni*.

Other *opere buffe*, now rarely performed, were great successes in their day. Domenico Cimarosa's *L'italiana in Londra* (1779)(W300) has characters from different parts of the world, with the Polidoro, one of the protagonists, singing in the Neapolitan style. This *intermezzo* was so popular that it was even produced by Haydn at Esterházy. Giovanni Paisiello's *Il barbiere di Siviglia* (1782)(W395), composed for the Russian court of Catherine the Great, employs the same libretto as Rossini's famous opera. Vicente Martín y Soler's *Una cosa rara* (1786)(W358) is quoted in *Don Giovanni*, a sign of its extraordinary popularity. Paisiello's *Nina* (1789)(W396) is an example of sentimental-moral comedy influenced by the developments in English literature led by Richard Steele. The heroine undergoes various trials that manifest her virtue. Cimarosa's *Il matrimonio segreto* (1792)(W302) was his masterpiece. This tuneful opera is ultimately based on William Hogarth's series of etchings *Marriage à la mode*. Its extraordinary success can be ascribed to its rich orchestration, sentimental plot (about the adventures of a young couple), and memorable arias.

SATIRES AND BURLESQUES

At times *opere buffe* critiqued the genre itself, offering a provocative glimpse into the production-performance world of the time. Examples are Pergolesi's *Il maestro di Musica* (1731)(W398), Haydn's *La cantarina* (1766)(W315), Mozart's *Der Schauspieldirektor* (1785)(W370), and Cimarosa's *Il maestro di cappella* (1790)(W301). Pergolesi's *Il maestro di Musica* includes an aria, "Le virtuose," which lambasts singers' devices and is notable for the large leaps, high tessitura, and extensive trills. Paisiello's *Socrate Imaginario* (1775)(W397) parodies Gluck's *Orfeo* (1762), especially the scene with the Furies.

The burlesque, extravaganza, and pantomime flourished in England in the late 18th and early 19th centuries. Arrangements of songs and incidental music were featured in takeoffs on serious operas that appealed to a broad audience. Often the same performers and composers were used for both.

OTHER OPERATIC FORMS

In France the *vaudeville* and the *comédie mêlée d'ariettes* drew on melodies from well-known sources. In Spain, the terms *comedia armónica, sainete*, and *tonadilla* refer to light opera, with short scenes from the lives of common people. Ultimately, however, the word *zarzuela* was the preferred designation. The German *singspiel* anticipates Romanticism through natural melody and folklike stories.

However, the *singspiel* took on symphonic features, often sharing stylistic traits with *opera buffa*. Mozart's two later masterpieces, *Die Entführung aus dem Serail* (1782)(W367) and *Die Zauberflöte* (1791)(W371), show this connection with *opera buffa* but also represent diverse types in the history of the genre. The first, written in German at the behest of Emperor Joseph II, is an instance of a Turkish opera, whereas *Zauberflöte* is a complex fairy story with magical elements—a popular type in later 18th-century Vienna. Johann Adam Hiller was one the most influential *singspiel* composers of the later 18th century. *Lisuart und Dariolette* (1766)(W355) includes an aria, "Bald die Blonde, bald die Braune," in the style of a patter song. Carl Ditters von Dittersdorf's *Doktor und Apotheker* (1786)(W307) dominated the Viennese stage. The comic "Schlaflied des Sturmwald" is sung by one the major characters as he falls asleep. Other works that demonstrate the popular tone of the *singspiel* are Johann Standfuss's *Der Teufel ist los* (1752)(W406), based on Charles Coffey's ballad opera *The Devil to Pay*, and Ignaz Umlauf's *Der Dorfbarbier* (1796)(W407), which anticipates the operetta of the Romantic period in its easily remembered melodies.

Popular in Vienna's suburbs from the 1780s into the early 19th century, "magic" opera flourished because of folkloric roots and fantastic stories. Important examples include Philipp Hafner's *Megära, die förchterliche Hexe* (1764)(W314) and Paul Wranitzky's *Oberon, König der Elfen* (1789)(W410)—the latter on the same subject as Carl Maria von Weber's *Oberon* (1826)(W642).

Puppet operas began to appear in 17th-century Venice, but the genre reached its high point in 18th-century London and Vienna, where small-scale operas, often involving slapstick, were composed for particular companies of marionettes. Puppet plays involving music, called *fantoccini*, were usually mock-heroic or satiric. Often performance included dances, songs, and instrumental selections. A work ascribed to Haydn, *Die Feuerbrunst* (c. 1775)(W316), illustrates the kind of puppet opera performed at the elaborate marionette theater constructed at Esterházy.

Opéra comique also evolved during the 18th century. As Manfred Bukofzer points out: "After 1715 the *vaudeville* became also known as *opéra comique*—a term that had originally a parodistic connotation since it applied to parodies of serious operas. Le Sage's *Télémaque* (1715), for example, parodies the opera of the same name by Destouches" (B37, 257). The French philosopher Jean-Jacques Rousseau epitomized the *opéra comique* in *Le devin du village* (1752)(W272). Mozart's *Bastien und Bastienne* (1768)(W364) was inspired by Rousseau's work in plot and conception. François Philidor's *Tom Jones* (1765)(W400) is based on Fielding's famous novel.

André-Ernest Grétry was the most important French opera composer of the later 18th century. Among his many contributions to the genre of *opéra comique*, *La Rosière Républicaine ou La Fête de la vertue* (1794)(W313), satirizes the Catholic church. Included are a parody of the Mass and even a *Carmagnole* danced by nuns. At one point the "Pater Noster" and "Ave Maria" are sung simultaneously as a malicious tease of Catholic liturgy.

Charles Dibdin, an interesting but neglected English comic opera composer, anticipates Gilbert and Sullivan. Dibdin's *The Padlock* (1768)(W306) features a role for Mungo, a black servant, a part Dibdin himself played with great success. *The Padlock*, like the contemporary *burletta* tradition, took Italian *opera seria* as its basis for parody. The Irishman Kane O'Hara, active in London in the 1760s, is a principal figure in the creation of *burlettas,* which are close in spirit to the burlesque and pantomime types mentioned.

Antonio Rodríguez de Hita developed Spanish national opera in conjunction with the writer Don Ramón de la Cruz. *Las Labradoras de Murcia* (1769)(W402), his most famous opera, includes Spanish national dances. *La ópera casera* (1799)(W360) by Pablo del Moral is a charming example of *zarzuela*. *La ópera casera*, like some of the works cited, critiques opera conventions. The plot revolves around the search for a good bass singer to take the lead in a little opera for three voices.

Other European nations participated in the development of national opera as a way of promoting nationalism. J.I. Fomin's *The Postman* (1787)(W309) is one of many Russian operettas written during the period of Catherine the Great. This work emphasizes choruses for women and folklike melodies. Jan Antoš's *Operetta o sedlekej svoboda* (1779)(W291) reveals a Slavic character and an emphasis on the lower classes.

THE COMIC CANON

Originally, as we have seen, the canon was used to demonstrate musical erudition. By the 18th century, however, it was a favorite vocal form to convey humor. Antonio Caldara, a composer mentioned in the previous chapter, wrote hundreds of canons, apparently as a musical pastime. "Questi son canoni" (early 18th century)(W178) makes it clear that these canons were meant to make people laugh rather than to be learned exercises. Haydn, Mozart, and Beethoven all contributed amusing examples, which at times were satiric or were dedicated to a particular person. Haydn set Gottfried Lessing's "Auf einen adeligen Dummkopf" (c. 1791)(W324) about a noble nitwit, whereas "Aus Nichts wird nichts" (c. 1791)(W325) is a play of words about various meanings of nothing. Some of Mozart's canons are scatological. "Leck mich im Arsch" appears in a setting for six voices (c. 1782)(W373) and three voices (c. 1782). "Difficile lectu mihi Mars" (1788)(W372) is on a garbled Latin text with vulgar connotations, and "Lieber Freistädler" (1787)(W374) pokes fun at a friend.

Beethoven's comic canons are closely related to those of Haydn and Mozart. "Schuppanzigh ist ein Lump" (1823)(W420), is a light-hearted dedication to a favorite violinist; "Ta ta ta lieber Mäzel" (1812)(W421) imitates the ticking of Mälzel's famous metronome. This canon was used as the basis of the slow movement of the Symphony No. 8 (1812)(W433). Several canons cannot be dated with certainty. "Signor Abate," in honor of Beethoven's friend the Abbé Stadler (W421), and the detailed instruction on how to sing a scale, "Ich bitt'dich," (W419) are further instances.

COMIC PART-SONGS AND GLEES

William Billings, the most important American composer of the 18th century, wrote several satiric part-songs, including "Jargon" (1781)(W295) and "Modern Music" (1781)(W296), the latter an extended jest on musical composition. Glees, a genre mentioned previously, were written in a style simple enough that even amateurs could easily sing them at sight. Major English composers of the type include Samuel Webbe (senior and junior) and Benjamin Cooke. Cooke's "Hark! Hark, the Lark" (1774)(W304), from Shakespeare's *Cymbeline*, is homophonic; Samuel Webbe's drinking song "Now I'm Prepar'd" (early 18th century)(W290) has a fugal close.

FOLK SONGS

Robert Burns fitted his own lyrics to Scottish folk songs in *The Scots Musical Museum* (1787) (W299). Thomas Moore did the same for Irish folk songs in *Irish Melodies* (1808–34)(W359). Johann Schulz published *Lieder in Volkston bey dem Klavier zu singen* (1782)(W405), an early collection in a deliberately folklike style.

SOLO SONGS

Songs for voice and keyboard also develop into an important genre. *Die Singende Muse an der Pleisse* (1736)(R30) was a collection of dancelike keyboard pieces with the addition of texts. The simple, strophic style of this anthology influenced the development of the solo song throughout the century. Many of Haydn's earlier songs, often on texts by minor poets, participated in this simple style. Haydn, however, set Gottfried Lessing's "Lob der Faulheit" (1781)(W326) more elaborately. Disjointed phrases, a simple chordal accompaniment, and slow rhythms are used to portray laziness. "Ein 'ssehr gewöhnliche Geschichte" (1781)(W329) represents the insistent lover's knocking at the door through repeated notes. During his visits to England, Haydn composed twelve English songs (1794–95) on texts by Anne Hunter. Several of the texts are humorous, including "The Mermaid's Song" (W327) and "The Sailor's Song" (W328).

Mozart, like Haydn, usually selected lesser poets and participated in the strophic tradition of the earlier 18th century. Toward the end of his career, however, he set Goethe's "Das Veilchen" (1785)(W376) in a richly expressive style. This little song about a violet that falls in love includes expressive changes of accompaniment and harmony. "Ich möchte wohl der Kaiser sein" for bass and orchestra (1788)(W375) satirizes military pomposity.

Francis Hopkinson's "The Battle of the Kegs" (c. 1776)(W356), sung to the tune of "Yankee Doodle," grew out of an incident of the American Revolution and contrasts with the generally serious American songs of that time.

BROADSIDES

Broadside ballads were an important form of popular expression in 18th-century England. Ballads employed narrative verses, printed on one side of a folio page, that detailed current events. Broadsides, as they came to be known, were sung to well-known tunes and often included in such ballad operas as *The Beggar's Opera*. In addition, broadsides frequently were satiric, the humor heightened by their use of familiar tunes (W298).

A BURLESQUE MASS

Hans Joachim Moser discusses an extraordinary "comic" Mass by Joseph Aumann, a composer associated with Sankt Florian in Austria who died around 1795. Aumann's *Juxmesse* or *Practical Joke Mass* (later 18th century)(B164, 90–91) uses a syllabic style in quick note values so that the Latin text of the Mass sounds like stuttering. Individual syllables are sung separately, making nonsense out of the text. Furthermore, this Mass ends with odd dissonances similar to the ending of Mozart's *A Musical Joke* (W384), to be discussed at the end of the chapter.

SYMPHONIES

Increasingly by the end of the 18th century, composers grouped symphonies into cycles. Thus Mozart's last three symphonies (Nos.39-41)(Ww380-2) in E-flat major, G minor, and C major (1788) contrast comedy and tragedy. The conclusion of the Symphony No. 39 is in the hilarious style associated with Haydn, whereas the Symphony No. 40 is tragic. On the other hand, the Symphony No. 41 (*Jupiter*) combines, as we have seen, comic and heroic gestures. Many specific connections between instrumental music and *opera buffa* can be found. The finale of Mozart's Symphony No. 35 (*Haffner*) (1782)(W378) is related thematically to Osmin's aria "Solche hergelauf'ne Laffen" from Act 1 of *Die Entführung aus dem Serail*, written in the same year. The Symphony No. 38 (*Prague*) (1786)(W379), composed the year before *Don Giovanni*, anticipates many features of the opera.

On the other hand, most symphonies evidence a looser connection to the procedures of comic opera. Thus, for example, Mozart's Symphony, No. 33 in B-flat major (1779)(W377) includes a scherzolike minuet with abrupt phrase patterns followed by a finale that anticipates Rossini's patter songs. The finale of Haydn's Symphony No. 90 in C major (1788)(W339), to cite just one of many possible examples, includes comic techniques of extensive pauses and distant key juxtapositions. Elaine R. Sisman has shown that some of Haydn's symphonies of the 1770s were performed as incidental music for plays (B772). The Symphony No. 60 in C major (1774)(W335), known as *Il Distratto*, is derived from incidental music Haydn wrote for a 6 January 1776 performance of *Der*

Zerstreute, which was a German translation of *Le Distrait* by Jean François Regnard. The symphony reveals its theatrical origins in many ways: the presence of five rather than four movements and sudden tempo and character changes within the movements. Unusual effects, such as the *perdendosi* in the first movement and the *scordatura* in the last, also are found.

Haydn's Symphony No. 45 in F-sharp minor (*Farewell*) (1772)(W334) was written to remind Haydn's employer that his musicians needed a vacation. The last movement requires the orchestra to leave the stage one by one, thus employing a quasi-operatic effect. Steven Everett Paul (B328, 337) has pointed out that Paul Wranitzky's *Sinfonia Quodlibet* (c. 1798)(W411) was inspired by Haydn's work. This symphony includes a second movement based on popular operatic arias and an opening movement that is an "arrival" in which the players are given directions when to enter. The last movement, clearly inspired by the Haydn example, also gives cues for the musicians' exits. In addition, the first movement begins with a series of tunings in all the strings, similar to the procedures of the finale of Haydn's *Il Distratto* symphony.

Descriptive symphonies were written throughout the 18th century. Haydn's early cycle of symphonies: *Le matin*, *Le midi*, and *Le soir* (c. 1761) (Ww330–32) describes the passage of time from morning to evening, including a lazy afternoon and a thunderstorm at night. Of the over 120 symphonies written by Carl Dittersdorf, several are programmatic. Thus the twelve symphonies on Ovid's *Metamorphoses* (c. 1787, six of which are extant)(W308) describe passages from Ovid, with quotations included in the score. Johann Vanhal's *Sinfonia comista* (c. 1767–85)(W408) ends with a movement marked "L'allegrezza"; Luigi Boccherini's symphony *Della Casa del Diavolo* (1771)(W297) includes quotations from Gluck's ballet *Don Juan* (1761) in its finale. Leopold Mozart wrote *Sinfonia burlesca* in G (1760)(W361), whose two concluding movements are entitled "Il Signor Pantalone" and "Harlequino."

PIANO CONCERTI

Like the symphony, the solo concerto often included comic moments, particularly in finales. Haydn's Harpsichord Concerto in D major (1784)(W346) ends with a "gypsy" or "Hungarian" rondo in which the minor mode and appoggiaturas are featured. Mozart's Concerto No. 17 in G major (1784)(W386) concludes with variations on a melody said to have been sung by his pet starling. The earlier Concerto No. 9 in E-flat major (1777)(W385) begins with an unexpected interruption by the solo piano; the finales of the Concerti No. 18 in B-flat major (1784) and No. 19 in F major (1784)(W387–88) feature hunting calls and military allusions, respectively. Beethoven's first two piano concerti are quite Mozartian; thus the finales of these works are humorous. The finale of the Piano Concerto No. 1 (1795)(W436) mocks the military style and has a central gypsy-like episode; the Piano Concerto No. 2 (1798)(W437) concludes with a hunting horn finale. Again the central episode is in the gypsy style with strong syncopations. The magnificent finale of the Piano Concerto No. 3 (c. 1800)(W438) is clearly in the manner of Hungarian gypsies, with its offbeat accents and swinging rhythms.

THE TURKISH STYLE

The "alla turca" instrumental movements of the 18th century also implied comedy. Characteristics of the style were minor mode, quick appoggiaturas, and chromatic passing tones. The side drum, triangle, and cymbal were often included as extra percussion. These stylistic features and percussion instruments were intended to imitate Turkish janissary or military bands heard in 18th-century Vienna. Many so-called gypsy or Hungarian movements also imitate these instruments. The famous Turkish rondo finale of Mozart's Piano Sonata in A major (1783)(W393) was sometimes performed during the 18th century on pianos with a special pedal attached to a drum. The finale of the Violin Concerto in A major (1775)(W389), as mentioned, features a central episode in the Turkish style. The opening movement of Mozart's Piano Sonata in A minor (1778)(W392), a more subtle instance, employs the dissonance and quick appoggiaturas associated with the style.

Haydn's Symphony No. 100 (*The Military*) (1793–94)(W342) adds side drum, cymbal, and triangle for both the slow movement and the finale. Beethoven's Overture to *The Ruins of Athens* (1811)(W439) continues this tradition, as does the central episode in the finale of the Symphony No. 9 (1824)(W434).

DANCE STYLES

Certain dances were in the lighter style and could at times even connote comedy. For example, the bourrée, gigue, contredanse, and ländler were of the "low" style, rustic and buoyant. Although the minuet and polonaise were originally stately, Leonard Ratner writes, "Minuets and Polonaises grew livelier toward the end of the century, reflecting both a more frivolous life style and restlessness of the times" (B194, 9). As we have seen, in the later 18th century the minuet could be comic. Often movements not so designated used a dance style and its implications; thus many finales of the later 18th century continue to use gigue patterns.

LIGHTER INSTRUMENTAL STYLES

Such titles as *divertimento, cassation* (a term of uncertain origin), and *serenade* imply entertainment. Works of this nature go beyond the three- or four-movement norms of symphonies and concerti by including several dances and/or marches. Haydn's *Scherzandi* (c. 1760)(W345) fulfill the implications of the title through short clearly structured movements without extensive motivic development. Gregor Joseph Werner's programmatic *Musicalischer Instrumental-Calender* (1748)(W409) describes the seasonal qualities of each month.

The *Toy* Symphony in C major (c. 1760)(W363) ascribed to both Leopold Mozart and Michael Haydn, is actually a seven-movement cassation with parts for toy trumpet, drums, and rattle. Leopold Mozart's *Sinfonia da caccia* (1756)(W362), also a burlesque, is striking for its suggested addition of bugle, hunting horn, "dog yelps," "human cries," and gunshots. The first movement has the instruction "Several dogs should be barking, the others howling together, 'ho, ho,' but only for six bars."

NICKNAMES

Haydn's symphonies and quartets are notable for their sometimes humorous nicknames, usually given during the 19th century. These reflect a salient comic feature of the work. The finale of the Symphony No. 82 (*The Bear)* (1786)(W337) has a sustained drone over which a cumbersome tune is heard—like a bear dancing. The Symphony No. 83 (*The Hen)* (1785)(W338) features henlike clucking in the second idea of the first movement. The popular Symphony No. 94 (*The Surprise)* (1791)(W341) gets its nickname from an unexpected drum stroke at the beginning of the second movement. Similarly, the Symphony No. 101 (*The Clock)* (1793–94)(W343) has a ticking accompaniment in the slow movement.

The String Quartet in E-flat major (*The Joke)* (1780)(W347) ends with a movement that constantly toys with phrase lengths and sudden changes of direction. The String Quartet in D major (*The Frog)* (1787)(W348) places "croaking" appoggiaturas in the finale's main idea. The String Quartet in G minor (*The Rider)* (1793)(W349) features a propulsive rhythm in the last movement.

THE CAPRICCIO

In an article for *Clavier* (B405), I discussed the importance of the 18th-century keyboard capriccio. Continuing the tradition of the Baroque, the capriccio of the Classic period emphasized either description or structural irregularity. Haydn's Capriccio in G major (1765)(W352), based on an Austrian folk song with the title "The Castration of a Boar," is one of his most important keyboard compositions of the 1760s. This vigorous melody is presented in various keys and with contrasting keyboard figurations.

Other composers of the late Classic and early Romantic period, such as Beethoven (W442), Carl Czerny (W305), and Muzio Clementi (W303), also wrote capricci that employ distant key relations and unusual formal designs. Beethoven's Capriccio in G major (1798)(W442) was originally entitled "Alla ingharese, quasi un Capriccio," but is best known as "The Rage over a Lost Penny."

This capriccio is similar in design and style to Haydn's Capriccio just discussed, and is, I believe, influenced by it. Domenico Scarlatti's hundreds of keyboard sonatas (W404) often feature descriptive and humorous traits, sudden changes of mode or texture, and unexpected dissonance. The early sonatas of the 1730s were entitled *essercizi* but are close to the capricci because of their unusual contrasts of texture and harmony. In addition, Scarlatti's years in Spain (after 1729) inspired guitaristic effects and references to Spanish dance types. The celebrated *Cat Fugue* (c. 1730)(W403), Scarlatti's most famous sonata, has a subject based on odd intervals, which legend says was inspired by Scarlatti's cat's walking across the keyboard.

BATTLE PIECES

Continuing the tradition of the Renaissance *battaglia*, several composers wrote "battle" pieces for solo piano, inspired by famous battles of the later 18th century. James Hewitt's *The Battle of Trenton* (1792)(W354) has the step-by-step descriptions typical of the genre. F. Kocžwara's *The Battle of Prague* (c. 1788)(W357) includes ad libitum parts for violin, drum, and cello to heighten the effect. Mozart's Piano Sonata in D major (1789)(W394) begins with a trumpetlike theme and thus also alludes to the battle tradition.

VARIATIONS

Often popular arias from comic operas were chosen as themes for variations for solo piano. One of Mozart's most important sets, "Unser dummer Pöbel meint" (1784)(W391) from Gluck's opera *La Recontre imprévue* (1764), is based on a German translation of Osmin's aria "Les hommes pieusement." Mozart here explores a wide range of musical and emotional connotations, including variations emphasizing the minor mode and chromaticism.

Beethoven also composed solo variations for piano on comic arias to show off his pianistic virtuosity. Like Mozart, Beethoven preferred rhythmically active and symmetric melodies. These allowed for many and often extreme transformations. The monumental set of Variations on a Waltz by Diabelli, Op.120 (1823)(W444), although written in his late period, sublimates 18th-century practice. There are many comic moments in this titanic work, including references to Leporello's aria from Mozart's *Don Giovanni*. Beethoven's late Variations for piano trio on "Ich bin der Schneider Kakadu" from Müller's *Die Schwestern von Prag* (1803)(W445) are also related to 18th-century procedures. Each instrument of the ensemble is highlighted as the variations proceed.

MOZART'S COMIC DIVERTIMENTI

One of Mozart's earliest orchestral works is a quodlibet for orchestra composed in the Hague while he was on the way to London. The *Galimathias musicum* (W383)(1766) is an eighteen-movement divertimento that begins with an overture in the Italian style and continues with short movements based on folk melodies. No. 18 includes a fugue on the Dutch National Anthem. This work is closely related to and influenced by Leopold Mozart's burlesques (Ww361–63) and anticipates the most famous of all burlesques—Mozart's own *Ein musikalischer Spass*.

Mozart's *Ein musikalischer Spass* (1787)(W384) sums up the humorous devices discussed in this chapter. Aptly entitled "A Musical Joke," it was also referred to by Mozart as a *Dorfmusikanten-Sextett*, "a sextet for village musicians." This divertimento parodies the compositional techniques of a mediocre composer of Mozart's day. Endless sequences, repeated two-bar phrases, and compositional clichés abound. For example, the trio for the minuet includes extraneous high notes. The first and last movements employ obvious structures with trite ideas repeated without development. The thematic material of the slow movement is vapid and is supported by thin harmonies. The work ends with a surprising dissonance—as if Mozart were sticking his tongue out at all that had happened previously.

SATIRES ON MUSIC

Antonio Eximeno satirized academic musical practice in *Don Lazarillo Vizcardi* (1806)(B76). A musical novel in the manner of *Don Quixote*, *Don Lazarillo* describes the adventures of a musician deranged by his study of counterpoint. Eximeno is particularly critical of Pietro Cerone's *El Melopeo y Maestro* (1613), the treatise cited in the Renaissance chapter:

> But, everything in its place, one should speak more of the fruit of the pear tree of Bergamo, of Cerone, who belonged to the school of Nassarre. Cerone was an organist at birth and blind by profession. "It should be the other way around," said Lazarillo. "He was blind at birth and an organist by profession." "That was a *lipsus languae*," responded Agapito. But Lazarillo retorted, "You mean to say a *lapsus linguae*." (44)

DISCUSSIONS OF MUSICAL HUMOR

Samuel Johnson and Immanuel Kant analyzed the philosophic implications of wit, humor, and comedy (B249, 140 and 198). Johann Georg Sulzer's influential *Allgemeine Theorie der schöner Künste* (1798)(B230) compared the expressive potential of the arts.

Composers also were involved in this intellectual debate. Carl Ditters von Dittersdorf (B496) distinguished comic style as follows:

> Just as the serious composer must seek to interest [his audience] chiefly through the newness of his ideas, so too—I dare say it flatly—so too will the comic composer succeed to the extent that he knows how to write pieces that are easy for the public to comprehend and easy to hum afterwards. (B249, 39)

Musical humor was seen to be extravagant, original, and the product of genius. North German critics criticized Haydn for disturbing the serious nature of instrumental music, particularly because of his inclusion of the minuet within the symphonic cycle. But others saw Haydn's use of humor as a consequece of his genius.

Heinrich Cristoph Koch distinguished three styles in the *Musikalisches Lexikon* (1802): church, chamber, and theater. According to Koch: "The comic in music consists in a particular use of melodic and harmonic artfulness whereby the feeling of the laughable is raised" (B249, 235, ftnt.18). Francesco Galeazzi in the *Elementi teorico-practici de musica* (1791–96) (B82) singled out 6/8 meter for it "serves only for the expression of the comic and humorous" (B249, 38).

Karl Ludwig Junker's *Zwanzig Componisten: Eine Skizze* (1776)(B123) includes an entry on Haydn that "becomes the occasion for a lengthy excursion on the subject of musical humor" (B249, 46). In 1807, Christian Friedrich Michaelis, a student of Kant's, wrote an article entitled "Über das Humoristische oder Launige in der musickalischen Komposition," which includes the following characteristic statement:

> The humorous composer distinguishes himself through curious fancies that provoke smiles; he disregards the conventional, and without violating the rules of harmony—indeed often with the finest use of contrapuntal art— his imagination sets in motion such an amusing game with the melody and accompaniment that one is astonished at the newness, the uniqueness, the unexpected; and because all the bold modulations and lively variety combine in a beautiful, interesting whole, it is attractive and delightful. (B249, 196)

Chapter 6

The Romantic Period

ITALIAN COMIC OPERA

Strong relationships exist between 18th- and 19th-century Italian comic opera, of which the following are the principal:

1. The use of secco recitative
2. Clear divisions between the sections
3. The use of the ensemble finale to climax acts
4. Libretti based on *commedia dell' arte*
5. The occasional use of Turkish subjects
6. Coloratura arias for the principal characters
7. The use of the *basso buffo* with large leaps
8. Repeated cadence patterns and formulas at the ends of arias
9. The occasional use of a smaller orchestra than was typical of the early 19th century

Rossini's *Il Barbiere di Siviglia* (1816)(W563) and Donizetti's *L'elisir d'amore* (1832)(W494) and *Don Pasquale* (1843)(W493), for example, continue the light harmonic style, the emphasis on flowing melody, and libretti derived from *commedia dell' arte* of 18th-century comic opera. Donizetti's *La fille du régiment* (1840)(W495) first appeared as an *opéra comique* in Paris and then was turned into an *opera buffa* with the title *La figlia del reggimento*, illustrating the connection between the two types. This work is notable for its mixture of military tunes and elegant arias. Rossini's *Il Barbiere,* on the same libretto as that used by Paisiello in the 18th century, established a brilliant model for later comic operas. Originally a failure, *Il Barbiere* quickly became the most successful comic opera of the century, largely because of its memorable patter-song arias and exuberant finales. Rosina's delicious aria "Una voce poco fa" is characteristic of the work's elegance.

Other Rossini operas were immediately popular. *L'italiana in Algeri* (1813)(W567), the first of his major operas in two-act form, is typical of the lighthearted exoticism favored in the early part of the 19th century. *La Cenerentola* (1817)(W564) is based on the Cinderella story, but with some significant changes in the characters (the wicked stepmother, for example, becomes a father). The mezzo-soprano lead has one of the most challenging roles in the operatic literature. Rapid ornamentation and rhythmic energy highlight this brilliant masterpiece, which has recently received increasing attention. *La gazza ladra* (1817)(W566) is an example of the *semiseria* genre, or comedy mixed with serious elements, thus continuing the tradition of some of the later comic operas of Haydn and Mozart. It also continues the kind of sentimental comedy found in Paisiello's *Nina* (W396). *Le Comte Ory* (1828)(W365) was originally a one-act *vaudeville*, based on the exploits of a real-life adventurer named Count Ory. Notable in this opera are the extended ensembles and the powerful delineation of the principal character, reminiscent of Mozart's Don in *Don Giovanni* (W366). The scene in which the count and his men are disguised as nuns alternates carousing and prayer and thus inspires parody of Catholic ritual.

GERMAN COMIC OPERA

The *Liederspiel* was an early 19th-century effort to stem what was felt to be the unnaturalness of much contemporary opera. Inspired by aesthetics of Goethe, Johann Friedrich Reichardt's *Lieb und Treue* (1800)(W559) uses folk texts as the basis for simple songs. Although this genre was short-lived, it continued to influence the German 19th-century *Singspiel*. Carl Maria von Weber's *Peter Schmoll und seine Nachbaren* (1803)(W643) and *Abu Hassan* (1811)(W644) already suggest their composer's talent. *Abu Hassan,* still known because of its charming overture, continues the tradition of the Turkish comic opera. Schubert wrote many short comic operas, including *Die Verschworren* (1823)(W575). In addition, Mendelssohn wrote five *singspielen* and an opera based on Cervantes's *Don Quixote, Die Hochzeit des Camacho* (1827)(W538), his only complete opera.

Wagner's *Die Meistersinger von Nürnberg* (1863)(W637) is derived from actual events from the history of mastersingers of 16th-century Germany. Striking are the many imposing choruses and the deft treatment of Hans Sachs, the protagonist. Wagner employs musical parody at several points of the score—the most famous occurs in Beckmesser's song in the last act with its excessive melismas and odd melodic contours. The "Tailor's Chorus" parodies Rossini's *Tancredi* (1813), reflecting Wagner's contempt of Italian opera. However, Wagner's Ring Cycle includes several interludes and characters that are, at least in part, humorous. For example, at the opening of *Siegfried* (1876)(W638), the third opera of the cycle, a scene occurs between Siegfried and the dwarf Mime during which Mime tries to trick a rather simple-minded Siegfried into believing that he loves him as a father.

Albert Lortzing's *Zar und Zimmermann* (1837)(W535), close in structure and style to operetta, includes sentimental songs that ensured its popularity. Peter Cornelius's *Der Barbier von Bagdad* (1885–88)(W485), one of the most brilliant comic operas of the 19th century, continues the 18th-century tradition of Turkish opera while employing the full resources of the Romantic orchestra. Engelbert Humperdinck's *Hänsel und Gretel* (1893)(W519), on a fairytale by Grimm, uses leitmotifs and rich chromaticism to capture the magic of the original story.

Mahler's completion of Carl Maria von Weber's *Die drei Pintos* (1888)(W640) was his only operatic effort. Mahler's operatic imagination is evident in his realization of this charming comic masterpiece. Hugo Wolf's *Der Corregidor* (1896)(W645), based on a story by the Mexican writer Pedro Antonio de Alarcón, is, by the composer's own admission, based on *Meistersinger*.

OPERAS BASED ON SHAKESPEARE

Shakespeare's plays inspired many comic operas. For example, Otto Nicolai's *Lustigen Weiber von Windsor* (1849)(W550) features Falstaff, a major character in *The Merry Wives of Windsor* and *Henry IV*. Nicolai's charming work anticipates the energy and subject matter of Verdi's *Falstaff* (1893)(W632). Wagner's early opera *Das Liebesverbot* (1836)(W636) is based on *Measure for Measure*; Berlioz's *Béatrice et Bénédict* (1862)(W447) employs *Much Ado About Nothing*. Verdi's *Falstaff*, based on a masterly libretto by Arrigo Boïto, is the period's major setting of a Shakespeare comedy. This opera is notable for its complex harmonies and cohesive large-scale design. The final scene in the garden reflects Mendelssohn's music for *A Midsummer Night's Dream* (W540), and the opera ends with a brilliant fugue whose text states that all the world is a joke. Also notable is a humorous quotation from *La Traviata* in Act 1. The rarely performed earlier opera, *Un giorno di regno* (1840)(W633), is Verdi's only other comic opera.

FRENCH COMIC OPERA OF THE 19TH CENTURY: *OPÉRA COMIQUE* AND OPERETTA

Opéra comique and, later, operetta dominate the French operatic stage of the 19th century. The 1817 Paris performance of Rossini's *L'Italiana in Algeri* (1813)(W567) inspired his French contemporaries. Daniel-François-Esprit Auber's *Fra Diavolo* (1820)(W415) includes rhythms from the polka and gallop, dances just coming into vogue. François Boieldieu's *La dame blanche*

(1825)(W456), based on a novel by Walter Scott, emphasizes melodious arias, simple accompaniments, and climactic ensembles.

Charles Gounod captured the spirit of *commedia dell' arte* in *Le Medecín Malgré Lui* (1858)(W512), based on Molière's play by that name. Camille Saint-Saëns composed several comic operas. Perhaps the most important are *La princesse jaune* (1872)(W572) and *Phryné* (1893)(W571). *La princesse jaune* is set in Japan and employs a number of authentic melodies.

PARODIES

Johann Nestroy (1801–62), an actor, playwright, and singer, played a major role in the development of opera parodies by taking well-known tunes from operas and substituting comic texts. For example, a parody was written on Wagner's *Tannhäuser* in 1857 with music by Carl Binder. Berlioz's *Le damnation de Faust* (1846)(W448) includes a tavern scene in which drunken students sing a sterile fugue on the word *Amen*, thus spoofing academic and religious music. As we have seen, Rossini's *Le Comte Ory* (W365) includes a similar scene.

NATIONALISM AND OPERA

Mikhail Glinka's *A Life for the Czar* (originally *Ivan Susanin*) (1836)(W506) sparked operatic nationalism. Glinka highlighted the energy of the opera with various instrumental interludes, including the celebrated *Dance of the Comedians* for the final act. The libretto for Glinka's later opera *Ruslan and Ludmila* (1842)(W507) is based on a poem by Alexander Pushkin, an author whose work was also used as the basis of operas by Tchaikovsky and Rimsky-Korsakov. Rimsky-Korsakov's *Le Coq d'Or* (1909)(W561) blends oriental color with a clever satire about the Russian-Japanese War of 1905–8.

Modeste Mussorgsky left *Sorochintsy Fair* (1874–80)(W542), based on a story by Nikolai Gogol, incomplete at the time of his death, but it was finished by Nikolai Tcherepnin and others. Perhaps the most significant comic opera within the nationalistic tradition, Bedřich Smetana's *The Bartered Bride* (1866)(W607), is striking for its sparkling orchestration. The brilliant and popular overture sets the tone for this opera, which explores the often amusing marriage arrangements of the 19th century. *The Kiss* (1876)(W608) maintains the brilliance of *The Bartered Bride*.

OPERETTA AND MUSICAL COMEDY

Related to such previous types as *singspiel*, *intermezzo*, and ballad opera, operetta was influenced by cabaret music in London, Vienna, and Paris. Jacques Offenbach's *Orphée aux Enfers* (1858)(W553) and *La belle Hélène* (1864)(W551) both satirize Greek mythology; *La Périchole* (1868)(W554), based on the life of a famous Peruvian actress, includes exoticism. Offenbach also continued the French tradition of poking fun at opera. Thus *Orphée* parodies an aria from Gluck's *Orfeo* and includes a cancan for the gods, and *Belle Hélène* features a patriotic chorus based on a chorus from Rossini's *Guillaume Tell* (1829). Emmanuel Chabrier's *L'Etoile* (1877)(W476) continues the Offenbach tradition of *opéra bouffe* with a satiric story about sedition and public executions.

Until 1871, Suppé's operettas held the Viennese stage, but in that year Johann Strauss's *Indigo und die vierzig Raüber* (W613) established the Viennese type. *Die Fledermaus* (1874)(W612), with its New Year's theme and melodious waltzes, is still one of the most popular of all operettas. Many operettas imitate this charming example—Franz Lehár's *Die lustige Witwe* (1905)(W521) is an instance. This nostalgic masterpiece features an exquisite waltz as its main idea. Franz von Suppé's *Boccaccio* (1879)(W628) deals with the opposition between a brilliant hero and the world around him. Michael Balfe's *The Bohemian Girl* (1843)(W416) was the most popular English operetta before the works of Gilbert and Sullivan. It explores the superficial exoticism then in vogue. However, Gilbert and Sullivan's operettas soon dominated the English-speaking world. *Cox and Box* (1866)(W621) and *Trial by Jury* (1875)(W627)—the first operetta created by this team—already reveal a gift for gently satirizing contemporary practices. Such later operettas as *H.M.S Pinafore* (1878)(W622) and *The Mikado* (1885)(W623) epitomize Victorian England. The former mocks English naval practices, and the latter lampoons colonialism and orientalism.

Gilbert and Sullivan's operettas also parody opera. For example, *The Pirates of Penzance* (1879)(W625) contains a mock-heroic duet in the Verdian style. Mabel's Waltz Song is a takeoff on the coloratura aria, and the Major-General's aria satirizes fugues. Vigorous refrain choruses often frame these arias or ensembles, creating structures that parallel those of grand opera. Patter songs attained popularity as individual numbers because of their clever wordplay and catchy rhythms. "My Name Is John Wellington Wells" from *The Sorcerer* (1877)(W626), the Major-General's song from *The Pirates of Penzance*, and Colonel Calverly's "If You Want a Receipt" from *Patience* (1881)(W624) are memorable examples.

RELATED OPERATIC TYPES

By the late 18th century, the *zarzuela* led to such comic offshoots as the *tonadilla*—considered in a previous chapter. Like operetta, the *zarzuela* includes dialogue, satire, and nationalistic dances—often on typical Spanish rhythms. Francisco Barbieri's *El Barbarillo de Lavapiés* (1874)(W417) remains one of the most popular, with its energetic "La Paloma" often sung on concert recitals. Countless other *zarzuelas* by such composers as Pablo Luna, Ruperto Chapí, and Federico Chueca still hold the Spanish stage. Isaac Albéniz, principally known for his piano compositions, wrote *Pepita Jiménez* (1896) in the *zarzuela* tradition (W412).

AMERICAN MUSICAL COMEDY

The origins of musical comedy lie in the minstrel show and vaudeville. By the end of the 18th century, *olios* connected songs by a general theme. The minstrel show, appearing in the United States in 1843, employed a troupe of entertainers who portrayed members of the underclass—particularly blacks—through stereotypes and exaggerated features. Minstrel shows combined song with comic episodes, each having autonomy. The musical sources for these shows were many: popular melodies of the time, favorite tunes from Ireland and England, and Italianate melodies. Blackface, or white performers in vivid clothing and in heavy black makeup, was also typical. Dan Emmett, a major figure at the end of the 19th century, composed such still-popular songs as "Dixie" (W503) and "Turkey in the Straw" (W502) .

The Black Crook (1866)(W455), a parody of Gounod's *Faust* (1859) and the first musical comedy, includes songs by several composers. Edward E. Rice's *Evangeline* (1874)(W560) was the first musical comedy whose songs were all written by the same composer. These early examples, composed about the same time as Gilbert and Sullivan's and Offenbach's operettas, rely on the popular styles of the day. Music was clearly secondary to the loosely constructed action, which relied heavily on broad humor and farce. Musical comedy was also indebted to vaudeville. By the later 19th century, vaudeville mixed popular songs, dancers, comedians, and acrobats into a series of vignettes. Like the minstrel show, vaudeville featured lilting songs with slapstick and sometimes vulgar humor. In general, vaudeville was associated with cities, principally those in the North, and was less directly related to the slave experience.

Such works as John Philip Sousa's *El capitan* (1895)(W609) and Victor Herbert's *Babes in Toyland* (1903)(W516) and *Naughty Marietta* (1910)(W517) began the American tradition. Whereas Herbert's musical comedies employ many elements of the Viennese operetta, Sousa's *El capitan* features vigorous "American" marches.

GERMAN COMIC SONGS

The development of the lied through more complex structures, richer accompaniments, and varied harmonies invited comic expression. One of Beethoven's earliest songs, "Elegie auf den Tod eines Pudels" (c. 1790)(W424), laments the death of a poodle. The two settings of "L'amante Impaziante" (1798)(W423)—the one serious, the other marked *arietta buffa*—reveal how a musical setting can change the meaning of a text. "Das Flohlied aus Faust"

(1809)(W425), on a text from Goethe's *Faust*, features short motives and appoggiaturas to depict flea bites.

Schubert created the narrative-dramatic song cycle. *Die schöne Müllerin* (1823)(W581) consists of twenty lively songs on poems by Wilhelm Müller. Individual songs are often striking for their humor. "Heiden Röslein" (1815)(W583), on a folklike poem by Goethe, narrates a conversation between a young man and a hedge rose with a simple melody and repeated chord accompaniment." "Die Forelle" (c. 1817)(W582) is a humorous song about a trout splashing through the waves, depicted by a repeated ascending figure in the piano. This song is featured in a set of variations for the final movement of the Quintet for Piano and Strings (1819)(W588).

Robert Schumann's interest in Robert Burns's folk poems is reflected in a set of songs that appears in a collection known as *Myrthen* (1840). "Jemand" and "Niemand" (W595), both after Burns, form a contrasting set that captures the irony of the poetry. "Räthsel" (W597), from the same collection, is based on a setting after Byron. Featured here is a play on words, each beginning with the letter *h* (the German abbreviation for *B* natural). "Der Hidalgo" (1840)(W594) begins with the text "It is sweet to jest with songs." "Die beide Grenadiere" (1840)(W592) narrates the fabulous exploits of the two soldiers. "Der Contrabandiste" (1849)(W593) begins with the text "I am a smuggler. I know how to scare everyone. So I am merry." Among other humorous songs by Schumann, one could cite "Ein Jungling liebt ein Mädchen" (W596) and "Schlusslied des Narren" (W598).

Carl Loewe's large-scale ballades offered many opportunities to depict humorous or dramatic texts with elaborate piano accompaniments. "Die Katzenkönigin" (1837)(W533) is, as the title implies, about the queen of the cats; "Hochzeitslied" (1832)(W532) "Die Wandelnde Glocke" (1832)(W534) are settings of humorous poetry by Goethe.

Johannes Brahms often employed folklike texts by minor poets. "Vergebliches Ständchen" (1882)(W466) is a serenade of a young man to his girlfriend, who refuses him the door. "Blinde Kuh" (1871)(W462), a representation of blind man's buff, has a busy sixteenth-note accompaniment supporting the narrative. "Der Schmied" (1858)(W464), about a blacksmith, presents a triadic melody over an energetic accompaniment descriptive of the anvil's blows. Other humorous examples include "Den Wirbel schlag ich" (1877)(W463), a song about playing the tambourine, and "Unüberwindlich" (1876)(W465).

Hugo Wolf grouped his lieder according to sources of poetry. His settings of poetry by Eduard Möricke (1889), for instance, include several humorous songs. "Abschied" (W648) ends with a parody of waltz style; "Elfenlied" (W650) plays on *Elf* and *Elfen*, or elf and the German word for eleven. "Der Tambour" (W652) is about a drummer boy whose mother is a witch. "Nimmersatte Liebe" (W651), from the same collection, alternates short phrases between piano and voice part to imply the yearning of unsatisfied love. Wolf set folk poetry from the collections known as the *Italienisches Liederbuch* (1892, 96) and *Spanisches Liederbuch* (1891). "Mausfallen Sprüchlein" (W647), a song about how to catch a mouse, is found in this latter collection. The *Spanisches Liederbuch* includes one of Wolf's best known songs, "Auf dem Grünen Balkon" (W649), a serenade in which the piano imitates the sound of a guitar. "Mein Liebster ist so klein" (W646) from the Italian collection describes the beloved with small intervals and pianissimo dynamics.

Mahler often used texts from *Des Knaben Wunderhorn* (1888–1900), folk poetry collected in the early 19th century by Arnim and Brentano. "Des Antonius von Padua Fischpredigt" (W832) typifies Mahler's humor and employs, as is often the case, a folklike melody. It later appeared in the third movement of the Symphony No. 2 (1894)(W838). "Lob des hohen Verstands" (W833) is about a contest between a cuckoo and a nightingale, with a donkey awarding the prize to the cuckoo. Other humorous songs from *Des Knaben Wunderhorn* include "Rheinlegendchen" (W834) and "Wer hat dies Liedlein erdacht" (W835).

COMIC SONGS IN OTHER LANGUAGES

Modeste Mussorgsky's *The Nursery* (1870)(W543) reflects a child's view of the world. In addition, Mussorgsky composed a setting of Goethe's "Song of the Flea" (1880)(W547) on the text also used by Beethoven. An extended song in the manner of a scene, "The Puppet Show" (1870)(W545) satirizes Mussorgsky's critics. Included is a parody of typical Italian opera cadential formulas. "The Seminarian" (1870)(W546), a song about a young love-struck seminarian who cannot concentrate on his Latin, mixes Latin and Russian texts.

Rossini, Donizetti, and Verdi composed some songs in dialect; others are serenades, or street and gondola songs. In 1836, Donizetti published a collection of songs with the title *Nuits d'été à Pausilippe*. "A mezzanotte" (W497) is a midnight serenade in which the lover speaks of the presence of a third person namely, love; "La Connochia" (W496), a song in the Neapolitan dialect, tells of a young woman who parades in front of a window when she wants her young man to notice her. Verdi's *Sei Romanze* of 1845 set texts by Felice Romani, famous as an opera librettist. "Lo spazzacamino" (W634) is about a chimneysweep who scares little children. The accompaniment, which employs a waltz style, highlights the hidden irony of the text. "Stornello" (1869)(W635), on an anonymous text, describes a young women's absolute freedom.

Rossini's "La regata veneziana" (c. 1830)(W565) is cantatalike because of its many sections and narrative development. Each event of the regata is described in a separate song, with the influence of the barcarolle evident throughout. Giacomo Puccini often wrote songs for special occasions. "Avanti Urania" (1896)(W557) praises Puccini's boat, *Urania*; "E'l'ucellino" (1899)(W558) is an example of a *ninna-nanna*, or lullaby.

As Frits Noske (B174, 35) points out, the term *chansonette* implied a short French song on a light text. Obviously influenced by this tradition, Richard Wagner wrote the song "Les deux grenadieres" (1840)(W639), a French version of the Heine poem set by Schumann. Like Schumann, Wagner quotes "La Marseillaise" at the end. Georges Bizet's "La coccinelle" (1868)(W452) is based on a fable by Victor Hugo. Léo Delibes was an important comic song writer as well as opera composer. Noske writes: "Among Delibes's youthful works are a number of comic chansons and *chansonettes* (e.g., 'Les animaux de Granville,' [W487] 'Le code fashionable,' [W488] and 'La taxe sur la viande' [W491]). They appeared between 1850 and 1860 in various journals such as *Paris Magazine* and *Le Journal des dames et des demoiselles*" (B174, 209). Of the songs that are more generally accessible, "Les filles de Cadiz," also known as "Chanson espagnole," from *Trois mélodies* (1863)(W490), uses a habanera rhythm. Édouard Lalo's "Ballade à la lune" (1860)(W520) is on a text by Alfred de Musset. Noske writes: "He courageously assaults that moon, which no one had dared to set to music, and makes of it a masterpiece" (B174, 240).   Emmanuel Chabrier's wit and sense of musical parody are evident in the "Ballade du gros dindons" (1890) (W477), which quotes the serenade from *Don Giovanni*.

SKITS AND ROASTS

By the mid-19th century, German beer gardens spawned music for entertainment, and 19th-century social clubs devoted to satire also included skits with humorous songs (B232). The *Liedertafel*, or song table, was a social organization that influenced the development of songs for male quartet. The first was founded by Carl Friedrich Zelter in 1809 for music and drinking; with the 1848 Revolutions, these organizations sang lieder that often had ironic undertones.

Founded in 1885, the American Gridiron Club served as a model for many subsequent organizations that sponsored "roasts," or humorous parodies of famous persons or professions. Popular songs, often with new texts suitable to the occasion, were always featured. This development of social music is mirrored in the vocal repertory considered in the next few sections.

SONGS FOR MUSIC HALLS

British songs for music halls employ texts that are humorous or sentimental, supported by simple accompaniments and strophic structures with piano interludes (Rr31–32). "Bacon & Beans" (R31) is described as "Original Songs Composed and Sung by Mr. Sam Cowell with immense applause at his popular concerts throughout England, Ireland, & Scotland." Another song typical of this type, "Champagne Charlie," is a multistanzaic narrative, which highlights the refrain "Champagne Charlie is my name, good for any game at nights, my boys" (R32).

CANONS AND PART-SONGS

About 1817, Schubert wrote several canonic May songs, such as "Willkommen, lieber schöner Mai" (W577) and "Der Schnee zerrint, der Mai beginnt" (W576). Mendelssohn's canon "Freund Felix ist ein guter Mann" begins: "Friend Felix is a good man. He teaches all he can: Canon, Fuga, Basso Ostinato, Passacaglio. Eviva, Contrapunto" (c. 1840)(W539). Schumann's convivial drinking canon "Gebt mir zu trinken," (1847)(W590) is one of eight canons in the German folksong tradition. Two of Brahms's canons use dialect: "Sitz a shön's Vogelrn auf'm Dannabaum" (c. 1860–63)(W459) and "Ein' Gems auf dem Stein" (c. 1860–63)(W458).

Schubert composed comic part-songs, of which "Die Advokaten" (1812)(W578) is an example. "Edit nonus, edit clerus" (1825)(W579) is a setting of a 14th-century drinking song for unaccompanied male quartet; "Trinklied im Mai" (1816) (W580) is also a drinking song. Robert Schumann's "Der Rekrut" (1844)(W591), on a German translation of a Robert Burns poem, highlights the text's play of words on soldiering.

Peter Cornelius uses ironic wordplay in "Nichts ohne Liebe" (1842)(W486). Brahms wrote many part-songs, including "Erlaube mir, feins Mädchen" (c. 1880)(W461) and "Da unten im Tale" (c. 1880)(W460), the latter example's sing-song verse caught through the symmetry of Brahms's setting.

Rossini's "Toast pour le nouvel an" (1824)(W569) is a New Year's drinking song for a capella ensemble. This is one of many such ensemble songs stylistically akin to his opera choruses. The "Duetto buffo di due gatti" (W568), ascribed to Rossini, is the most famous part-song of the period. It is a vocalise for two voices that imitates the sounds of cats' meowing, but according to Philip Gossett, this work is not by Rossini. He writes: "Its first section is a 'Katte-Cavatine' written earlier in the century by the Danish composer Christoph Ernst Friedrich Weyze. Both the second and third sections are adaptations from Rossini's opera seria, *Otello* (1816). The arranger is one G. Berthold, a German musician active in the 1820's and 1830's" (B546).

COMIC BALLET

The Nutcracker (1892)(W630), a whimsical treatment of a story by E.T.A. Hoffmann, is Tchaikovsky's only ballet with touches of comedy. The well-known suite from this work, premiered in the same year as the ballet, highlights the various toys that come to life in the child's dream of Christmas. Particularly striking is the "Dance of the Clowns" at the end. A story by E.T.A. Hoffmann also inspired Léo Delibes's *Coppélia* (1870)(W492), one of the most important French ballet scores of the period. This work mixes comedy with fantasy and features a mechanical doll, also a device in one of the episodes of Offenbach's opera *Les contes d'Hoffmann* (1881)(W552).

Other comic ballets were created from preexistent music, often for piano. For example, Schumann's *Carnaval* (1835)(W600), to be discussed later in this chapter, served as the basis for *Le Carnaval*, first produced in St. Petersburg in 1910 with choreography by Michel Fokine. The loosely organized scenario refers to Schumann's life as well as the *commedia dell' arte* characters implicit in Schumann's original piano work.

COMEDY IN BEETHOVEN'S INSTRUMENTAL MUSIC

The composer-theorist Ferruccio Busoni was the first 20th-century author to emphasize Beethoven's comic powers. His essay "Beethoven and Musical Humor" (B450) offers a provocative look at a composer who is generally thought exclusively serious or tragic.

As we have seen in the previous chapter, Beethoven often participated in the witty techniques of Haydn and Mozart. The Serenade in D, Op. 8 (1797)(W440) reflects the 18th-century tradition in its ebullient dances and comic turns of phrase. It begins and ends with a humorous march. The Piano Trios, Op. 1 (1795)(W441), include scherzi with unexpected changes of register, quick tempi, and playful thematic material. The minuet of the Symphony No. 1 (1800) is actually a scherzo (W426). The *Eroica* Symphony (1803)(W428) features an expansive scherzo with humorous contrasts, particularly in the raucous horn trio. All nine of Beethoven's symphonies (Ww426–34) include comedy. Thus the last movement of the Symphony No. 1 (1800) begins with a halting introduction, and the finale of the Symphony No. 2 (1802) is imbued with the spirit of *opera buffa*. The Symphony No. 4 (1806) presents a humorous solo for bassoon just before the rushing scales at the conclusion; the heroic Symphony No. 5 (1808) has a comic trio in the scherzo with gruff scales for the double basses.

Composed in 1812, the Symphony No. 8 strongly contrasts with the Symphony No. 7 (1812) not only in dimension but in emotional tone. In addition, all the movements reflect traits of Italian comic opera. For example, the first movement concludes with a sudden piano cadence after a brief quotation of the opening idea. The second movement is based on Beethoven's own canon (W422), mentioned previously in this chapter. The repeated staccato chords of the canon become the movement's pervasive feature. The finale, the most hilarious of all, is dominated by a busy repeated-note idea. Throughout this movement the bassoon and timpani have odd duets based on the octave leap. An extended crescendo occurs toward the end, followed by a cadence that delays the conclusion with many false starts and stops. The Battle Symphony (*Wellington's Victory*) (1813)(W435) is replete with cannon effects and quotations of "God Save the King," "Rule Britannia," and the French marching tune that we know as "For he's a Jolly Good Fellow." This descriptive work, clearly intended to please the public, continues the tradition of battle pieces begun, as we have seen, in the Renaissance.

String quartets and piano sonatas of a given opus often include one comic work to contrast with the other, more serious compositions. The Piano Sonatas Op. 31 (1802) in G major, D minor, and E-flat major serve as an example. The central sonata is flanked by sonatas that are lighter. The third sonata of the series (W443) emphasizes short phrases, unexpected contrasts, and staccato articulations. The second movement sounds like a German student song; the tarantella-like finale has a sometimes erratic accompaniment.

On a smaller scale, the *Bagatelles* Op. 126 (1824)(W446) suggest such Viennese popular styles as the waltz and contredanse. The last bagatelle contrasts a slow, meditative section with an explosive series of chords—a technique found in many later string quartets and piano sonatas.

MENDELSSOHN'S *A MIDSUMMER NIGHT'S DREAM*

Mendelssohn's incidental music to Shakespeare's *A Midsummer Night's Dream* (W540) was completed in 1843. Its celebrated overture, however, was composed in 1826, when Mendelssohn was only seventeen. Both the overture and the scherzo from the incidental music emphasize pianissimi and quick string figurations and repeated chords. These techniques, used to conjure up Shakespeare's world of fantasy and mystery, are typical of many other Mendelssohn scherzi, such as that for the Octet for Strings (1825)(W541).

THE SYMPHONY

Schubert's Symphony No. 6 (1818)(W584), known as *The little C major*, emphasizes high-spirited comedy. Bizet's popular Symphony in C (1855)(W453) is clearly modeled on the *buffa* style. Although Brahms's Symphony No. 4 (1885)(W467) is generally tragic, its scherzo is notably energetic and playful as is the march movement in Tchaikovsky's Symphony No. 6 (*Pathetique*) (1893)(W629). William Henry Fry, the American composer, wrote a *Santa Claus* symphony (1853)(W505), which includes parts for saxophone, whip, and sleigh bells. String glissandi are used to depict the howling of the winds.

Franz Berwald's Symphony No. 2 (*Capricieuse*) (1842)(W451) has a finale that features startling changes of pattern. Similarly, Schumann's *Overture, Scherzo, and Finale* (1840)(W599), actually a symphonic work, contrasts with his other symphonies by reason of its lighter orchestration and emphasis on staccato articulation. Ludwig Spohr's symphonies continue the tradition of the 18th-century programmatic symphony: No. 6 (*Historical*) (1839)(W610) is a self-conscious reflection of past styles verging on caricature; No. 9 (*The Seasons*) (1847)(W611) continues the descriptive approach of Vivaldi and Haydn.

Parody, sometimes involving toy instruments, is found in a number of instrumental works. Etienne-Nicolas Méhul featured toy instruments in the *bur-*

lesque grotesque (early 19th century)(W536), one of several works of the time that imitate the 18th-century "Toy" symphony.

DANCES

In Germany and Austria, such composers as Joseph Lanner and the Strauss family wrote many dances for chamber groups or orchestra. Not only waltzes, but also polkas, quadrilles, and marches bore individual titles, referring to persons, contexts, or styles. This is seen in the following examples by Johann Strauss II (from the 1860s and early 1870s)(Ww614–20):

> *Die Jovialen* Op. 34
> *Motor-Quadrille* Op. 129
> *Tritsch-Tratsch Polka* Op. 241
> *Wiener Bonbons* Op. 307
> *Freut euch des Lebens* Op. 340
> *Tik-Tak Polka* Op. 365
> *Kuss-walzer* Op. 400

Dance styles and rhythms often inspired lighter instrumental music intended for concert performances. For example, Emmanuel Chabrier's *Bourrée Fantasque* (1891)(W479) transforms the rhythm of the Baroque dance. Dances from comic operas provide *divertissements* and plangent color. The *Furiant-Polka-Dance of the Comedians* from Smetana's *The Bartered Bride* (1866) (W607) illustrates this, as do the dances from Glinka's *Life for the Tsar* (1836)(W506) and Borodin's *Prince Igor* (1887)(W457).

SERENADES AND OVERTURES

Brahms's first two orchestral works were serenades influenced by Haydn: Serenade No. 1 in D major (1858)(W468) and Serenade No. 2 in A major (1859)(W469). Dancelike and energetic movements prevail in these works. Wolf's *Italienische Serenade* (1892)(W653) evokes the atmosphere of Italy through tarantella rhythms.

Berlioz's overture *Le carnaval romain* (1841)(W450), inspired by a stay in Rome during his student years, describes the hurly-burly of a carnival through brilliant string figurations and sudden changes of texture. Brahms's *Academic Festival Overture* (1880)(W470) was dedicated to the University of Breslau in recognition of the honorary doctorate awarded him in 1879. It quotes a number of melodies associated with German student life, including "Gaudeamus igitur." Wagner's Prelude to *Meistersinger* (1868)(W637) telescopes the major ideas of the opera, from the magnificent opening to the satiric diminution of the main idea with staccato bassoon accompaniment.

Rossini usually prefaced an opera with a preexistent overture. Such Rossini overtures as those for *Il barbiere di Siviglia* (1816)(W563) and *La gazza ladra*

(1817)(W569) emphasize mercurial figurations and sustained crescendi. Schubert's two *Overtures in the Italian Style* in C and D major (1817)(W586), influenced by Italian comic opera, are similar to the overtures of Rossini.

CHAMBER MUSIC

Schubert's Quintet for Piano and Strings (1819)(W588), *Die Forelle*, uses his own song (W582) as the theme for light-hearted variations that form the fourth movement. The Octet in F major (1824)(W587) reflects the divertimenti of Haydn and Mozart in its multimovement organization and wind instrumentation. Mendelssohn's Octet for Strings (1825)(W541) includes, as we have seen, a scherzo reminiscent of his music for *A Midsummer Night's Dream*.

Dvořák's Piano Quintet in A major (1887)(W500) was clearly modeled on Schubert's Piano Quintet in tonality, style, and restrained treatment of the piano. Brahms's String Quartet No. 3 in B-flat major (1876)(W471), in contrast to the two previous quartets, is good-natured and bucolic. In the article "Humour in Chamber Music," for *Cobbett's Cyclopedic Survey of Chamber Music* (B367), the editor Walter Willson Cobbett lists a number of humorous chamber works by obscure composers. These include Carl Friedrich Graf's *Economical Duet for Two Performers on One Violin*, Op. 27 (W514), and J. Holbrooke's *Pickwick Quartet* (W518). Cobbett further writes of M. Kassmayer: "Spoken of by Riemann as a musical humorist of the first order. [He wrote] thirteen humorous settings in counterpoint for string quartet of folk-songs of various nations" (B367, v. 1, 580).

CAPRICES: ORCHESTRAL AND FOR SOLO VIOLIN

In the 19th century, the term *capriccio* implied a brilliant, often descriptive work, with striking instrumental effects. Thus Tchaikovsky's *Capriccio italien* (1880)(W631) is inspired by Italian street songs, while Dvořák's *Scherzo capriccioso* (1883)(W499) combines two comic genres. Mikhail Glinka's *Capriccio brillante on the Jota aragonesa* (1845)(W508), written while he was in Madrid, features guitarlike effects and the Spanish *jota*. Rimsky-Korsakov's *Capriccio Español* (1887)(W562) uses many authentic Spanish dance styles and instrumental colors.

Anthony Philip Heinrich, the so-called American Beethoven, delighted in prolixity and exaggeration. Most of his compositions are in the tradition of the capriccio because of their bizarre contrasts, such as the orchestral tone poem *Pushmataha, a Venerable Chief of a Western Tribe of Indians* (1831)(W515), which concludes with a quotation of "God Save the King."

Nicolò Paganini's Capricci for Solo Violin (c. 1805)(W555) explore advanced and innovative techniques for the instrument and became models for many later composers. Both Schumann and Liszt wrote piano arrangements that emphasized the extreme virtuosity of the originals.

THE PIANO MUSIC OF SCHUMANN

Schumann's piano works, grouped into sets with poetic titles, reveal his imaginative humor. One of his first great successes, *Papillons* (1831)(W605), juxtaposes changing pianistic patterns and melodic ideas, suggested by its "butterflies" title. Almost every cycle of piano pieces by Schumann includes a humorous work. Thus *Grillen* from *Phantasiestücke* (1837)(W606) is, as the title implies, a study of humor.

Carnaval (1835)(W600) has its roots in the poetic, fantastic world of E.T.A. Hoffmann and *commedia dell' arte*. *Carnaval* includes movements entitled "Florestan," "Pantalone et Columbine," "Chopin," and "Paganini." In addition, Schumann used the musical notes associated with SCHA (E-flat-C-B-A) and ASCH (A-E-flat-C-B) as recurrent melodic cells. SCHA was associated with Schumann's own name; ASCH was the name of the hometown of Ernestine von Fricken, a pupil of Friedrich Wieck's and a girlfriend of Schumann's.

Davidsbündlertänze (1837)(W601) depict Schumann's war against the "Philistines," or minor composers of Schumann's generation. Eighteen dances with such indications as "lively" and "with humor" are included. *Faschingsschwank aus Wien* (1839)(W602) is also related to *Carnaval*, but does not employ titles. The five movements are longer than the sections of *Carnaval* and full of vivid contrast, implying the different sights and scenes of a carnival. The first movement quotes the "Marseillaise," forbidden at the time by the censors.

As the title implies, Schumann's *Humoreske* (1839)(W603) portrays a variety of moods, despite its thematic unity. Both the title and the shaping of this work reflect the writings of Jean Paul. Like Mozart's *Musical Joke* and Haydn's *Il Distratto* symphony, Schumann's *Humoreske* demonstrates that purely instrumental music can be humorous.

PIANO MUSIC BY OTHER COMPOSERS

The second of Max Reger's *Fünf Humoreske* (1896)(W904) transforms the first movement of Mozart's celebrated Sonata in C major K.545 through references to jazz. Antonin Dvořák's *8 Humoresken* (1894)(W501) are based on melodies he gathered during his American visit. Richard Strauss's brilliant *Burleske* for piano and orchestra (1884)(W966) contrasts elegant lyricism with dialogues between the piano and timpani. Max Reger wrote many burlesques, including *6 Burlesken* for Piano four-hands (1901)(W905).

Children's pieces abound during the Romantic period. Schumann's *Kinderscenen* (1838)(W604) have imaginative and appropriate titles, such as "Traumerei" or "dreaming." Mrs. H.H.A. Beach's *Children's Carnival* (1894)(W418) includes such pieces as "Columbine," "Pantalone," and "Pierrot and Pierrette." Georges Bizet's *Jeux d'enfants* (1871)(W454) and Gabriel Fauré's *Dolly* (1897)(W704) are also suites that comprise short, descriptive pieces. Anatoly Liadov's *The Music Box* (1893)(W824) uses the high register of the piano in a waltzlike pattern.

Chabrier's Impromptu in C major (1873)(W481) burlesques the waltz style, and the *10 Pièces pittoresques* (1881) includes many scherzolike compositions. Chabrier's colorful harmonies and evocative rhythms deeply influenced Debussy and Ravel in their humorous piano works. Charles-Valentin Alkan's *Le festin d'Estope* from the Twelve Etudes (1857)(W413) is a brilliant virtuoso description of a spider's feast. Rossini's *Album for Adolescent Children* (1857–68)(W570) anticipates the piano works of Erik Satie through clever and ironic titles, frequently simple textures, and musical parody. This collection contains such works as the *Thème Näif et Variations, idem,* which contrasts sections in octave virtuosity with a chordal melody. The *Valse lugubre* constantly shifts from minor to major mode and features odd chromaticism. The *Prélude Convulsif* is an extended work in many sections, with octave passages contrasting with polyphonic imitation.

Saint-Saëns's *Le carnaval des animaux* (1886)(W573) for two pianos and orchestra, perhaps the period's humorous masterpiece, depicts various animals, from the ferocious lion to the gentle swan. "Fossiles," with its indication of *Allegro ridicolo*, is a parody of Saint-Saëns's own *Danse Macabre* (W574). "Pianistes" makes fun of the pianistic warmup passages then fashionable, and "L'Elephant" satirizes excerpts from both Berlioz's *Damnation de Faust* (W448) and Mendelssohn's *Midsummer Night's Dream* (W540). "Personnages a Longues oreilles" includes large leaps to depict "persons with large ears." Ogden Nash, the 20th-century American poet, wrote texts to be recited during the performance of these pieces.

NATIONALISM AND HUMOR IN SOLO PIANO MUSIC

Louis Moreau Gottschalk, both a pianist and a composer, traveled widely in Latin America, where he found inspiration for many of his compositions. *The Banjo* (1854)(W510) and *Souvenir do Porto Rico* (1857)(W511) mix Lisztian pyrotechnics with syncopated rhythms.

Ignacio Cervantes, a Cuban contemporary of Gottschalk's, wrote a number of short descriptive pieces between 1875 and 1895. *La Carcajada* (W473) features energetic descending scales to illustrate laughter, the title's meaning. *Zig-Zags* (W475) includes passages moving in contrary motion, and *Pst!* (W474) ends with a sudden pause.

Mussorgsky's famous suite for piano, *Pictures at an Exhibition* (1874)(W549), describes ten paintings by Victor Hartmann. Several of its sections are comic. "Tuileries" depicts quarreling children in this famous French garden. "Ballet of the Chicks" illustrates chicks in various roles and costumes. "Limoges, the market place" describes arguing women, and "The Hut on Fowl's Legs" depicts the witch Baba Yaga's hut.

FANTASIES, ARRANGEMENTS, AND VARIATIONS FOR PIANO

Fantasies, arrangements, and variations for solo piano often transformed themes from comic works. Typically, melodies from the major arias were highly embellished, followed by elaborate, freely composed interludes. Liszt introduced many comic works through his arrangements, as illustrated by the following selected examples (Ww528–31):

> *Grand Fantasie sur la Tyrolienne de l'opéra La Fiancée* (1839) (Auber)
>
> *Soirée musicales* (1837) (Rossini)
>
> *Reminiscences de Don Juan* (1841) (Mozart)
>
> *Wedding March and Dance from A Midsummer Night's Dream* (1849–50) (Mendelssohn)

Favorite arias were often grist for virtuosity. For example, Chopin's Variations on Mozart's "La ci darem la mano" from *Don Giovanni* for Piano and Orchestra (1829)(W484) elicited Schumann's celebrated exclamation "Hats off Gentlemen, A Genius!"

MACABRE HUMOR

Berlioz's *Symphonie fantastique* (1830)(W449) concludes with a "Witches' Sabbath," which turns the symphony's idée fixe into a can-can and includes references to the "Dies Irae" chant from the Gregorian Requiem Mass. Saint-Saëns's *Danse Macabre* (1874)(W574) parodies waltz rhythm to portray a dancing skeleton. Similarly, Mussorgsky's *Night on Bald Mountain* (1867)(W548) depicts the wild orgy of witches. Gounod's popular *Funeral March of a Marionette* (1872)(W513) has mock-spooky figurations in the winds. Alkan's *Scherzo diabolico* (1857)(W414) shows the influence of Liszt.

Liszt was a master of the macabre. *Totentanz* for piano and orchestra (1865)(W527) is a set of variations on the "Dies Irae," and the *Mephisto Waltz* (orchestral version–1858)(W526) was inspired by the Faust legend. The finale of the *Faust-Symphonie* (1857)(W523) employs thematic distortion to describe Mephistopheles. Liszt wrote two masterpieces inspired by Dante's *Divine Comedy*: the *Dante* Sonata (1849)(W522) and the *Dante* Symphony (1857)(W524). Both depict Dante's *Inferno* through tonal ambiguity and driving rhythms. The Sonata in B minor (1853)(W525)–one of the central works for solo piano of the century—includes a diabolic central motive.

THE COMIC POTENTIAL OF SPECIFIC INSTRUMENTS

The violin symbolizes death in Saint-Saëns's *Danse Macabre* (1879)(W574), where its use of the tritone (the so-called diabolic interval) heightens the effect. Mahler also used scordatura for the violin in the scherzo of the Symphony No. 4 (1900)(W839) in order to imply the surreal. Earlier we have seen the violin employed to imitate animals in Carlo Farina's *Capriccio Stravagante* (1636)(W208). The double bass is first used by Beethoven as a solo instrument in the famous spot in the scherzo of the Symphony No. 5 (1808)(W430) mentioned previously in this chapter. Later composers treat strings in parodistic ways, as in Alfred Schnittke's *Sonata; MozART à la Haydn* (1977)(W939), cited in the next chapter.

Haydn introduced an unexpected forte note on the bassoon with great comic effect toward the end of the slow movement of the Symphony No. 93 (1791)(W340). As mentioned previously, Beethoven employed the bassoon in the last movement of the Symphony No. 8 in an octave dance with the timpani (W433). The bassoon implies Beckmesser's pedantry in *Die Meistersinger* (W637), and the same instrument connotes the feverish energy of the apprentice in Dukas's tone poem *The Sorcerer's Apprentice* (1897)(W758), considered in the next chapter. The flute and oboe are often employed to convey bird calls, most strikingly in Haydn's oratorio *The Seasons* (1801)(W323) and Beethoven's Symphony No. 6 (1808)(W431), but many later composers, such as Wagner, Mahler, and Messiaen, also used these instruments in a similar way. The flute also portrays the mechanical doll in the first act of Offenbach's *Les contes d'Hoffmann* (W552) and implies an automatic music box in the orchestral version of Liadov's *The Music Box* (W824).

The rambunctious qualities of the horn are explored by Richard Strauss in *Till Eulenspiegels lustige Streiche* (1895)(W965), mentioned in the next chapter. Wagner also used the horn in a playful manner in *Siegfried* (W638). The connotation of hunting horns is frequently used by Haydn and Beethoven–the lively finale of Haydn's Symphony No. 73 (c. 1782)(W336) is one of many instances. Leopold Mozart's *Sinfonia da caccia* (1756)(W362), discussed in the previous chapter, likewise employs high horn parts to convey the joys of the chase.

Weber, Bruckner, Wagner, and, of course, Mahler continuously explored these features of the horn. The scherzo of Bruckner's Symphony No. 4 (last version 1888)(W472), for example, is based on a repeated hunting horn figure. In the aria "Aprite un po'ques'occhi" from Act 4 of *Le nozze di Figaro* (W369), the horns are used to imply the "horns" of a cuckold—Mozart here subtly playing with the meaning of the word.

The tuba, introduced into the orchestra in the later 19th century, is of all brass instruments the richest in comic implications because of its size and low range—both features explored by Walt Disney in key scenes of *Fantasia* (1940)(W752). Saint-Saëns selected the xylophone to depict bones knocking together in *Danse macabre* (1874)(W574); Humperdinck featured the instrument in *Hänsel und Gretel* (W519). Tchaikovsky introduced the glockenspiel into *The Nutcracker* (W630), as did Mozart in *Die Zauberflöte* (W371) for the arias of Papageno.

The side drum, triangle, and cymbal implied Turkish instruments and were added for special effects in the repertory discussed earlier. Beethoven employed these instruments in *The Ruins of Athens* (1811)(W439) as well as the central march episode in the finale of the Symphony No. 9 (1824)(W434). Berlioz used additional percussion to convey grotesque humor in the finale of the *Symphonie fantastique* (W449). Bells, for example, accompany the intoning of the "Dies Irae" chant.

The piano conveys hellish shrieks through repeated glissandi in Liszt's *Totentanz* (1865)(W527)—a work that profoundly influenced such later composers as Busoni, Rachmaninov, and Prokofiev. The harpsichord is used to imply the spirit of 18th-century *opera buffa*, as in Stravinsky's *The Rake's Progress* (1951)(W975), discussed in the next chapter.

THE SCHUMANN-KEFERSTEIN CONTROVERSY ON COMIC MUSIC

Robert Schumann, Gustav Keferstein, and Stephan Schütze debated the possibility of expressing comedy in music (B762). Schütze had written an article for the 19th-century journal *Caecilia* (vol. 51) about the impossibility of comedy in instrumental music. This position was refuted by an article by Keferstein in *Caecilia* 60 (1833): 221–66 and supplemented by an article by Schumann for the *Neue Zeitschrift für Musik* 1 (1834): 10, entitled "Das Komische in der Musik." Schumann vigorously defended music's ability to convey comedy. His *Humoreske* (W603) sums up, as we have seen, music's humorous potential, thus becoming the musical equivalent to his landmark article.

The following translation of Schumann's article was made with the assistance of Elfriede Blanco-González, Ph.D.:

I intend to reply to the article "The Comical in Music" by C. Stein in vol. 60 of *Caecilia* a second time later, as well as to write about the topic itself. But for the present, I will write just this much. In general, less educated persons tend to hear in textless music only sorrow, joy, or (somewhere in between) nostalgia. However, they are incapable of distinguishing the finer shades of emotion, such as, on the one hand, fury, anger, and remorse. On the other hand, they do not recognize the pleasant, leisurely, and comfortable. For that reason, it is impossible for them to understand masters like Beethoven or Franz Schubert, who are able to translate any experience into the language of sound. Thus, I believe one can recognize in certain *Moments Musicals* by Schubert even the incident of a tailor's bill he was unable to pay—there is such a sense of a distaste for the bourgeois that floats above it. In one of his marches, one sees the whole Austrian militia marching, with pipes in front and bayonets in the back.

I turn now to purely comic instrumental effects. I cite the kettle-drums tuned in octaves in the scherzo of the D minor Symphony. There is also the horn effect (Ex.1) in the A major Symphony. In general, the various entries in D major in a slow tempo are retained and three times startle the listener. Also, the entire last movement of this symphony is the most humorous that instrumental music can offer. Then there is the effect of the pizzicato in the scherzo of the C minor Symphony, although a low, resonant sound is in the background. There is also that spot in the last movement of the F major Symphony, where a whole famous and experienced orchestra started to laugh because it recognized in the bass figure (Ex.2) the name of a valued member (Belcke). Also the questioning figure (Ex.3) in the double basses in the C minor Symphony has a humorous effect. The figure (Ex.4) in the heavenly slow of movement of the B-flat Symphony is either in the basses or timpani—a proper Falstaff. Someone wanted to hear in it a maybug humming around a pair of lovers in a charmed moonlit night—but this description is far-fetched and too specific. A purely humorous impression is also produced by the finale of the Quintet, Op.29, beginning with that insolent figure (Ex.5) up to the 2/4 time, which fervently tries to suppress the opposing 6/8. It is certain that in the *Andante scherzoso* Beethoven himself enters (as perhaps Grabbe with a lantern in his comedy), or engages in a conversation with himself, which may start: "Heaven, what have you done there? This will make the wigs shake their heads." (In reality, the other way around.) Very entertaining are the closing bars of the scherzo of the A major Symphony, or the Allegretto of the Eighth. One can virtually see the composer throwing away the pen which most likely was in pretty bad condition. Then there is that spot for the horns at the end of the scherzo of the B-flat Symphony, that with (Ex.6) they seem as if they want to "hit it" one more time.

How much of the comic is found in Haydn's music (less in idealistic Mozart's). Among the newer composers one must mention (aside from Weber) especially Marschner—whose talent for the comic seems greatly to surpass that for the tragic.

I reserve developing all of this more clearly in the future. I shall call this future essay "Of Humor in Music." Fn. (=Florestan)

Example 1

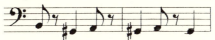

Example 2

Example 3

Example 4

Example 5

Example 6

Chapter 7

The Contemporary Period

Artistic 20th-century revolutions involving humor shaped new aesthetics. Dada, which appeared in Zürich in 1916, emphasized protest and absurdity. Futurism, initiated by F.T. Marinetti in 1909, featured music by F.B. Pratella and Luigi Russolo with *intonarumori* or "noise-makers." George Antheil combined elements of jazz, noise, and repetition in the *Airplane Sonata* (1922)(W660) and *Ballet mécanique* (1925)(W661)—the latter work written for an ensemble of pianos, percussion, and airplane propellers.

COMIC OPERA IN THE 20TH CENTURY

Richard Strauss's *Der Rosenkavalier* (1911)(W961), Sergei Prokofiev's *The Love for Three Oranges* (1921)(W881), and Igor Stravinsky's *The Rake's Progress* (1951)(W975) relate to older operatic traditions. *The Rake's Progress* parodies major aspects of *opera buffa*, including secco recitative, da capo arias, and refrain choruses. Strauss drew on the mores of 18th-century Vienna for *Rosenkavalier*, but the musical style employs waltz rhythms and soaring melodic lines. Prokofiev's *The Love for Three Oranges*, based on a play by Carlo Gozzi, includes *commedia dell' arte* figures in a complex plot, although Prokofiev's style is dissonant and brutal, with little reference to the musical procedures of the 18th century.

After the success of *Der Rosenkavalier*, Strauss turned to the traditions of *commedia dell' arte* for *Ariadne auf Naxos* (1912, rev. 1916)(W960), on a libretto by Hugo von Hofmannsthal. This "opera within an opera" often refers to the 18th-century style. *Arabella* (1933)(W959) is a domestic comedy, and *Die schweigsame Frau* (1935)(W962) employs a libretto by Stefan Zweig after Ben Jonson's comedy *Epicoene*.

Kurt Weill's and Bertold Brecht's brilliant collaboration climaxed in the 1920s and 1930s. *Die Dreigroschenoper* (1928)(W1016) updated Gay's *The*

Beggar's Opera by highlighting contemporary political and social corruption. Alexander Zemlinsky's *Kleider machen Leute* (1910)(W1021) anticipates the social commentary of Weill and Brecht.

Ernst Krenek's *Jonny spielt auf* (1927)(W822) juxtaposes fantasy and realism, jazz and Romantic lyricism. Donald J. Grout termed it "a combination of fantasy and gross realism set to exuberant rhythms and catchy tunes in jazz style with just enough dissonance to give the impression of daring 'modernism'" (B93, 547).

Paul Hindemith's *Neues vom Tage* (1929)(W785) portrays the sensationalism of newspaper reporting. *Hin und Zurück* (1928)(W784), only twelve minutes in duration, is based on a plot whose second half is the reverse of the first. Ferruccio Busoni, associated with the German school during this period, based *Arlecchino* (1918)(W707) on *commedia dell' arte* and older operatic structures. *Die Brautwahl* (1912)(W708) employs an E.T.A. Hoffmann fantasy; *Turandot* (1916)(W709), in contrast to Puccini's famous setting, is satiric. Arnold Schoenberg's *Von heute auf morgen* (1928)(W940) influenced by Strauss's *Intermezzo* (1924), is autobiographical. It is also a critique of the Neoclassicism then in vogue.

Giacomo Puccini's *Gianni Schicchi* (1918)(W556), part of the three operas that make up *Il trittico*, shows his comic ability. The style, influenced by 18th-century *opera buffa*, is lighter than that found in his serious operas, although the popular aria "O mio bambino caro" demonstrates a touching lyricism. Pietro Mascagni was, like Puccini, one of the most famous *verismo* composers of the period, but *L'amico Fritz* (1891)(W842) is comic. Ermanno Wolf-Ferrari's *Il segreto di Susanna* (1909)(W1018)—Susanna's secret is that she smokes—is also a delightful comedy, whose overture has remained in the orchestral repertory.

Luciano Berio's *Un Re en Ascolto* (1984)(W681) employs a libretto by Italo Calvino and the composer. Loosely based on Shakespeare's *The Tempest*, *Un Re* is an opera within an opera. This complex score, one of the most important comic operas of the century, includes many references to such past masters as Mahler. Manuel De Falla's *El retablo de maese Pedro* (1923)(W763), based on an episode from Cervantes's *Don Quixote* and strongly influenced by Stravinsky, is an example of Spanish Neoclassicism. Xavier Montsalvatge's *El Gato con Botas* (1948)(W853), termed "an opera of magic and mystery in five scenes," likewise emphasizes a chamber texture and clearly defined structures.

French composers, although influenced by Neoclassicism, have also continued traditions of *opéra comique*. An early—and undated—opera by Erik Satie, *Genevièvr de Brábant* (1899)(W920), based on a 13th-century legend, was originally intended for shadow theater and was performed by puppets. Maurice Ravel wrote two comic operas: *L'heure espagnole* (1911)(W898) and *L'enfant et les sortilèges* (1925)(W897). Grout notes that the *L'heure espagnole* has a "libretto in which the art of *double-entendre* is carried to a height worthy of

Favart" (B93, 503). *L'enfant et les sortilèges* uses a libretto by Colette and is, like its companion opera, rich in references to popular styles. Jacques Ibert's *Angélique* (1927)(W803) is influenced by the style of vaudeville. Francis Poulenc's *Les mamelles de Tirésias* (1947)(W870) has an absurdist libretto by Guillaume Apollinaire.

Stravinsky's satiric *Mavra* (1922)(W972) emulates the Russian folk tradition. Prokofiev's *The Duenna* (1939–40)(W879) is a witty comedy based on a play by Sheridan; *The Gambler* (1917)(W880) is full of the strong dissonance typical of *The Love for Three Oranges* (W881). Dmitry Shostakovich's *The Nose* (1930)(W947), based on Nikolai Gogol's story, is likewise satiric and features a brittle, dissonant score. Virgil Thomson's *Four Saints in Three Acts* (1934)(W994), on a text by Gertrude Stein, explores the complex wordplay and many levels of meaning of Stein's text. Thomson's musical style combines simplicity and subtlety. Although Gian Carlo Menotti is best known for his continuation of the *verismo* tradition, he also is a successful comic opera composer. Two chamber operas illustrate this: *The Old Maid and the Thief* (1939)(W843) and *The Telephone* (1947)(W844), the latter for single character.

Domenick Argento's *Casanova's Homecoming* (1985)(W662), set in the Carnival season in Venice in 1774, employs Casanova's own memoirs, with a libretto by the composer. Tonal references and motivic-rhythmic echoes of the 18th century create a subtle transformation of the *opera buffa* style. John Corigliano's *The Ghosts of Versailles* (1987)(W734) had a brilliant première at the Met in 1991. Originally *The Ghosts of Versailles* was conceived as a completion of the Figaro trilogy by Beaumarchais, but the final version of the opera only borrowed characters from *La mère coupable*. In a surrealistic blending of the theatrical, historical, and ghostly, *The Ghosts of Versailles* rethinks history. Musical references to Mozart, Rossini, Strauss, and the Turkish style of the 18th century enrich the work.

Gustav Holst began his career as an operatic composer with *The Perfect Fool* (1923)(W800) and continued it with an opera based on Shakespeare's *Henry IV: At the Boar's Head* (1925)(W799). Ralph Vaughan Williams also composed comic operas, beginning with *Hugh the Drover; or, Love in the Stocks* (1925)(W1005), which imitates ballad opera. His later *Sir John in Love* (1929)(W1006) is based on Shakespeare's *Merry Wives of Windsor* and thus is related to Verdi's *Falstaff* (W632).

Benjamin Britten celebrated Elizabeth I in *Gloriana* (1953)(W700), in which vivacious dances in the Renaissance style contrast with the more somber love story. *A Midsummer Night's Dream* (1960)(W702) is a fantasy based on Shakespeare's play. Britten also composed operas for children: *The Little Sweep* (1949)(W701) and *Noye's Fludde* (1958)(W703). *Albert Herring* (1947)(W699) is full of parody and caricature. Thea Musgrave's *Masko the Miser* (1962)(W855) is entitled "A Tale for children to mime, sing, and play."

Operas for children have become an important genre. Carl Orff composed several fairy operas, including *Der Mond* (1939)(W861), *Die Kluge* (1943)(W860), as did Werner Egk in *Die Zaubergeige* (1935)(W761) and *Der Revisor* (1957)(W760). Two operas of the century's most charming operas are inspired by a comic strip and a popular comic character from French literature: Leoš Janáček's *The Cunning Little Vixen* (1924)(W813) and Krzysztof Penderecki's *Ubu Rex* (1990–91)(W864). Penderecki's *Ubu Rex* reflects a Postmodernist simplification of style and a return to tonality. References to musical comedy and parodies of Wagner, marches, and dances are included.

BALLET

Of the three early ballets Stravinsky wrote for Sergei Diaghilev, *Petroushka* (1911)(W973) most clearly refers to Russian folk music. This ballet includes a caricature of a waltz as well as music descriptive of its main character, the bittersweet figure of a clown. A clown is also featured in Prokofiev's ballet *Chout (The Tale of a Buffoon)* (1920)(W882), likewise written for Diaghilev.

Stravinsky's *L'histoire du Soldat* (1918)(W970) is a theater piece in two parts "to be read, played, danced" to a French text by C.F. Ramuz. Based on a Russian folktale related to the Faust legend, *L'histoire* uses a chamber orchestra and a solo violin, which stands for the devil. Ragtime, waltzes, and marches enliven this highly satiric work. *Pulcinella* (1920)(W974) is the touchstone work for Neoclassicism. This score transforms music ascribed to Pergolesi, using figures drawn from *commedia dell' arte*. *Pulcinella* was partly inspired by the success of Vincenzo Tommasini's *The Good-Humored Ladies* (1916)(W1002), based on orchestral transcriptions of Domenico Scarlatti's keyboard sonatas. Stravinsky's *Jeu de cartes* (1937)(W971), described as a ballet "in three deals," depicts card games. Allusions to Rossini's *Il Barbiere* (W563) contribute to the work's wit. *Le baiser de la fée* (1928)(W968) cites the music of Tchaikovsky, one of Stravinsky's favorite composers, to create a score that is both sentimental and witty. *Circus Polka* (1942)(W969) parodies instruments commonly heard in the circus as well as popular dance styles.

Debussy's *Jeux* (1913)(W746), one of this composer's most experimental compositions, was inspired by the moves of a tennis match. *La boîte à joujoux* (1913)(W745), a children's ballet, contrasts with *Jeux* by reason of its simplicity. Manuel de Falla's *El sombrero de tres picos* (1919)(W764), presented by Diaghilev with decor by Picasso, combines the influence of Stravinsky with the flamenco style. Shostakovich's *The Age of Gold* (1930)(W946) is full of dissonance and musical satire—illustrated by its popular polka.

Ravel's ballet *Ma mère l'oye* (1912)(W899) captures the childlike wonder of the Mother Goose stories, especially in the exquisite "Beauty and the Beast," with its contrasting of high and low sonorities. The ballet also includes an evocation of the Orient in the "Empress of the Pagodas" and "The Fairy Garden."

Falla's *Sombrero de tres picos* (1919)(W764), produced by Diaghilev with designs by Picasso, reveals a Stravinskian influence and a strong Spanish nationalism, especially in the set dances in the *gitano* style. Francis Poulenc's *Les biches* (1923)(W868) cites music and texts from French popular songs. Like *Pulcinella*, this work combines dance and ensemble singing. Erik Satie's *Relâche* (1924)(W921) was written in collaboration with Francis Picabia and Marcel Duchamp. It exists also in a film version.

THE INFLUENCE OF POPULAR ART

Popular art clearly impacted such composers as Satie, Poulenc, and Milhaud. The 1917 premiere of Satie's ballet *Parade* (W922) was the occasion for many French writers, composers, and painters to reevaluate their positions on Impressionism. Jean Cocteau's manifesto *The Cock and the Harlequin* (1918)(B183) attacked the solemn aesthetics of Wagner. He proposed that the sounds of the cabaret, music hall, cinema, and circus act as stimuli for composers. In addition, he wrote the libretti for Fokine's *Le Dieu bleu* (1912) and Massine's *Parade* (1917) and *Le Boeuf sur le toit* (1920), with music by Milhaud (W848).

Nancy Perloff's Art and the Everyday: Popular Entertainment and the Circle of Erik Satie (B183) discusses the use of popular idioms by Satie, Milhaud, and their French contemporaries. These composers frequented a type of establishment called *cabaret artistique*. The Chat Noir, founded in 1881 by Rodolphe Salis, was the first cabaret artistique to achieve fame. Performers engaged in songs, poetry readings, and dramatic recitations to create a varied evening's experience.

Debussy's celebrated prelude for piano *General Lavine-eccentric* (1914)(W750) was inspired by a particular acrobat at the Cirque Médrano. In addition, many of the compositions written by Milhaud, Poulenc, and their French contemporaries imitated the cabaret idiom by combining divergent sounds and melodies. Banality is deliberately employed, as illustrated by Debussy's *La soirée dans Granade* and *Les collins de Anacapri* (1912–13)(W750).

Darius Milhaud's ballet *Le boeuf sur le toit* (1918)(W848) (later a name for a popular Parisian nightclub) includes a Latin American tune with "wrong" notes in the harmony and unusually brittle orchestration—even "squeaks" from the E-flat clarinet are featured. Popular rhythms are filtered through polytonality, which itself becomes a playing of key against key.

George Gershwin's *An American in Paris* (1928)(W772) includes taxi horn effects and imitation of street noises. Jacques Ibert's *Divertissement* (1930)(W805) imitates a horse's laugh by the use of muted trumpets. Francis Poulenc's ballet *Les biches* (1924)(W868), mentioned previously, cites cabaret songs.

Stravinsky's *Renard* (1916)(W976), a "burlesque" in song and dance, combines mime and singing to reflect the energy of a circus. Stravinsky composed two suites for orchestra: No. 1 (1917-25) and No. 2 (1921)(Ww978–79). The second suite ends with a polka that describes Diaghilev's whipping his dancers into action. Silvestre Revueltas, the Mexican composer, was notable for his sense of humor. *8 × Radio* or *Ocho por Radio* (1933)(W907) has a title obliquely referring to mathematics, but also to its instrumentation for octet. Revueltas combined Mexican popular styles with complex rhythms and textures, creating a surrealist blend.

William Walton's *Façade* (1922)(W1012), for two narrators and chamber group, is based on poems by Edith Sitwell. Modeled on Schoenberg's *Pierrot Lunaire* (1912), *Façade* combines witty poetry, quick declamation, and musical references to dance rhythms. Hindemith's *Plöner Musiktage* (1932)(W786) includes a sprightly section for speaker and chamber group.

Schoenberg's *Pierrot Lunaire* (1912)(W942) employs *Sprechstimme*, complex textures, and popular references. Within its lurid Expressionism one finds moments of mordent satire, such as "Valse de Chopin" and "Serenade," with their caricature of Romanticism. Even the boldly experimental String Quartet No. 2 (1908)(W943) includes humorous quotations of the Austrian popular song "Ach, du lieber Augustin." The combination of madness and satire found in *Pierrot* remained a hallmark of Viennese Expressionism, as exemplified by Alban Berg's operas *Wozzeck* (1925)(W680) and *Lulu* (1935)(W679).

JAZZ AND POPULAR DANCES

The complex history of jazz parallels that of the cabaret idiom. Ragtime, with its steady beat in the left hand against which syncopations occur in the right, influenced many composers at the turn of the century. Irving Berlin's song "Alexander's Ragtime Band" (1911)(W683), although strictly speaking not a ragtime, influenced the creation of a lively ragtime-jazz style. Blues, a style that implied melancholy and employed a repeated harmonic bass, nonetheless could be ironic. Ferdinand Morton's *Jelly Role Blues* (1915)(W854) typifies the frequent enigmatic and humorous connotations of titles.

One of the first works to evidence the jazz influence, John Alden Carpenter's *Krazy Kat* (1921)(W721), is based on the then-popular comic strip by that name. Stravinsky's *Dumbarton Oaks* concerto (1938)(W982), Copland's *Danzón Cubano* (1942)(W728), and Wallingford Riegger's *Dance Rhythms* (1955)(W908) are likewise jazz-influenced. Darius Milhaud's *La création du monde* (1923)(W849), based on an African creation myth, combines jazz with sensuous colors. In addition, Copland's Piano Concerto (1926)(W732), and Clarinet Concerto (1948)(W731), the latter written for the jazz great Benny Goodman, reveal a characteristically American energy and good humor. Even Bernstein's *Chichester Psalms* (1965)(W687) evidences the ebullience of jazz.

Ragtime and cakewalk, the latter marked by strutting and flamboyant costumes, were immensely popular in Paris of the 1920s (B245, 100). Debussy's celebrated "Golliwog's Cakewalk" from the *Children's Corner Suite* (1906–8)(W748) demonstrated the satiric qualities of this dance. The Shimmy, introduced in the *Ziegfield Follies* (1922), was almost immediately employed by Hindemith, who includes this dance in the *Suite 1922* for Piano (W797). The Charleston, striking for its "stumbling" bass, which interrupts the previous even flow of rhythm, found its way into Virgil Thomson's *Four Saints in Three Acts* (1934)(W994). Josephine Baker, the American dancer who made Paris her home, helped popularize these dances. Glen Watkins writes: "Baker's versions of the charleston and shimmy, which gave her audiences a memorable visual message, and her concluding savage dance with Joe Alex proved that *la danse nègre* or *step afroamericaine* was capable of engendering controversy" (B245, 135).

MUSICAL COMEDY

The popularity of Lehár's *Die lustige Witwe* caused composers to imitate its style; thus such successes as Victor Herbert's *Naughty Marietta* (1910)(W517) and Rudolf Friml's *Rose Marie* (1924)(W769) are linked to Viennese operetta. By the 1920s, the influence of ragtime, and jazz and the extraordinary importance of Tin Pan Alley moved musical comedy from a European to an American orientation. George Gershwin wrote a string of musical comedies with lyrics by his brother, Ira Gershwin. *Lady, Be Good!* (1924)(W771) created a sensation. One of the hits of the show, "Fascinating Rhythm," reveals Gershwin's gifts of melodic profile and catchy rhythms. Jerome Kern's *Show Boat* (1927)(W818), one of the most colorful and influential musical comedies of this time, evokes 19th-century life on the Mississippi.

Marc Blitzstein played an important role in the development of serious American theater. His first major success, *The Cradle Will Rock* (1937)(W694), showed that musical comedy could be a medium for controversial issues. Cole Porter, one of the most important song composers of the mid-20th century, extended the range of musical comedy's sophistication. *Kiss Me Kate* (1948)(W867), based on Shakespeare's *Taming of the Shrew*, includes such universal hits as "So in Love" and "Wunderbar."

By the 1940s, musical comedy resonated the experiences of the Depression and World War II, through either stories based on particular incidents or depictions of a rural America of the past. Rodgers and Hart, and later Rodgers and Hammerstein, produced a series of musical comedies that defined the genre. Rodgers and Hammerstein's *Oklahoma!* (1943)(W913) combines song, dance, and choral sections into a cohesive whole. *South Pacific* (1949)(W914) highlights exoticism in a story that mixed tenderness and humor. The lush harmonies of "Bali H'ai" evokes the mysteries of the East, and "Some Enchanted Evening," recurrent throughout the show, became one of the most popular songs of its time.

Leonard Bernstein's *On the Town* (1944)(W689) and *West Side Story* (1957)(W690) include many independent dance episodes. The latter work also shows the strong Hispanic influence on Bernstein at that time. *Candide* (1973)(W688), based on Voltaire's novel, bridges musical comedy and opera through a highly sophisticated plot and elegant music. Andrew Lloyd Webber's eclecticism is illustrated by *Cats* (1981)(W1014) and *The Phantom of the Opera* (1986)(W1015), both emphasizing startling multimedia effects. *Cats* uses a text based on a work by T.S. Eliot for a series of fantasy scenes. Stephen Sondheim, perhaps the most successful composer of musical comedies of the 1970s, began his career as a lyricist, collaborating in Bernstein's *West Side Story* (W690). *A Little Night Music* (1972)(W956) explores the mores of the upper class, whereas *Sweeney Todd* (1979)(W958) is set in London's lurid underworld. *Sunday in the Park with George* (1984)(W957), based on a famous painting by Georges Seurat, is striking for its tender lyricism.

AMERICAN POPULAR SONG AND TIN PAN ALLEY

Berlin's *Easter Parade* (made into a film in 1948)(W759) became a touchstone for its musical variety. Most American songs of the 1920s, however, are sentimental or topical. Vincent Youman's "Tea for Two" (1924)(W1020) is one of the rare humorous songs from this time. New popular styles appeared in the 1950s. "Rock Around the Clock," created in 1955 by Bill Haley and the Comets (W781), revolutionized American popular music. Later Elvis Presley shocked audiences with his renditions of "You Ain't Nothing but a Hound Dog" (1956)(W874). The Beatles, an English group formed in Liverpool in 1956, attracted world attention in the 1960s because of their blend of subtle lyrics and a provocative eclecticism. *Sergeant Pepper's Lonely Heart's Club Band* (1967)(W678), for example, employs modality and intricate textures.

MUSICAL SATIRE

As mentioned in the Introduction, Victor Borge combines slapstick with a considerable knowledge of music (Bb28–29)(Dd42–46). Anna Russell created audacious, though often quite accurate, narratives of Wagner's *Ring Cycle* (Dd2–4). Michael Flanders and Donald Swann were British songwriters and performers in the 1950s and 1960s who continued the tradition of Gilbert and Sullivan (D7). Sometimes they added lyrics to famous pieces of Classical music, such as the last movement of Mozart's Horn Concerto in E-flat major (1787).

The American composer Leroy Anderson wrote many gently humorous orchestral works that anticipate Peter Schickele in their clever titles. Among the most popular of these are *Syncopated Clock* (1945)(W659) and *The Typewriter*

(1950)(W658). Joseph Horovitz's *Horrortorio* (1974)(W802) is likewise in the Schickele tradition. Peter Schickele—also known as P.D.Q. Bach—has become the leading satiric composer of the contemporary period. He illustrates his musical acumen in such works as *Last Tango in Bayreuth* (c. 1974)(W936) and the *Erotica* Variations (date uncertain) (W935). A recent work, *The Little Pickle Book* (1996)(W937), was inspired by Bach's *Orgelbüchlein* (1708–17).

P.D.Q. Bach's *The Seasonings* (c. 1973)(W938), humbly edited by Professor Peter Schickele, satirizes 18th-century oratorio style. At the opening of the score one reads: "*THE SEASONINGS* is, as far as is known, the only oratorio written by P.D.Q. Bach (1807–1742)? and we must thank God for small favors." This parody of Baroque style includes arias, recitatives, and Handelian choruses. Highlighted is a fugue with an excessively long subject, which stops at the beginning of the second entry. Here one reads the warning "Forget it!" in the score. Also included is the chorus "By the leeks of Babylon." In a 1971 interview conducted by Linda Lowry (B318, 89f.), Schickele noted that his favorite subjects for satire are the 17th and 18th centuries. Popular sounding phrases are mixed with standard Baroque patterns. Passages are created in which the performers sound lost in the complexity. Timing of the musical events, the creation of pyramids of funny references, and incongruous incidents are also important. In concerts, such visual aspects as slapstick and miming supplement the music. Titles are humorous derivations of those for well-known classics, thus triggering connections between the parent work and the work it satirizes (see Dd19–39).

CHORAL SONGS

Carl Orff's *Carmina Burana* (1937)(W862) employs texts from the medieval collection discussed in the first chapter (W12). Energetic rhythms, hypnotic repetitions, and powerful choral climaxes are here found. The collection *Music for Children* (1930–35, revised 1950–54)(W863) demonstrates Orff's pedagogical interests.

Ernst Toch's clever *Geographical Fugue* (1930)(W999) is based on famous city and country names. The rhythm of the names of these various places creates the illusion of counterpoint. Alexander Tcherepnin's *Four Russian Folk Songs* (1969)(W989) includes "Shali-Vali" and "Nonsense Song." Ivan Tcherepnin the son of Alexander, composed *Noel, Noel* (1980–87)(W993), an a capella Christmas song in which "Noel" and "O Hell" are heard in the various voice parts simultaneously.

Gian Carlo Menotti's *Moans, Groans, Cries and Sighs ("A Composer at Work")*(c. 1981)(W845)describes how to compose, with madrigalesque questions and answers between the groups of voices. "Work, Gian Carlo, work" is a key phrase. The work ends with the statement "But, thank God, this piece is finished. I hope someone will like it." Virgil Thomson's *Capitals Capitals*, for four male voices (1927)(W995) on a text by Gertrude Stein, captures the word play of the text. Ralph Vaughan Williams frequently composed for choir, including the madrigalesque *Three Shakespeare Songs* (1951)(W1007), on poems from *The Tempest* and *A Midsummer Night's Dream*.

On a larger scale, Menotti's *The Unicorn, the Gorgon and the Manticore or Three Sundays of a Poet* (1956)(W846) is described by the composer as "A Madrigal Fable for Chorus, Ten Dancers and Nine Instruments." This fable is set in medieval-style music that features extensive instrumental interludes and narrative sections for the chorus. Bartók's *Four Slovak Folksongs* (c. 1907)(W668) are early instances of his fascination with ironic folk texts. More recently, György Ligeti's *Night/Morning* (1955) (W825), on a text by Sándor Weöres, consists of two short choruses for a five-part texture. The second of the set imitates birdcalls, employing devices used in the Middle Ages and Renaissance.

Schoenberg's *Drei Satiren* (1925)(W941) includes an attack on Stravinsky's Neoclassicism. The following is my translation of Schoenberg's satiric poem:

> Who is beating the drum
>
> Why, it is little Modernsky.
>
> His hair is cut in the old-fashioned style.
>
> It looks nice.
>
> Like false hair.
>
> Like a wig.
>
> Just like (as Modernsky likes to imagine)
>
> Papa Bach.

NARRATIVES, SOLO SONGS, AND ENSEMBLES FOR SOLO VOICES

Prokofiev's well-known *Peter and the Wolf* (W878) was written in 1936, a few years after *Lieutenant Kijé*, and likewise highlights simple textures and naive good humor. Each character in the story has its own leitmotiv, always given to the same instrument. Francis Poulenc's *L'histoire de Babar (le petit éléphant)* (1940–45)(W869) is in a similar style. Prokofiev's *The Ugly Duckling* (1914)(W876), entitled a "song drama," is based on the story by Hans Christian Andersen. This cycle, similar to and probably inspired by Mussorgsky's *The Nursery*, uses a declamatory voice part and imaginative dissonance in contrasting textures. Stravinsky's "The Owl and the Pussy Cat" (1966)(W967) demonstrates this composer's continuing interest in humor.

Erik Satie's *Trois poèmes d'amour* (1914)(W918) set his own texts. These are in simple rhythms and parody the foursquare phrasing prescribed by academic pedagogy. *Trois melodies* (1916)(W917) is based on nonsense poetry. "La Chapelier," for example, employs the Mad Hatter episode from *Alice in Wonderland*. The third song of the cycle, marked *genre Gounod*, parodies Gounod's operas. Debussy used Verlaine texts for *Fêtes galantes* (1894 and 1904)(W744). "Fantoches" refers to *commedia dell' arte* figures.

Ravel's *Deux Épigrammes* (1896)(W894), based on the poetry of Clemens Marot, show Ravel's wit. *Histoire naturelle* (1906)(W896) reflects Saint-Saëns's *Carnaval* as well as the old literary tradition of the bestiary. Four animals were selected for description: "The Peacock," "The Cricket," "The Swan," and "The King-Fisher." The first song imitates the pompous style of the French Baroque to satirize the peacock's vainglory; "The Cricket" has a chirping accompaniment in the piano's upper register. "The Swan" is a description of that animal's efforts to catch food as it glides smoothly across the waters. Poulenc's *Le bestiaire* (1918–19)(W871) likewise employs the old bestiary tradition. Ravel's *Don Quichotte à Dulcinée* (1933)(W894) has an interesting history. Originally Ravel was asked to write film music for *Don Quixote*. When he did not complete this project in time, Jacques Ibert wrote the background music as well as five songs (W804) for Fyodor Chaliapin, who starred in the film. The remnants of this project formed Ravel's cycle, each parodying a different Spanish rhythm. The final drinking song, for example, reflects the *jota*.

Enrique Granados composed a set of *tonadillas* (1916)(W780), or short songs for voice, about the *majos* and *majas* of Madrid at the time of Goya. Manuel de Falla's *Siete Canciones Populares* (1914)(W765), inspired by the gypsy *cante hondo* style, also mixes tragic and comic texts; Alberto Ginastera's *Cinco Canciones Populares Argentinas* (1943)(W774) reflects Argentine dance and popular rhythms. "Chacarera," the opening song, plays with the word *ñata* or "snub."

Bartók's *Ungarische Volkslieder* (1929)(W669) illustrates the Hungarian folk idiom. Benjamin Britten chose a text by Thomas Hardy for "Wagtail and Billy (A Satire)" (1968)(W698) for a Purcellian treatment. Paul Bowles set a series of poems by Tennessee Williams entitled *Blue Mountain Ballads* (1946)(W696), which captures the simplicity of rural America. The final song of this set, "Sugar in the Cane," is blueslike.

Samuel Barber's *Hermit Songs* (1952–53)(W665), based on old monastic texts, include several humorous examples. For example, "Promiscuity" (No. 7 from this cycle) is based on a 9th-century poem. Virgil Thomson's "Preciosilla" (1927)(W996) is on an extensive Gertrude Stein text. Nicolas Slonimsky used well-known advertising slogans for *Five Advertising Songs* (c. 1988)(W954) Lee Hoiby's *Songs for Leontyne, Six Songs for High Voice and Piano* (c. 1985)(W798) concludes with a setting of "The Serpent" by Theodore Roethke. Ned Rorem's *Four Dialogues for Two Voices and Two Pianos* (1954)(W915) are on texts by Frank O'Hara. The composer himself described the set: "Not as Pop Art, however, so much as vaudeville is my feeling for these Dialogues." William Bolcom composed two volumes of *Cabaret Songs* (1979)(W695), on texts by Arnold Weinstein. Although quasi-popular, these songs are intricate, with difficult accompaniments and extremely disjunct voice parts. "Amor," the opening song of the cycle, begins with a text about a traffic policeman.

Ivan Tcherepnin wrote *5 Songs* (1979)(W992) on a commission from WFMT, the classical music station in Chicago, as part of a project on 20th-century song. These songs use a variety of texts, including quotations from James Joyce. In discussing the first song, the composer writes: "The solfége syllables that are presented at the beginning of the song gradually begin to resemble familiar words, to the point that they 'take off,' forming verselets—ditties which float on the surface of nonsense" (B786).

Charles Ives's *114 Songs* (late 19th century into the 1920s)(W806) constitute the most important collection of songs by an American composer. These songs were written over a long period and in a variety of styles—from the simple and sentimental to the most outrageously complex. "Charlie Rutlage," No. 10, evokes a frontier ballad. A steady beat accompaniment highlights the homespun text. No. 28, "On the Counter" (1920) has a note by the composer beneath the song: "Though there is little danger of it, it is hoped that this song will not be taken seriously, or sung, at least, in public." No. 53, "In the Alley" (1896), also has a note: "This song (and the same may be said of the others) is inserted for association's sake—on the grounds that it will excuse anything; also, to help clear up a long disputed point, namely: which is worse the music or the words?"

SONGS FOR VOICE AND ORCHESTRA

Hans Werner Henze's *Voices* (1973)(W782) combines twenty-two songs in various languages. Some are clearly in the style of the Viennese serialists; others, such as "Recht und Billig," parody popular music. Lukas Foss's *Time Cycle* (1960)(W767) plays, as the title implies, on various notions of time. David Del Tredici's cycle on *Alice in Wonderland* (W751) conjures up the world of Lewis Carroll. This cycle includes *Pop-Pourri* (1968), *An Alice Symphony* (1969), *Adventures Underground* (1971), *Vintage Alice* (1972), *Final Alice* (1976), and *Child Alice* (1981). Tonal gestures—often an ascending sixth—returning melodies, and a childlike innocence are typical traits. Peter Maxwell Davies's *Eight Songs for a Mad King* (1969)(W742), based on statements by King George III of England, contain sections of horrific humor. Joachim Volkman's *Komponisten auf Abwegen* (1973)(W1011) is a musical parody (the title means "Composers Going the Wrong Way") in the style of Bach through Hindemith and Stravinsky.

TONE POEMS

Richard Strauss's *Till Eulenspiegel's Merry Pranks* (1895)(W965) high-lights the horn to stand for this comic villain's adventures; *Don Quixote* (1897)(W963) uses the cello to refer to Cervantes's hero. Paul Dukas's *The Sorcerer's Apprentice* (1897)(W758), based on Goethe's poem, paints the apprentice's feverish attempts to stop his master's pails filling with water.

Anatoly Liadov's *Baba Yaga* (1904)(W823) describes the famous Russian witch through brusque chords and colorful changes in orchestral texture. Edward Elgar's *Falstaff* (1913)(W762) depicts the Shakespearean clown. Busoni's *Rondo Arlecchinesco* (1915)(W707), inspired by the *commedia dell' arte* figure of Harlequin, refers to the thematic material of his opera *Arlecchino* (W707), mentioned previously.

OTHER ORCHESTRAL FORMS

Max Reger's *Variations and Fugue on a Merry Theme of Johann Adam Hiller* (1907)(W903), based on a tune from Hiller's *Der Ärndkranz* (1771), works out all the humorous implications of this theme through motivic fragmentation, harmonic variety, and orchestral color. Hindemith's early *Lustige Sinfonietta* (1916)(W788) reveals a characteristic sense of humor. Nonsense poems of Christian Morgenstern are used before each movement, including one that satirizes fugal practice. *Ragtime for Orchestra* (1921)(W789) parodies Bach's C minor fugue from *The Well-Tempered Clavier*. Hindemith said of this work: "If Bach were alive today, perhaps he would invent the Shimmy." *Symphonic Metamorphosis on Themes of Carl Maria von Weber* (1943)(W790), on the other hand, cites fragments from Weber's incidental music to Turandot (1809).

Alfredo Casella's *Pupazetti* (1916)(W723) was originally written as an accompaniment for a marionette play, with futuristic puppets. The work ends with a grotesque polka. The same composer's *Paganiniana* (1941–42)(W722) cites little-known works by Paganini. A macabre Tarantella ends this virtuoso study. Ravel's *La Valse* (1920)(W900) brilliantly parodies waltz style through exaggeration of gesture and subtle color variation. Copland's *El Salón México* (1936)(W729) is a takeoff on Mexican popular dances.

Zoltan Kodály's opera *Háry János* (1926)(W820) portrays the adventures of the Hungarian folk hero and braggart by that name. In 1927, Kodály created a suite (W821) for orchestra from the materials of the opera. The suite begins with a sneeze in the orchestra and includes the famous description of a Viennese musical clock and the battle with Napoleon.

Ives wrote several large-scale instrumental works with comic passages. *Symphony: Holidays* (W807), *Decoration Day* (1912), and *Fourth of July* (1913) form a set that quote American tunes to describe these major festivities. Multiple layers of musical activity and references to the American popular idiom are common in these works. Henry Cowell's *Saturday Night at the Firehouse*

(1948)(W737) reveals an Ivesian humor. Deems Taylor, notable for his interest in musical humor, was inspired by Lewis Carroll in *Through the Looking Glass* (1917)(W988). Each of the five sections of this work portrays a particular section of Carroll's fantasy.

Walter Piston's suite from the ballet *The Incredible Flutist* (1938)(W865) satirizes various dance styles, including a minuet, Spanish waltz, siciliana, and tango. John Corigliano's *Gazebo Dances* (1981)(W735) was suggested by pavilions where public band concerts were given on summer evenings. As the composer notes in the preface to the score: "The delights of that sort of entertainment are portrayed in this set of dances, which begins with a Rossini-like overture, is followed by a rather peg-legged waltz, a long-lined Adagio, and finishes with a flouncy Tarantella."

Bernstein's *A Musical Toast* (1980)(W691) is a joyful tribute to André Kostelanetz, based on the rhythm of this conductor's name. At the climactic point the entire orchestra sings his name, accompanied by tutti chords. Stravinsky celebrated the 80th birthday of Pierre Monteux with a *Greeting Prelude* (1955)(W983), which is a pointillistic transformation of "Happy Birthday."

Britten's *The Young Person's Guide to the Orchestra* (1946)(W705), a series of variations based on a melody from Purcell's incidental music for *Abdelazer*, features a different instrument or section of the orchestra in each variation. Dmitry Kabalevsky's suite *The Comedians* (1940)(W817) comprises a series of short movements, each of which reflects a humorous dance. Respighi's *Gli Uccelli* (1927)(W906), mentioned in the discussion of the Baroque, employs various "bird" pieces from the 17th and 18th centuries.

OVERTURES

Barber's *Overture to The School for Scandal* (1931–33)(W666), for the comedy by Sheridan, was this composer's first success. Shostakovich's *Festive Overture* (1954)(W952) was clearly intended as a popular piece with an immediately accessible style. William Walton's *Scapino (comedy overture)* (1940)(W1013) highlights sprightly rhythms and textures to mirror Jonson's play. George Gershwin's *Cuban Overture* (1932)(W773) evokes the tropical connotations of its title; Gordon Jacob's *The Barber of Seville Goes to the Devil Overture* (1960)(W812) is based on Rossini's masterpiece (W563).

Alberto Ginastera's *Overture to the Creole Faust* (1943)(W775) portrays the impressions of a gaucho on seeing Gounod's *Faust*. Fragments from the opera are combined with the rhythm of the *zamba*, an Argentine dance. Bernstein's *Candide* has been mentioned, but its overture, including many of the major ideas of this work, has become an independent concert favorite (W688). Ernst Toch's *Circus Overture* (1953)(W1000) depicts the roaring of animals by allowing the horns, trumpets, and trombones to play freely against the steady beat of the conductor.

CONCERTI

The scherzo from Prokofiev's Violin Concerto No. 1 (1917)(W887) emphasizes large leaps, "off-key" sections, and rhythmic shifts. The scherzo from the
Piano Concerto No. 2 (1913)(W885) employs Lisztian diabolic effects. The Piano Concerto No. 5 (1932)(W886) is the shortest of Prokofiev's concerti and the
most satiric. Similarly, Shostakovich's Piano Concerto No. 2 (1957)(W953)
ends with an exciting takeoff on Hanon exercises in which the soloist speeds up
against the orchestra. The American composer Rudolph Ganz begins his Piano
Concerto No. 1 (1941)(W770) with a deft scherzo-march.

Stravinsky's *Concerto for Piano and Winds* (1924)(W981) combines references to the French Baroque with spiky rhythms and staccato patterns for the
piano and wind orchestra. The *Capriccio for Piano and Orchestra*
(1929)(W980), as the title implies, is marked by strong contrasts and complex
thematic relationships.

Carl Nielsen's Flute Concerto (1926)(W857) and Clarinet Concerto
(1928)(W856) explore the comic potential of the solo instruments. Ravel's Piano
Concerto No. 2 (1931)(W901) is jazz-inspired and has a *moto perpetuo* finale.
More recently, Witold Lutosławski's Cello Concerto (1970)(W830) makes the
cello a comic protagonist. John Corigliano's *Pied Piper's Fantasy*
(1981)(W736) for flute and orchestra, written for James Galway, involves the
audience as the flutist "leads the children off the stage."

Hindemith's *Kammermusik* No. 4 for Violin (1925)(W792) concludes with
a satiric waltz that ends pianissimo. *Der Schwanendreher* Concerto for Hindemith's own instrument, the viola (1936)(W793), is a modern example of a
quodlibet. *The Four Temperaments* for piano and strings (1940)(W791) includes
a second movement that depicts the sanguine mood through humorous dialogues.

The term *concertino* implies a shorter, lighter work for solo instrument. Arthur Honegger's *Concertino for piano and orchestra* (1925)(W801) reminds one
of music for a Chaplin film because of its staccato textures. Walter Piston wrote
a *Concertino for piano and orchestra* (1937)(W866) that reflects French clarity
and energy. Jean Françaix's *Concertino for piano and orchestra* (1934)(W768)
typifies this composer's wit.

Ernst von Dohnány's *Variations on a Nursery Song* for piano and orchestra
(1914)(W756), based on "Twinkle, Twinkle Little Star," begins with a solemn
introduction, after which the piano innocently presents the main theme. Sergei
Rachmaninov's popular *Rhapsody on a Theme of Paganini* (1934)(W893) transforms Paganini's caprice theme, balancing serious and comic episodes.

Britten's *Diversions* for Piano Left Hand and Orchestra (1942)(W706) was
written for Paul Wittgenstein. This is a theme and variations in different styles
leading to a Tarantella finale. Notable is the "Burlesque" variation No. 8. Boris
Blacher's *Variationen über ein Thema von Muzio Clementi* (1961)(W693) is
based on the opening five-finger study from Clementi's *Gradus ad Parnassum*
(1817–26). These variations satirize technical exercises.

Bartók's *Concerto for Orchestra* (1943)(W670) includes a second movement entitled a "Game of Pairs." The fourth movement introduces a sudden laugh in the orchestra followed by a satiric quotation from Shostakovich's Symphony No. 7 (1941). Also to be found in this movement are references to the aria "Da geh'ich zu Maxim" from Lehar's *Die Lustige Witwe* (W521). Lutosławski's *Concerto for Orchestra* (1954)(W831), inspired by Bartók's masterpiece, includes a surrealistic scherzo performed at a breathless pace and pianissimo dynamics.

SYMPHONIES AND SERENADES

Gustav Mahler's symphonies often mix grotesque irony and black humor. Thus, for example, the Symphony No. 1 (1888)(W837) has a slow movement based on a lugubrious variant of "Frère Jacques" and references to the sounds of a Jewish klezmer band. The Symphony No. 4 (1900)(W839) includes a "dance of death" scherzo with a scordatura violin and concludes with a child's view of heaven based on a text from *Des Knaben Wunderhorn*. The third movement of the Symphony No. 2 (1894)(W838) transforms the song "Des Antonius von Padua Fischpredigt" from *Des Knaben Wunderhorn*. The central movements of the Symphony No. 5 (1902)(W840) parody the Viennese waltz. The Symphony No. 9 (1909)(W841) includes a scherzo-burleske that alternates wild dissonances and extraordinary tranquility.

Shostakovich's symphonies manifest the influence of Mahler in their juxtaposition of serious and macabre movements. Shostakovich's Symphony No. 1 (1925)(W948) refers to Stravinsky's *Petroushka* and popular music. The comic Symphony No. 9 (1945)(W949) strikes a typically ironic tone. Symphony No. 15 (1971)(W951) includes quotations from Rossini and Wagner and ends with a coda that sounds like music from a toy shop. Shostakovich's Symphony No. 13 (*Babiy Yar*) (1962)(W950) calls for special commentary because of its bleak humor. The second movement, marked "humor," is a grotesque combination of scherzo and march.

Prokofiev's Symphony No. 1 (*Classical*) (1917)(W884) mirrors the high spirits of the symphonies of Haydn and Mozart and includes a Gavotte. The Symphony No. 7 (1952)(W885) reflects his ballet *Cinderella* (1945) through its waltzlike lyricism and frequent flashes of humor.

Stravinsky's Symphony in C (1940)(W977) shows the influence of Beethoven, Rossini, and his own *Pulcinella* (W974). The bouncy rhythms and repeated-note motives are immediately apparent, but the symphony also plays with the structural and stylistic patterns of the Classic period.

Strauss's *Sinfonia Domestica* (1903)(W964) describes domestic life in detail, including the sounds of a vacuum cleaner. Nielsen wrote two symphonies with comic episodes. The Symphony No. 2 (*The Four Temperaments*) (1902)(W858) ends with a joyous depiction of the sanguine temperament. The

Symphony No. 6 (*Sinfonia Semplice*) (1925)(W859) satirizes Webern pointil-
lism. The second movement emphasizes large leaps and percussion passages.
The third movement is marked "serious response," and the last movement is a
series of comic variations on a theme announced by the bassoon.

Britten's *Simple Symphony* (1933–34)(W704) for String Orchestra expands
on works Britten wrote between nine and twelve years of age. The presence of
such titles as "Boisterous Bourée" and "Frolicsome Finale" implies the spirit of
the work. Albert Roussel's Symphony No. 4 (1934)(W916) is notable for its
conclusion, which caricatures the march style. Henry Cowell was a prolific sym-
phonist. His Symphony No. 11 (1953)(W738) has a fourth movement entitled
"ritual of dance and play," which emphasizes percussion in giguelike rhythms.

Composers of the contemporary period also continue the serenade tradition
of the previous centuries. Alexander Tcherepnin's *Serenade for Strings*
(1964)(W990), for example, juxtaposes ironic humor and violent dissonance in
short movements.

WORKS FOR PIANO

Satie composed short piano compositions grouped into sets with witty titles.
Beginning with the celebrated *3 Gymnopédies* (1888)(W928) and *3 Gnossiens*
(1890)(W927), an emphasis on modality, simple textures, and unconventional
chord successions appears. *Vexations* (c. 1893)(W933) anticipates the Minimalism of the later part of the century by requiring the pianist constantly to repeat a
short phrase. *Morceaux en forme de poire* (1903)(W929) for piano duet is thus
entitled (*Piece in the form of a Pear*) as a response to Debussy's suggestions that
the work have some particular form.

Works often employ unusual titles, as the following illustrate:

> *Chapitres tournées* (W923)
>
> *Croquis et agaceries* (W924)
>
> *Embryons déséches* (W926)
>
> *Préludes flasques* (W930))
>
> *Vieux sequins et vieilles cuirasses* (W934)

Descriptions automatiques (1913)(W925) reflects the interest in automatic
response found among the Surrealists. *Sports et divertissements* (1914)(W932)
includes performance directions like the well-known injunction to play "softly,
like a nightingale with a toothache." At times, Satie employs a particular model,
as in the *Sonatine bureaucratique* (1917)(W931), based on a Clementi sonatine.

Debussy's frequently humorous titles and style mirror Satie's influence. *The Children's Corner* (1906–8)(W748) begins with an etude, "Dr. Gradus ad Parnassum," referring to Clementi's famous 19th-century collections of studies. It concludes with "Golliwog's Cakewalk," based on the American dance style popular in Paris. A key phrase from Wagner's *Tristan und Isolde* appears unexpectedly in the middle of the movement. The piano prelude *Hommage à Pickwick* (1912–13)(W750) depicts the famous character from Dickens's novel and quotes the English national anthem. The Etudes (1915)(W749) opens with a mock-etude *Pour les cinq droits apres Monsieur Czerny* in the style of a Czerny study.

Heitor Villa-Lobos's *Prole do bebé* (1918)(W1010) describes different kinds of dolls found in a child's collection, including Punch. Alexander Tcherepnin's *Le Monde en Vitrine* (1946)(W991) was inspired by the glass menagerie of his patron. Each movement depicts a particular animal, including the crab, described through contrary motion dissonant chords.

Prokofiev's fascination with mockery is found in even his earliest pieces, such as the *Suggestion diabolique* (1908)(W892) and the *Sarcasms* (1914)(W891). The Piano Sonatas Nos. 6 and 7 (1940, 1942)(Ww889–90) imply macabre humor through repeated notes and dissonant chords in different registers of the piano.

Stravinsky's Neoclassic *Sonata* (1924)(W985) has the same wit and energy found in the Symphony in C (W977). *The Piano-Rag-Music* (1919)(W987) reflects the fascination with American popular idioms that we have found already in Debussy. *The Five Fingers* (1921)(W986) explores permutations of five-finger exercise patterns.

Bartók's *3 Burlesques* (1908–11)(W674) explore polytonality and strident dissonance. "Quarrel," the second movement of the set, is both a quarrel of keys as well as a description of a dispute. Continuing the tradition of Schumann, Bartók wrote many pieces for children in *Mikrokosmos* (1926–39)(W675), a series of increasingly difficult studies in rhythms and textures. *From the Diary of a Fly*, one of the best known works from this series, features overlapping patterns in the two hands that form cluster dissonances. Bartók's larger works for piano, particularly the suite *Out of Doors* (1926)(W676), frequently manifest brutal humor.

Influenced by jazz and rags, Hindemith's *Suite 1922* (W797), as we have seen, includes "Shimmy," "Boston," and "Ragtime." In addition, many fugues of *Ludus Tonalis* (1943)(W795) feature comedic subjects. The title "tonal play" is reflected in Hindemith's playing with tonal relations. The Piano Sonata No. 3 (1936)(W796) contrasts somber movements with a pompous march and an energetic fugue.

Casella composed a set entitled *À la maniere de* (1911)(W725), in which the musical styles of Wagner, Fauré, Brahms, Debussy, Strauss, and Franck are caricatured. In 1913, a second volume, which contains two numbers by Casella and two by Ravel, appeared.

Lord Berners (his original name was Gerald Tyrwhitt-Wilson) has been called the "English Satie." Many piano works up to 1920 are satiric or specifically parodistic, as implied in such titles as *Trois petites marches funèbres* (1914)(W685) and *Fragments psychologiques* (1915)(W684). *Valses Bourgeoises* (1917)(W686) satirize different waltzes by the Strauss family. Percy Grainger's compositions appeared for various instrumental combinations. *Molly on the Shore* (1918)(W779) and *Handel in the Strand* (1912)(W778) are examples of what Grainger referred to as "fripperies."

Scott Joplin's rags have beguiling titles that evoke America of the first decades of the century. *The Entertainer* (1902)(W815) and *Mapleleaf Rag* (1899)(W816)—the most popular—feature syncopated patterns in the right hand supported by a steady beat in the left. Ives's *Three-Page Sonata* (1905)(W811), so called because the work originally occupied three pages, is actually on a large scale. Like many of Ives's compositions, this sonata quotes a variety of popular melodies within a thickly dissonant texture. The monumental *Concord Sonata* (1915)(W810), whose movements are named after figures in the New England Transcendentalist movement, also includes moments of comic relief.

Copland's *The Cat and the Mouse* (1920)(W733) contrasts registers to depict these two animals. Virgil Thomson's series *Portraits* (1927–40)(W997) portrays his friends and associates. This is a collection of forty short pieces in five books—each piece meant to reflect a salient trait of the individual portrayed. Samuel Barber's *Excursions* (1944)(W667) ends with a description of a barn dance, including an imitation of a solo fiddler.

George Rochberg's *Carnival Music for Piano* (1971)(W911), a five-movement suite, reflects the title's meaning through strong contrasts of mood, tonality, and atonality. The last movement, "toccata-rag," features a transformation of the rag style through metric changes and sudden leaps.

Satire and irony led to innovative uses of the piano. Cowell's *The Advertisement* (1914)(W739) is an early use of clusters; *The Aeolian Harp* (1923)(W740) and *The Bandshee* (1925)(W741) employ strumming of the piano strings for special effects. John Cage continued these experiments, using what he termed a "prepared piano," or a piano modified to create new sounds. *Bacchanale* (1940)(W714) is the first work for prepared piano. *Water Music* (1952)(W718) and *Cheap Imitation* (1969)(W715) illustrate the use of clever titles that obliquely refer to the nature of the composition.

CHAMBER WORKS

Debussy's Sonata for Cello and Piano (1915)(W747)—the first of three sonatas for various combinations which reflect the French Rococo—contains a serenade movement influenced by *commedia dell' arte*. Ravel's Sonata for Violin and Cello (1922)(W902) includes a second movement marked *Très vif* on a simple tune presented in odd bitonality.

Schönberg's *Serenade* (1923)(W944) involves instruments associated with popular music and bass voice together with references to the 18th-century serenade, made incongruous because of the serial idiom. The third movement is a set of variations, each variation a caricature.

Bartók's *Contrasts* for violin, clarinet, and piano (1938)(W673) were written for Benny Goodman. Each of the three dances that this work comprises has quasi-improvisatory passages. The last, entitled "Fast Dance," employs tritones in the violin to create the effect of an off-tune fiddle. The six String Quartets include many satiric or comic episodes. The fifth (1935)(W671) and sixth (1939)(W672) are particularly heterogeneous. The Presto finale of the fifth quartet features a banal passage which sounds like a barrel organ; the sixth quartet has a grotesque "Burletta" with strange instrumental effects.

Hindemith's String Quartet in E-flat major (1943)(W794) includes a second movement with a punctuated march rhythm. This quartet ends with humorous pizzicati. Stravinsky's Octet for Wind Instruments (1923)(W984) is the most important of his Neoclassic chamber works. The "Tema con variazioni" satirizes styles and sounds of the waltz, military march, and street band. Ives's sense of humor is evident in the early Scherzo for String Quartet (1903)(W808) and the *Halloween* for string quartet, piano, and bass drum (1906)(W809), which employs clusters and complex percussive effects. Sir Eugene Goossens's *Two Sketches* for String Quartet (1916)(W777) ends with a humorous "Jack o'Lantern" featuring polytonal chords. Paul Bowles's *Music for a Farce* for clarinet, piano, trumpet, and percussion (1938)(W697) reveals his interest in the popular style as does Hans Werner Henze's *Fragmente aus einer Show* for Brass Ensemble (1971)(W782). Heitor Villa-Lobos's *Assobio a jato* (1950)(W1009) for flute and violoncello reflects its title, which means "jet whistle," through many quick ascending passages and glissandi for the flute.

FILM MUSIC

Beginning with Al Jolson's *The Jazz Singer* (1924), sound played a dramatic and integral role in the development of a film's plot. Background music conveyed mood and highlighted character development; motivic references and orchestral colors created subtle markers for the audience. Charlie Chaplin, the greatest film comic of the century, studied composition around 1927, the time of the development of sound film. He later provided music for his own films, such as *Modern Times* (1936)(W850), including the song "Smile." Hindemith composed the music for the cartoon *Felix the Cat* (1927)(W787), which included a mechanical organ. As we have seen, Satie wrote the music for the surrealist fantasy *Relâche* (1924)(W921), in which he himself appeared.

Early comic films such as the Marx Brothers' *Monkey Business* (1931)(W852) featured music within the film itself. William Darby and Jack Du Bois note that some productions combined music from different sources: "An extreme example of this practice can be seen in the credits for *Abbott and Costello Meet the Keystone Cops* (1955), which has cues by Stein, Mancini, and William Lava as well as four seconds [!] of tracked music from Rozsa's *The Killers* and seven seconds lifted from Waxman's *Fury*" (B54, 190). Walt Disney allied music with animation, beginning with *Steamboat Willie* (1928)(W755) and continuing in the series of *Silly Symphonies* (1929)(W753). *Snow White and the Seven Dwarfs* (1937)(W754) employs songs to delineate the major characters, thus illustrating another technique used in animated films to integrate music. Disney's *Fantasia* (1940)(W752) featured Stravinsky's *The Rite of Spring* as a background for some of the most exciting imagery in the history of film. *Fantasia* combined other Classical masterpieces, led by Leopold Stokowski, with unexpected visual analogues to explore new areas of humor.

Music played a major role in the great fantasy *The Wizard of Oz* (1939)(W1017), in which Judy Garland's rendition of "Somewhere over the Rainbow" symbolized America's dreams for a better future. *My Fair Lady* (1956)(W828), the extraordinarily popular musical of Lerner and Loewe based on the Pygmalion myth, was turned into a film starring Rex Harrison. Burt Bacharach composed the score for *The Producers* (1968)(W875), about the production of a mythical musical entitled *Springtime for Hitler*.

Erich Wolfgang Korngold arranged Mendelssohn's incidental music for the film version of *A Midsummer Night's Dream* (1935)(W847). Copland caught the tenderness and fantasy of Thornton Wilder's *Our Town* in his film score composed in 1940 (W730). Prokofiev's *Lieutenant Kijé* (W888) was composed in 1934 for a film based on a story by Y.N. Tynyanov and later, as we have seen, turned into a suite in which the opening satiric march returns at key points.

42nd Street (1932-33)(W766), starring Fred Astaire and Ginger Rogers, highlights brilliant dance episodes in complex choreography by Busby Berkeley. These dance scenes with complex symmetries enlivened many film musical comedies of the 1930s. The Beatles's film *A Hard Day's Night* (1964)(W677) featured many of their imaginative songs. *Tommy* (W902), with music by the group The Who, led to *Lisztomania* (1976)(W827), a wild film biography of Liszt. The *Rocky Horror Picture Show* (1976)(W912), has become a cult classic. *Victor/Victoria* (1982)(W1008), with Julie Andrews, highlights sexual ambiguities and employs music from the British music hall tradition. *Kiss of the Spider Woman* (1993)(W828), on the story by the Argentine writer Manuel Puig, evokes the atmosphere of Argentina and uses evocative music to underline the sad-funny love story between the two principals.

More recently, the animated film *Babe* (1995)(W663), about the adventures of a "sensitive" pig, has a provocative score. The music for the hit Mexican film *Like Water for Chocolate* (1992)(W826) was composed by the important Cuban composer Leo Brower. Occasionally films use period music by major composers to underscore the film's general mood and style. *Three Worlds of Gulliver* (1960)(W998) is a surrealistic blend of images and sounds. *Tous le Matins du Monde* (1991)(W1004), the French film on the life of the 18th-century composer Marin Marais, uses his music as an integral part of the film.

CHANCE MUSIC

Aleatoric or "chance" compositions have challenged audiences to accept bizarre choices of instruments or performance style. Marcel Duchamp, more famous as an artist than a composer, wrote a number of "musical compositions" (early 20th century)(W757), which are Dadaist sketches involving chance. Indeterminacy, based on the *I-Ching Manual of Changes*, controlled most of John Cage's mature compositions, which influenced the next generation of American composers.

Cage's early *String Quartet in Four Parts* (1949–50)(W712) experiments with a simplification of texture and rhythmic movement. The *Sonatas and Interludes* (1946–48)(W717) for prepared piano, a 70-minute cycle of 16 sonatas and 4 interludes, explores a wide spectrum of emotions. *Aleatoric Music of Unfixed Medium. 4'33"* (1952)(W713) shows music's relationship to silence and Zen Buddhism. *Fontana Mix* (1958–59)(W716) was one of the first compositions for electronic media. Cage inspired many other composers to emphasize simplicity and humor. For example, Cornelius Cardew wrote a work entitled *1001 Activities from Scratch Music* (c. 1970)(W720). According to the composer: "Scratch Music is the basic music of the world, going on everywhere, all the time." This work consists of 1001 short phrases to suggest means of performance. Thus No. 657 reads: "Show them who's boss, then resign your position."

THIRD STREAM

"Third stream," a style especially popular in the United States, combined elements from cultivated music with references to jazz. Already found in Ives and Copland, "third stream" was espoused by Gunther Schuller and is exemplified in *Seven Studies on Themes of Paul Klee* (1959)(W945), notably in the witty "Twittering Machine" section.

MINIMALISM

Immediately after the post-Webernite intricacies of the 1960s and 1970s, Minimalism returned to direct expression and uncomplicated procedures by emphasizing pattern repetition, simple structures, and diatonicism. Terry Riley's *In C* (1964)(W909) highlights C within gradually expanding motivic patterns. John Adams's *The Chairman Dances: Foxtrot for Orchestra* (W654), drawn from his opera *Nixon in China* (1987), mirrors the opera's strange blend of comedy, tragedy, and references to an important historical event. Philip Glass's *Glassworks* (1982)(W776) combines Minimalism with elements of rock.

POSTMODERNISM

Glen Watkins points out that a direct relationship exists between Postmodernism and musical humor (B245, 443–74). Collage, parody, multiculturalism, and combinations of high and low art are typical, obscuring the divisions between esoteric and popular practice. Berio's *Sinfonia* (1969)(W682), originally written for the Swingle Singers, includes a third movement created from diverse musical citations (with emphasis on the scherzo from Mahler's Symphony No. 2), fragments of overlapping texts, and nonsense syllables.

Recent historicism can create unexpected and even jarring contrasts. Rochberg's String Quartet No. 3 (1971–72)(W910) is "multigestural" because of its juxtaposition of styles and mirroring of late Beethoven quartets. Maxwell Davies's *St. Thomas Wake* for orchestra (1969)(W743) combines three separate styles: a pavane by John Bull (the origin of the title of the piece), a foxtrot played by a dance band, and "serious" symphonic music played by the orchestra. Titles in the Postmodernist tradition not only are humorous in themselves, but sometimes imply how the work was conceived and/or how it is to be performed, providing analytic cues to the given work. Alfred Schnittke's *Quasi una sonata; Moz-ART à la Haydn* (1977)(W939), for two violins and string ensembles, deconstructs the classical idiom. Similarly, Osvaldas Balakauskas's *Alla Turca Once More* for two pianos (1987)(W664) dissects Mozart's *Turkish Rondo* (W393).

William Albright includes Iveslike juxtapositions in *The King of Instruments: A Parade of Music and Verse for Organ Solo and Narrator* (1979)(W656) and *Enigma Syncopations for organ, percussion, flute, and bass* (1982)(W655). Meredith Monk's *Our Lady of Late* (1972)(W851) for Soprano and Wine Glass filled with water is an hour-long work created from various types of vocal inflections. Tom Johnson's *Transitory Circumlocutions for Solo Trombone* (1973)(W814) and Claus Dieter Ludwig's *Humoristische variationen über ein Geburtstaglied* (1987)(W829)—the title means "humorous variations on a birthday song"—likewise have evocative titles. Laurie Anderson's *Duet for Violin and Door Jamb* (1977)(W657) "is performed on the threshold of a door between two rooms." Christian Wolff's *Looking North* (1973)(W1019) has the directive "Think of, imagine, devise, a pulse, any you choose, of any design."

In conclusion, the vast repertory of comic music, of which this book has explored only a small part, mandates a reevaluation of conventional music history. Ultimately, comedy and tragedy form twin poles of human experience—the one would be impossible without the other.

Bibliography

OVERVIEW

General Studies on Comedy in Music: B28, B55, B87, B118, B129, B146, B164, B224, B225, B316, B318, B329, B358, B394, B398, B413, B421, B426, B427, B439, B446, B454, B470, B483, B488, B517, B519, B522, B529, B535, B537, B544, B554, B574, B576, B592, B595, B601, B604, B606, B619, B629, B631, B644, B661, B667, B668, B673, B675, B676, B679, B684, B692, B700, B729, B731, B733, B741, B745, B748, B762, B779, B788, B797, B802, B808.

General Reference Sources: B378, B382, B383, B389, B390.

Caricature: B724.

Chamber Music: B367.

Choral Music: B110, B122, B238, B366, B373.

Comedy Types: B79, B117, B135, B141, B159, B160, B301, B303, B375 (Reference).

Comic Opera: B13, B18, B19, B62, B93, B98, B101, B130, B132, B148, B151, B166, B187, B240, B254, B424, B445, B481, B499, B513, B551, B577, B602, B635, B638, B639, B716, B734, B736, B768, B784, B798, B821, B828.

Comic Opera in General Reference Sources: B365, B370, B372, B379, B380, B383, B384, B388, B391.

Commedia dell' arte: B368.

Dance: B207.

Documents by Composers (Some Humorous): B247.

Drama: B392.

Etymology of Musical Terms: B377.

Grone's Dictionary: B38.

Hoffnung Companion: B111.

Jazz and Popular Music: B245, B369, B371, B376, B386, B387.
Musical Americana: B59.
Musical Theater: B374.
Pasticcio: B800.
Quodlibet: B164.
Satire: B71, B214, B232, B575.
Satirikon of Musical Instruments: B107
Sociology: B185.
Theorists Cited in the Narrative: B6, B25, B43, B44, B63, B82, B92, B123, B128, B154, B163, B173, B.176, B189, B191, B192, B231, B234, B259.

BOOKS

B1.   Allanbrooke, Wye J., ed. *Convention in Eighteenth-and Nine-teenth-Century Music: Essays in Honor of Leonard J. Ratner*. New York: Pendragon, 1992.

B2.   Altman, Rick. *La Comedie Musicale Hollywoodienne: Les Problems de Genre au Cinema*. Paris: Colin, 1992.

B3.   Anthony, James R. *French Baroque Music from Beaujoyeux to Rameau*. New York: W.W. Norton, 1974.

B4.   Antolini, Bianca Maria. *Napoli e il teatro musicale in Europa tra Sette e Ottocento: Studi in onore di Friedrich Lippmann*. Florence: Olschki, 1993.

B5.   Apel, Willi. *The History of Keyboard Music to 1700*. Translated and edited by Hans Tischler. Bloomington: Indiana University Press, 1972.

B6.   Arbeau, Thoinot. *Orchésographie*. Geneva: Slatkine Reprints, 1970.

B7.   Atlas, Alan. *Renaissance Music*. New York: W.W. Norton, 1997.

B8.   Austin, William. *Music in the 20th Century*. New York: W.W. Norton, 1966.

B9.   Ayre, Leslie. *The Gilbert and Sullivan Companion*. New York: Dodd & Mead, 1972.

B10.   Bailey, Leslie. *The Gilbert and Sullivan Book*. Rev. ed. New York: Coward-McCann,1957.

B11.   Balanchine, George. *Balanchine's Complete Stories of the Great Ballets*. Rev. ed. Garden City, N.Y.: Doubleday & Company, 1968.

B12.   Bateson, Frederick W. *English Comic Drama, 1700–1750*. Oxford: Clarendon Press, 1929.

B13.   Bauer, Rudolf. *Oper und Operette: Ein Führer durch die Welt der Musikbühne*. Berlin: Deutsche Buch-Gemeinschaft, 1959.

B14.   Bellman, Jonathan. *The Exotic in Western Music*. Boston: Northeastern University Press, 1997.

B15.   ——. *The Style Hongrois in the Music of Western Europe*. Boston: Northeastern University Press, 1993.

B16.   Benton, Jack. *The Blue Book of Hollywood Musicals*. Watkins Colen: Century House, 1953.

B17.   Bergson, Henri. *Laughter*. New York: Doubleday Anchor Books, 1956.

B18.   Bethléem, Abbé L. *Les Opéras, les opéras-comiques et le opérettes*. Paris: Editions de la Revue des lectures, 1926.

B19.   Biedenfeld, Ferdinand, Freiherr von. *Die komische Oper der Italiener, der Französer und der Deutschen*. Leipzig: Weigh, 1848.

B20.   Birkin, Kenneth. *Richard Strauss: Arabella*. Cambridge: Cambridge University Press, 1988.

B21.   Bloom, Ken. *American Song: The Complete Musical Theatre Companion 1877-1995*. 2d ed. New York: Schirmer Books, 1995.

B22.   Boardman, Gerald. *American Musical Comedy from Adonis to Dreamgirls*. New York: Oxford University Press, 1982.

B23.   ——. *American Operetta from H.M.S. Pinafore to Sweeney Todd*. New York: Oxford University Press, 1981.

B24.   Boileau, Nicolas. *Le Lutrin*. Los Angeles: University of California, 1967.

B25.   Bolte, Johannes. *Die Singspiele der englischen Komödianten und ihrer Nachfolger in Deutschland, Holland und Skandanavia*. Hamburg: L.Voss, 1893.

B26.   Bonafedé, Félix. *Rossini et son oeuvre*. Le Puy-en-Velay: Éditions de la Main de Bronze, 1955.

B27.   Borchmeyer, Dieter. *Mozarts Opernfiguren: Grosse Herren, Rasende Weiber, Gefährliche Liebschaften*. Bern: Haupt Verlag, 1991.

B28.   Borge, Victor. *My Favorite Comedies in Music*. New York: Evans, 1994.

B29.   ——. *My Favorite Intermissions*. New York: Evans, 1993.

B30.   Böttger, Friedrich. *Die "Comédie-Ballet" von Molière-Lully*. Berlin: Funk, 1931.

B31.   Branscombe, Peter. *W.A. Mozart: Die Zauberflöte*. Cambridge: Cambridge University Press, 1991.

B32.   Briard, Emanuel. *Le Comique en Musique*. Nancy: Crepin-Leblond, 1884.

B33.   Brion, Patrick. *Le comodie musicale du Chanteur de jazz a Cabaret*. Paris: La Martiniere, 1993.

B34.   Brown, Bruce Alan. *W.A. Mozart: Così fan tutte*. Cambridge: Cambridge University Press, 1995.

B35.   Brown, Howard Mayer. *Music in French Secular Theatre, 1400–1550*. Cambridge: Harvard University Press, 1963.

B36.   Budis, Ratibor. *Nápad Monsieura Offenbacha. Výpraven o Čestach Svetovoperety a Preslusnou Zasravkou v Parze.* Prague: Supraphone, 1970.

B37.   Bukofzer, Manfred. *Music in the Baroque Era.* New York: W.W. Norton, 1947.

B38.   Burnham, Howard. *Grone's Dictionary of Music, or A Golden Treasury of Musical Rubbish, or Misleading Lives of the Great Composers.* Yorkshire: Emerson, 1978.

B39.   Burt, George. *The Art of Film Music.* Boston: Northeastern University Press, 1994.

B40.   Calmus, Georg. *Zwei Opernburlesken der Rokokozeit.* Berlin: Liepmannsohn, 1912.

B41.   Carmody, Francis J. *Le Repertoire de l'opéra-comique en vaudevilles de 1708 à 1764.* Berkeley: University of California Press, 1933.

B42.   Carpenter, Nan Cooke. *Rabelais and Music.* Chapel Hill: University of North Carolina Press, 1954.

B43.   Castiglione, Baldassare. *Il Libro del Cortegiano.* Milan: Mursia, 1972.

B44.   Cerone, Pietro. *El Melopeo y Maestro.* Naples, 1613. See also B405.

B45.   Cessac, Catherine. *Marc-Antoine Charpentier.* Portland, Oregon: Amadeus Press, 1995.

B46.   Chailly, Luciano. *Il matrimonio segreto, guida musicale.* Milan: Istituto d'Alta Cultura, 1949.

B47.   Charlton, Andrew. *Music in the Plays of Shakespeare—a Practicum.* New York: Garland Publishing, 1991.

B48.   Clarke, Donald. *The Rise and Fall of Popular Music.* New York: St. Martin's Press, 1995.

B49.   Cockrell, Dale. *Demons of Disorder: Early Blackface Minstrels and Their World.* Cambridge: Cambridge University Press, 1997.

B50.   Cooper, Martin. *Opéra Comique.* New York: Chanticleer Press, 1949.

B51.   Cotarelo y Mori, Emilio. *Historia de la Zarzuela o sea El drama lirico en España, desde su origen a fines del siglo XX.* Madrid: Tipografia de Archivos, 1934.

B52.   Czech, Stan. Franz Léhar: *Schön ist die Welt: Franz Léhars Leben und Werk.* Berlin: Argon, 1957.

B53.   Danhill, Thomas F. *Sullivan's Comic Operas: A Critical Appreciation.* New York: Oxford University Press, 1928.

B54.   Darby, William, and Du Bois, Jack. *American Film Music: Major Composers, Techniques, Trends, 1915–1990.* Jefferson, Georgia: McFarland & Company, 1990.

B55.   Daschner, Hubert. *Humor in der Musik*. Wiesbaden: Breitkopf und Härtel, 1986.

B56.   Davis, Lee. Bolton and Wodehouse and Kern: *The Men Who Made Musical Comedy*. New York: Heineman, 1993.

B57.   Davison, Peter. *Songs of the British Music Hall*. New York: Oak Press, 1971.

B58.   Day, W.G. *The Pepys Ballads*. Rochester, N.Y.: University of Rochester Press, 1997.

B59.   Deak (C.T.), Martin. *Martin Deak's Book of Musical Americana*. Englewood Cliffs, N.J.: Prentice-Hall, 1970.

B60.   Decsey, Ernst. *Johann Strauss: Ein wiener Buch*. Vienna: Paul Neff Verlag, 1948.

B61.   Della Corte, Andrea. *L'opera comica italiana nel 1700*. Bari: Laterza & Fifli, 1923.

B62.   Dent, Edward J. *Foundations of English Opera*. New York: Da Capo, 1956.

B63.   Diderot, Denis. *Le neveu de Rameau*. New York: Theatre Communications, Group, 1988. Excerpts in *Strunk's Source Readings in Music History*. Vol. 5. Rev. ed. New York: W.W. Norton, 1998, 188–98.

B64.   Donington, Robert. *The Rise of Opera*. London: Faber and Faber Limited, 1981.

B65.   Drinkow, John. *The Vintage Musical Comedy Book*. Reading: Osprey, 1974.

B66.   Dronke, Peter. *The Medieval Lyric*. Rochester, N.Y.: University of Rochester Press, 1996.

B67.   Dua, Mohammed. *Nueva Colleción de Bombas Puertorriqueñas*. San Juan: Author, 1991.

B68.   Duault, Alain, ed. *Wagner, les maîtres chanteurs: Die Meistersinger von Nuremberg*. Paris: Avant-scene, 1989.

B69.   Einstein, Alfred. *The Italian Madrigal*. Princeton, N.J.: Princeton University Press, 1949.

B70.   Elders, Willem. *Studien zur Symbolik in der Musik der alten Niederländer*. Bilthoven: A.B. Creyghton, 1968.

B71.   Elliott, Robert C. *The Power of Satire: Magic, Ritual, Art*. Princeton, N.J.: Princeton University Press, 1960.

B72.   Engel, Lehman. *Words with Music*. New York: Macmillan, 1972.

B73.   Ewen, David. *All the Years of American Popular Music*. Englewood Cliffs, N.J.: Prentice-Hall, 1977.

B74.   ——. *The Complete Book of American Theater*. New York: Henry Holt & Co., 1959.

B75.   ——. *The Complete World of Musical Comedy*. New York: Holt, Rinehart & Winston, 1976.

B76.   Eximeno, Antonio. *Don Lazarillo Vizcardi*. Madrid: La Sociedad de Bibliofils Españoles, 1873.

B77.   Fiske, Roger. *English Theater Music in the Eighteenth Century*. London: Oxford University Press, 1973.

B78.   Font, Auguste. *Favart, l'opéra-comique et la comédie-vaudeville aux XVIIe et XVIIIe siècles*. Paris: Fischbacher, 1894.

B79.   Freud, Sigmund. *Jokes and Their Relation to the Unconscious*. London: Routledge, 1960.

B80.   Friedrich, Gerhard. *Die deutsche und italienische Gestaltung des Falstaffs Stoffes in der Oper*. Habelschwerdt: Graeger, 1941.

B81.   Gagey, Edmond McAdoo. *Ballad Opera*. Bronx: Benjamin Blom, 1965.

B82.   Galeazzi, Francesco. *Elementi teorico-practici de musica. 1791–96*. Excerpts in *Strunk's Source Readings in Music History*. Rev. ed. New York: W.W. Norton, 1998, 85–91.

B83.   Gänzl, Kurt. *The Musical: A Concise History*. Boston: Northeastern University Press, 1997.

B84.   Gatti, Guido Maria. *Le Barbiere de Seville de Rossini: Etude historique et critique, analyse musicale*. Paris: P. Mellottée, n.d.

B85.   Gilbert, William Schwenk. *The First Night Gilbert and Sullivan*. Rev ed. London: Chappell, 1976.

B86.   Glass, Paul. *The Spirit of the Sixties: A History of the Civil War in Song*. St Louis: Educational Publishers, 1964.

B87.   Glossy, Blanka and Haas, Robert. *Wiener Comödienlieder aus drei Jahrhunderten*. Vienna: Anton Schroll, 1924.

B88.   Goldschmidt, Hugo. *Studien zur Geschichte der italienische Oper*. Leipzig: Breitkopf und Härtel, 1909.

B89.   Gonzáles Ruiz, Nicolas. *La caramba vida alegre y muerte: ejemplar de una tonadilla del siglo XVIII*. Madrid: Ediciones Morata, 1944.

B90.   Green, Stanley. *Rogers and Hammerstein Fact Book*. New York: The Kynn Farnal Group, Inc.

B91.   ——. *The World of Musical Comedy*. New York: A.S. Barnes and Co., 1974.

B92.   Grimm, Friedrich Melchior. *Le petit prophete de Boemischbroda*. Paris, 1882. Excerpts in B227, 619–35.

B93.   Grout, Donald J. *A Short History of Opera*. 2d ed. New York: Columbia University Press, 1965.

B94.   Grün, Bernard. *Kulturgeschichte des Operette*. Munich: Langen, 1961.

B95.   Haar, James, ed. *Chanson and Madrigal 1480–1530: Studies in Comparison and Contrast: A Conference at Isham Memorial Library*. Cambridge: Harvard University Press, 1964.

B96.   Hadamowsky, Franz Heinz Otto. *Die Wiener Operette: ihre Theater und Wirkungsgeschichte*. Vienna: Bellria Verlag, 1947.

B97.   Hamm, Charles. *Yesterday's Popular Song in America*. New York: W.W. Norton, 1974.

B98.   Hammerschmidt, Wolfgang. *10. Jahre Komische Oper*. Berlin: Komische Oper, 1958.

B99.   Hammerstein, Reinhold. *Diabolus in Musica*. Bern: A. Franke AG Verlag, 1974.

B100.   ———. *Tanz und Musik des Todes*. Bern: Francke Verlag, 1980.

B101.   Harpner, Stefan G., ed. *Über Musiktheater: eine Festschrift gewidmet Arthur Scherle anlasslich seines 65. Geburtstages*. Munich: Ricordi, 1992.

B102.   Hasse, Max. *Peter Cornelius und seine Barbier von Bagdad*. Leipzig: Breitkopf und Härtel, 1904.

B103.   Heartz, Daniel. *Mozart's Operas*. Berkeley: University of California at Berkeley, 1990.

B104.   ———. *Pierre Attaingnant, Royal Printer of Music*. Berkeley: University of California at Berkeley, 1964.

B105.   Hepokoski, James A. *Giuseppe Verdi: Falstaff*. Cambridge: Cambridge University Press,1984.

B106.   Herrick, Marvin T. *Italian Comedy in the Renaissance*. Urbana: University of Illinois, 1966.

B107.   Herrmann, Ursula, and Buttner, Henry. *Satirikon der Musikinstrumente*. Wilhelmshaven: Noetzel Verlag, 1987.

B108.   Herrmann-Bengen, Irmgard. *Tempobezeichnungen: Ursprung und Wandel*. Tutzing: Hans Schneider, 1959.

B109.   Highet, Gilbert. *The Anatomy of Satire*. Princeton, N.J.: Princeton University Press, 1962.

B110.   Hines, Robert. *The Composer's Point of View: Essays on Twentieth-Century Choral Music by Those Who Wrote It*. Norman: University of Oklahoma Press, 1963.

B111.   Hoffnung, Gerard. *The Hoffnung Companion to Music*. New York: Dover Press, 1971.

B112.   Hol, Joan C. *Horatio Vecchi's weltliche Werke*. Leipzig: Heitz, 1934.

B113.   Hoppin, Richard H. *Medieval Music*. New York: W.W. Norton, 1978.

B114.   Hosler, Bellamy. *Changing Aesthetic Views of Instrumental Music in 18th Century Germany*. Ann Arbor, Mich.: UMI Research Press, 1981.

B115.   Hughes, Gervase. *Composers of Operetta*. Westport, Conn.: Greenwood Press, 1973.

B116.   ———. *The Music of Arthur Sullivan*. New York: St Martin's Press, 1960.

B117.   Huizinga, Johan. *Homo ludens: A Study of the Play Element in Culture*. Boston: Beacon Press, 1955.

B118.   Humphrey, Laning. *The Humor of Music and Other Oddities of Art*. Boston: Crescendo, 1971.

B119.   Hyman, Alan. *The Gaiety Years*. London: Cassell, 1975.

B120.   Istel, Edgar. *Johann Strauss und das neunzehnte Jahrhundert*. Amsterdam: Querido Verlag, 1937.

B121.   ———. *Die Komische Oper: eine historisch-ästhetische Studie*. Stuttgart: C. Grüninger, 1906.

B122.   Jacobs, Arthur. *Choral Music: A Symposium*. Baltimore: Penguin Books, 1963.

B123.   Junker, Karl. *Zwanzig Componisten: eine skizze*. Berne, 1776.

B124.   Kassel, Richard. *The Soul of Dimitri Shostakovich: The Complete String Quartets*. New York: Town Hall Foundation, 1989.

B125.   Keller, Otto. *Die Operette in ihrer geschichtliche Entwicklung*. Vienna: Stein-Verlag, 1926.

B126.   Kidson, Frank. *The Beggar's Opera: Its Predecessors and Successors*. Cambridge, Mass.: The University Press, 1922.

B127.   Kirby, Franklyn E. *Music for Piano: A Short History*. Portland, Oregon: Amadeus, 1995.

B128.   Kircher, Athanasius. *Musurgia Universalis*. Rome, 1650.

B129.   Klauwell, Otto. *Geschichte der Programmusik*. 2d ed. Leipzig: M. Ständig, 1968.

B130.   Klob, Karl Maria. *Beiträge zur Geschichte der deutschen Komischen Oper*. Berlin: "Harmonie," 1903.

B131.   Knepler, Georg. *Musikgeschichte des 19. Jahrhunderts*. Berlin: Henschenverlag, 1961.

B132.   Koch, Hans. *Das deutsche Singspiel*. Stuttgart: Metzler, 1974.

B133.   Koch, Heinrich. *Kurzgefasstes Handwörterbuch der Musik*. Reprint Hildesheim: Georg Olms, 1981.

B134.   ———. *Musikalisches Lexikon*. Frankfurt, 1802.

B135.   Koestler, Arthur. *The Act of Creation*. New York: Macmillan, 1964.

B136.   Kostelanetz, Richard. *John Cage (ex)plain(ed)*. New York: Schirmer Books, 1996.

B137.   Kracauer, Siegfried. *Orpheus in Paris*. New York: Alfred A. Knopf, 1928.

B138.   Kreuger, Miles, ed. *The Movie Musical from Vitaphone to 42nd Street*. New York: Dover Press, 1975.

B139.   Kuhnau, Johann. *Musicalische Quacksalber*. Berlin: E. Bock, 1900.

B140.   Lajoinie, Vincent. *Le basson n'est pas contagieux*. Paris: Van de Velde, 1993.

B141.   Langer, Suzanne K. *Feeling and Form: A Theory of Art Development from Philosophy in a New Key*. New York: Charles Scribner's Sons, 1953.

B142.   Layton, Robert, ed. *A Guide to the Symphony*. Oxford: Oxford University Press, 1995.

B143.   Lehmann, Dieter. *Russlands Oper und Singspiel in der zweiten Hälfte des 18. Jahrhunderts*. Leipzig: Breitkopf und Härtel, 1958.

B144.   Levarie, Siegmund. *Mozart's Le Nozze di Figaro*. Chicago: University of Chicago Press, 1952.

B145.   Levy, Lester. *Flashes of Merriment: A Century of Humorous Songs in America 1805–1905*. Norman: Oklahoma University Press, 1971.

B146.   Lissa, Zofia. *Aufsätze zur Musikasthetik: Eine Auswahl*. Berlin: Henschel, 1969.

B147.   Lister, Laurie-Jeanne. *Humor as a Concept in Music: A Theoretical Study of Expression in Music, the Concept of Humor and Humor in Music with an Analytic Example—W.A. Mozart, Ein musikalische Spass, KV 522*. Frankfurt: Peter Lang, 1994.

B148.   Loewenberg, Alfred. *Annals of Opera, 1597–1940*. Geneva: Societas Bibliographica, 1955.

B149.   Lomax, Alan. *The Folk Songs of North America*. New York: Doubleday & Co., 1960.

B150.   Maltin, Leonard. *Leonard Maltin's Movie and Video Guide*. New York: Signet, 1997.

B151.   Mamczarz, Irene. *Les Premiers Opéras en Europe et les Formes Dramatiques Apparentées: Actes du 4e-Seminaire International de la Societé Internationale d'Histoire Comparée de Theatre, de l'Opéra et du Ballet*. Paris: Klincksieck, 1992.

B152.   Mander, Raymond, and Mitcheson, Joe. *Musical Comedy: A Story in Pictures*. New York: Taplinger, 1970.

B153.   Maniates, Maria Rika. *Mannerism in Italian Music and Culture, 1480–1530*. Chapel Hill: The University of North Carolina Press, 1979.

B154.   Marcello, Benedetto. *Il teatro alla moda*. Venice: Tessier, 1887. B227, 518-31; also in *The Musical Quarterly* 32 (1946): 371–403 and 35 (1948): 85-105.

B155.   Masson, Alain. *Comedie Musicale*. Paris: Stock Cinema, 1981.

B156.   Mattson, Inger, ed. *Gustavian Opera: An Interdisciplinary Reader in Swedish Opera, Dance, and Theatre 1771-1800*. Stockholm: Kungliga Musikaliska Akademien, 1991.

B157.   Messing, Scott. *Neoclassicism in Music*. Rochester, N.Y.: University of Rochester Press, 1996.

B158.   Meyer, Bernhard. *Die Tonarten der Klassischen Vokalpolyphonie*. Utrecht: Oosthoeck, Schletema, & Holkema, 1974.

B159.   Meyer, Leonard. *Emotion and Meaning in Music*. Chicago: University of Chicago Press, 1956.

B160.   ——. *Music, the Arts, and Ideas*. Chicago: University of Chicago Press, 1967.

B161.   Meyer-Baer, Kathi. *Music of the Spheres and the Dance of Death: Studies in Musical Iconology*. Princeton, N.J.: Princeton University Press.

B162.   Miles, William. *Songs, Odes, Glees, and Ballads: A Bibliography of American Presidential Campaign Songsters*. Westport, Conn.: Greenwood Press, 1990.

B163.   Morley, Thomas. *A Plain and Easy Introduction to Practical Music*. New York: W.W. Norton, 1953.

B164.   Moser, Hans Joachim. *Corydon: Geschichte des Mehrstimmigen Generalbassliedes und das Quodlibets im Deutschen Barock*. 2d ed. Hildesheim: Georg Olms Verlagsbuchhandlung, 1966.

B165.   Müller, Karl-Josef. *Mahler: Leben, Werke, Dokumente*. Mainz: Schott, 1988.

B166.   Muraro, Maria Teresa. *L'opera tra Venezia e Parigi*. Florence: Olschki, 1988.

B167.   Murata, Margaret. *Operas for the Papal Court 1631–1668*. Ann Arbor, Mich.: UMI Research Press, 1981.

B168.   Nash, Bruce M. *The Wacky Top 40*. Holbrook: Bob Adams, 1993.

B169.   Neicks, Frederick. *Programme Music in the Last 4 Centuries*. London, 1907.

B170.   Neumeister, Sebastian. *Das Spiel mit der höfische Liebe: das altprovenzalische Partimen*. Munich: W. Fink, 1969.

B171.   Newman, William S. *The Sonata in the Baroque Era*. Rev. ed. New York: W.W. Norton, 1972.

B172.   Nicoll, Allardyce. *The World of Harlequin: A Critical Study of the Commedia dell' Arte*. Cambridge: Cambridge University Press, 1963.

B173.   Niedt, Freidrich Erhardt. *Musikalische Handleitung*. Hamburg, 1700, excerpts in B227, 453–70.

B174.   Noske, Frits. *French Song from Berlioz to Duparc: The Origin and Development of the Mélodie*. 2d ed. New York: Dover Publications, 1970.

B175.   Orledge, Robert. *Satie the Composer*. Cambridge: Cambridge University Press, 1990.

B176.   Ortiz, Diego. *Trattado de glosas*. Rome, 1553. Facsimile Edition: Kassel: Bärenreiter, 1936.

B177.   Osthoff, Wolfgang. *Theatergesang und darstellende Musik in der Italienische Renaissance*.Tutzing: Hans Schneider, 1969.

B178.   Palisca, Claude V. *Baroque Music*. 2d ed. Englewood Cliffs, N.J.: Prentice-Hall, 1981.

B179. Palmer, Roy. *"What a lovely war": British Soldiers' Songs from the Boer War to the Present Day*. London: Joseph, 1990.

B180. Pedrell, Felipe. *Teatro lírico español anterior al siglo XIX*. La Coruña: Berea, 1897–98.

B181. Pejovik, Roksanda, ed. *Baroque i Rokoko*. Belgrade: Fakultet Muzicke Umetnosti, 1985.

B182. Pellisson, Maurice. *Les Comédies-ballets de Molière*. Paris: Hachette, 1914.

B183. Perloff, Nancy. *Art and the Everyday Popular Entertainment and the Circle of Erik Satie*. New York: Oxford University Press, 1991.

B184. Peteani, Maria von. *Franz Lehár: Seine Musik, sein Leben*. Vienna: Glocken Verlag, 1950.

B185. Pflicht, Stephan. *"fast ein Meisterwerk": die Welt der Musik in Anekdoten, eine heitere Musik-Soziologie*. London: Schott, 1987.

B186. Pirandello, Luigi. *On Humor*. Chapel Hill: University of North Carolina Press, 1974.

B187. Pitou, Spire. *The Paris Opéra: An Encyclopedia of Operas, Ballets, Composers, and Performers*. Westport, Conn.: Greenwood Press, 1983.

B188. Pougnin, Arthur. *Molière et l'opéra comique*. Paris: J. Baur, 1882.

B189. Printz, Wolfgang Caspar. *Phrynix Mitilinaeus*. Freiburg, 1691.

B190. Querol Gavalda, Miguel. *La Música en las Obras de Cervantes*. Madrid: Union Musical Español, 1971.

B191. Rabelais, François. *Gargantua and Pantagruel*. New York: W.W. Norton, 1990.

B192. Ramos de Pareia, Bartolomé. *Musica practica*. Bologna, 1482. English translation by C. Miller. Stuttgart: American Institute of Musicology, 1993.

B193. Rastall, Richard. *The Heavenly Singing Music in Early English Religious Drama*. Rochester, N.Y.: University of Rochester Press, 1996.

B194. Ratner, Leonard, G. *Classic Music: Expression, Form, and Style*. New York: Schirmer Books, 1980.

B195. Reese, Gustave. *Music in the Renaissance*. Rev. ed. New York: W.W. Norton, 1959.

B196. Reichardt, Johann Friedrich. *Ueber die deutsche comische oper*. Hamburg: C.E. Bohn, 1774.

B197. Riis, Thomas Lawrence. *Just Before Jazz: Black Musical Theater in New York: 1890–1915*. Washington, D.C.: Smithsonian Institution, 1989.

B198. Rissen, David. *Offenbach ou le Rire en Musique*. Paris: Fayard, 1980.

B199. Robinson, Michael F. *Naples and Neapolitan Opera*. Oxford: Clarendon Press, 1972.

B200.   Roche, Jerome. *The Madrigal.* New York: Oxford University Press, 1990.

B201.   Rommel, Otto. *Die Alt-Wiener Volkskomödie: ihre Geschichte vom barocken Welt-Theater bis zum Tods Nestroys.* Vienna: Schrolls, 1953.

B202.   Rosand, Ellen. *Opera in Seventeenth-Century Venice: The Creation of a Genre.* Berkeley: University of California Press, 1991.

B203.   Rosen, Charles. *The Classical Style: Haydn, Mozart, and Beethoven.* 2d ed. New York: W.W. Norton, 1997.

B204.   Rourke, Constance. *American Humor.* New York: Harcourt Brace, 1931.

B205.   Rubsamen, Walter. *Literary Sources of Secular Music in Italy (c. 1500).* Berkeley: University of Califronia Press, 1943.

B206.   Sabol, Andrew J. *Four Hundred Songs and Dances from the Stuart Masque.* Providence: Brown University Press, 1978.

B207.   Sachs, Curt. *The World History of the Dance.* New York: W.W. Norton, 1937.

B208.   Salem, James M. *A Guide to Critical Reviews: The Musical from Rodgers and Hart to Lerner and Loewe.* Metuchen, N.J.: Sacrecrow Press, 1967.

B209.   Scherillo, Michele. *L'opera buffa napolitana durante il settecento.* 2d ed. Milan: R. Sundron, 1917.

B210.   Schering, Arnold. *Humor, Heldtum, Tragik bei Beethoven: Über einige Grundsymbole der Tonsprach Beethovens.* Strasbourg: Librarie Heitz, 1955.

B211.   Schlotterer, Reinhard, ed. *Musik und Theater im Rosenkavalier von Richard Strauss.* Vienna: Verlag der Österrechischen Akademie der Wissenschaften, 1985.

B212.   Schultz, William Eben. *Gay's Beggar's Opera: Its Content, History, Influence.* New Haven, Conn.: Yale University Press, 1923.

B213.   Schwed, Paula. *I've Got Tears in My Ears from Lyin' on My Back while I Cry over You: Country Music's Best (and Funniest) Lines.* Kansas City: Andrews & McKeel, 1992.

B214.   Seidel, Michael. *Satiric Inheritance: Rabelais to Sterne.* Princeton, N.J.: Princeton University Press, 1979.

B215.   Senechaud, Marcel. *Le Repertoire Lyrique d'Hier et d'Aujourd'hui: Opéras, Opéras-Comiques, Drames Lyriques, Comedies Musicales et Ballets Dramatiques.* Paris: Billaudot, 1971.

B216.   Simpson, Charles M. *The British Broadside Ballad and Its Music.* New Brunswick, N.J.: Rutgers University Press, 1966.

B217.   Smoldon, William L. *The Music of the Medieval Church Dramas.* London: Oxford University Press, 1980.

B218.   Solomon, Maynard. *Mozart: A Life*. New York: Harper Collins, 1995.

B219.   Sonneck, Oscar G. *Early Opera in America*. New York: Benjamin Bloom, 1963.

B220.   Srong, Roy. *Art and Power: Renaissance Festivals 1450-1650*. Rochester, N.Y.: University of Rochester Press, 1997.

B221.   Stambler, Irwin. *The Encyclopedia of Pop, Rock, and Soul*. New York: St. Martin's Press, 1974.

B222.   Steblin, Rita. *A History of Key Characteristics in the Eighteenth and Early Nineteenth Centuries*. Rochester, N.Y.: University of Rochester Press, 1996.

B223.   Stefan, Paul. *Die Zauberflöte: Herkunft, Bedeutung, Geheimnis*. Vienna: Reichner, 1937.

B224.   Steinecke, W. *Die Parodie in der Musik*. Wolfenbüttel: Moseler, 1970.

B225.   Stille, Michael. *Möglichkeiten des Komischen in der Musik*. Frankfurt am Main: Lang, 1990.

B226.   Strohm, Reinhard. *Die Italienische Oper im 18. Jahrhundert*. Wilhelmshaven: Heinrichshofen, 1979.

B227.   Strunk, Oliver. *Source Readings in Music History*. New York: W.W. Norton, 1951.

B228.   Subirá, José. *Historia de la música teatral en España*. Barcelona: Editorial Labor, 1946.

B229.   ———. *La tonadilla escenica*. Madrid: Tipografia de archivos, 1928–30.

B230.   Sulzer, Johann Georg. *Allgemeine Theorie der schönen Künste*. Frankfurt, 1798.

B231.   Surrans, Alain. *100 compositeurs de A a Z: Jeux de massacre*. Arles: Coutaz, 1988.

B232.   Test, George A. *Satire: Spirit and Art*. Tampa: University of South Florida Press, 1991.

B233.   Tibaldi Chiesa, Mary. *Cimarosa e il suo tempo*. Milan: A. Garzanti, 1939.

B234.   Tinctoris, Johannes. *Terminorum musicae*. New York: Da Capo, 1978.

B235.   Tinhorao, José Ramos. *Musica Popular: Teatro & Cinema*. Petropolis: Editora Vozes, 1972.

B236.   Tolksdorf, Cäcilie. *John Gay's Beggar's Opera und Bert Brecht's Dreigroschenoper*. Rheinberg: Sattler & Koss, 1934.

B237.   Toll, Robert. *Blacking Up: The Minstrel Show in Nineteenth-Century America*. New York: Oxford University Press, 1974.

B238.   Tortolano, William. *Original Music for Men's Voices: A Selected Bibliography*. 2d ed. Metuchen, N.J.: Scarecrow Press, 1981.

B239.   Trauberg, Leonid. *Zhak Offenbah i Drugie.* Moscow: Iskusstvo, 1987.

B240.   Upton, George Putnam. *The Standard Light Operas.* Chicago: A.C. McClurg, 1902.

B241.   Veidl, Theodore. *Der musikalische Humor bei Beethoven.* Leipzig: Breitkopf und Härtel, 1929.

B242.   Vitale, Roberto. *Domenico Cimarosa.* Aversa: Noviello, 1929.

B243.   Vladimirskaja, Alla, ed. *The Leningrad State Theater of Musical Comedy.* Leningrad: Muzyka, 1972.

B244.   Warrick, John. *Richard Wagner: Die Meistersinger von Nürnberg.* Cambridge: Cambridge University Press, 1994.

B245.   Watkins, Glen. *Pyramids at the Louvre: Music, Culture, and Collage from Stravinsky to the Postmodernists.* Cambridge, Mass.: Harvard University Press, 1994.

B246.   Webster, James, and Hunter, Mary, eds. *Opera Buffa in Mozart's Vienna.* Cambridge: Cambrige University Press, 1997.

B247.   Weiss, Piero, and Taruskin, Richard. *Music in the Western World: A History in Documents.* New York: Schirmer Books, 1984.

B248.   Werf, Hendrik van der. *The Chansons of the Troubadours and Trouvères.* Utrecht: Oostoek, 1972.

B249.   Wheelock, Gretchen A. *Haydn's Ingenious Jesting with Art: Contexts of Musical Wit and Humor.* New York: Schirmer Books, 1992.

B250.   Wilder, Alec. *American Popular Song—the Great Innovators 1900–50.* New York: Oxford University Press, 1972.

B251.   Wilkins, Nigel. *Music in the Age of Chaucer.* Rochester, N.Y.: University of Rochester Press, 1996.

B252.   Williamson, Audrey. *Gilbert and Sullivan Opera.* London: Rockliff, 1953.

B253.   ———. *Gilbert and Sullivan Opera: A New Assessment.* London: Rockliff, 1955.

B254.   Wolff, Hellmuth Christian. *Geschichte der komischen Oper: von der Änfangen bis zur Gegenwart.* Wilhelmshaven: Heinrichshofen, 1981.

B255.   Wolff, Stéphane. *Un demi-siècle d'opéra-comique (1900–1950).* Paris: A. Bonne, 1953.

B256.   Woll, Allen. *Black Musical Theatre from Coontown to Dreamgirls.* Baton Rouge: Louisiana University Press, 1989.

B257.   ———. *Songs from Hollywood Musical Comedies, 1927 to the Present: A Dictionary.* New York: Garland Press, 1976.

B258.   Worbs, Hans Christian. *Das Dampfkonzert: Musik und Musikleben des 19. Jarhunderts in der Karikatur.* Wilhelmshaven: Heinrichshofen, 1982.

B259.   Zarlino, Gioseffo. *Le istitutioni harmoniche*. Venice, 1558. Part 3 published as *The Art of Counterpoint*. Translated by G.A. Marco and C.V. Palisca. New Haven, Conn.: Yale University Press, 1968.

B260.   Zeman, Herbert, ed. *Wege zu Mozart: Don Giovanni*. Vienna: Holder-Pickler-Tempsky Verlag, 1987.

B261.   Zurita, Marciano. *Historia del género chico*. Madrid: Prensa Popular, 1920.

DISSERTATIONS

B262.   Adams, Michael Charles. "The Lyrics of Stephen Sondheim: Form and Function." Ph.D. dissertation, Northwestern University, 1980.

B263.   Appel, Bernhard R. "Robert Schumanns *Humoreske* für Klavier, op. 20: zum Musikalischen Humor in der ersten Hälfte des 19.Jahrhunderts unter besonderer Berücksichtung des Formproblems." Ph.D. dissertation, University of Saarbrücken, 1981.

B264.   Baker, Sarah Ellen. "An Annotated Translation and Analysis of Richard Strauss's *Kramerspiegel*." D.M.A. dissertation, Memphis State University, 1990.

B265.   Banducci, Antonia Louise. "*Tancrede* by Antoine Danchet and André Campra: Performance History and Reception." Ph.D. dissertation, Washington University, 1990.

B266.   Barnett, Christina Powers. "Charles Ives: *114 Songs* and Transcendental Philosophy." D.M.A. dissertation, The University of Texas at Austin, 1986.

B267.   Beagle, Nancy Sue. "The Theatres of La Foire in Early Eighteenth Century France: Analysis of *La Ceinture de Venus* by Lesage." D.M.A. dissertation, Stanford University, 1985.

B268.   Beer, Otto Fritz. "Mozart and das Wiener Singspiel." Ph.D. dissertation, University of Vienna, 1932.

B269.   Bilanchone, Victor Jr. "*The Unicorn, the Gorgon and the Manticore* by Gian Carlo Menotti: A Study of a Twentieth-Century Madrigal Fable." D.M.A. dissertation, University of Miami, 1977.

B270.   Böttger, Friedrich. "Die Comedie-ballets von Molière und Lully." Ph.D. dissertation, University of Berlin, 1930.

B271.   Braunlich, Helmut. "Satire in Music, 1900 to 1920." Ph.D. dissertation, Catholic University of America, 1966.

B272.   Cardamone, Donna Gina. "The *Canzone Villanesca alla Napolitana* and Related Italian Vocal Part-Music." Ph.D. dissertation, Harvard University, 1972.

B273.   Carr, Cassandra Irene. "Wit and Humor as a Dramatic Force in the Beethoven Piano Sonatas." Ph.D. dissertation, University of Washington, 1985.

B274.   Citron, Maria Judith. "Schubert's Seven Complete Operas: A Mu-sico-Dramatic Study." Ph.D. dissertation, University of North Carolina, 1971.

B275.   Clark, Walter. "Spanish Music with a Universal Accent: Isaac Al-béniz's Opera *Pepita Jiménez*." Ph.D. dissertation, University of California, Los Angeles, 1992.

B276.   Clifton, Keith. "Maurice Ravel's *L'Heure espagnole*: Genesis, Sources, Analysis." Ph.D. dissertation, Northwestern University, 1999.

B277.   Cothern, Leah Kathleen. "The Coon Song: A Study of American Music, Entertainment, and Racism." M.A. thesis, University of Oregon, 1990.

B278.   Curfagno, Simon A. "The Life and Dramatic Music of Stefano Landi with a Transliteration and Orchestration of the Opera *Sant'Alessio*." Ph.D. dissertation, University of California, Los Angeles, 1960.

B279.   Debly, Patricia Anne. "Joseph Haydn and the Dramma Giocoso." Ph.D.dissertation, University of Victoria, British Columbia, 1993.

B280.   Delorenzo, Joseph P. "The Chorus in American Musical Theater: Emphasis on Choral Performance." Ph.D. dissertation, New York University, 1985.

B281.   Dicus, Kent Timothy. "A Stylistic Analysis of Selected Piano Works of Louis Moreau Gottschalk." M.M. thesis, University of Arizona, 1988.

B282.   Diener, Betty Sue. "Irony in Mozart's Operas." Ph. D. dissertation, Columbia University, 1992.

B283.   Ericson-Roos, Catarina. "The Songs of Robert Burns: A Study of the Unity of Poetry and Music." Ph.D. dissertation, Uppsala University, 1977.

B284.   Fischer, Frederic Irwin. "A Study of Humor in Keyboard Music." D.M.A. dissertation, Eastman School of Music of the University of Rochester, 1963.

B285.   Fleck, Stephen Harlan. "Molière's Comedy-Ballets: A Dramatic and Musical Analysis." Ph.D. dissertation, University of California, Davis, 1993.

B286.   Flynn, Susan Jane. "The Presence of Don Quixote in Music." Ph.D. dissertation, University of Tennessee, 1984.

B287.   Frampton, William McLeod. "The Piano Music of Emmanuel Chabrier." D.M.A. dissertation, University of Cincinnati, 1986.

B288.   Fuch, Marianne. "Die Entwicklung des Finales in der italienischen Opera Buffa vor Mozart." Ph.D. dissertation, University of Vienna, 1932.

B289.   Gallagher, Patricia M. Louise. "Book by the Bard: A Study of Four Musical Comedies Adapted from Plays by William Shakespeare." Ph.D. dissertation, University of Missouri, 1985.

B290.   Garwood, Ronald Edward. "Molière's Comedies Ballets." Ph.D. dissertation, Stanford University, 1985.

B291.   Giebisch, Thomas. "'Take Off' als kompositionsprinzip bei Charles Ives." Ph.D. dissertation, Musikwissenscha, University of Cologne, 1993.

B292.   Gilman, Janet Lynn. "Charles Ives—Master Songwriter: The Methods Behind His Madness." Ph.D. dissertation, University of Southern California, 1994.

B293.   Godsalve, William Herbert Louis. "Opera from Comedy: Britten Remakes Shakespeare's *Dream*." Ph.D. dissertation, University of Saskatchewan, 1990.

B294.   Goehring, Edmund J, Jr. "The Comic Vision of *Così fan tutte*: Literary and Operatic Traditions." Ph.D. dissertation, Columbia University, 1993.

B295.   Glasow, E. Thomas. "Molière, Lully, and the Comedy-Ballet." Ph.D. dissertation, State University of New York at Buffalo, 1985.

B296.   Graves, James Blackmon. "A Theory of Musical Comedy Based on the Concepts of Susanne K. Langer." Ph.D. dissertation, University of Kansas, 1981.

B297.   Grout, Donald J. "The Origins of *Opéra Comique*." Ph.D. dissertation, Harvard University, 1939.

B298.   Gustafson, DonnaMae Jenon. "Giovanni Croce's *Mascarate piacevoli et ridiculose per il carnevale*: A Contextual Study and Critical Edition." Ph.D. dissertation, University of Minnesota, 1992.

B299.   Hartmann, Donald Conrad. "The *Don Quichotte à Dulcinée* of Maurice Ravel and the *Chansons de Don Quichotte* of Jacques Ibert: A Study of Two Song Cycles for the Film *Don Quixote*, which Starred Feodor Chaliapin." D.M.A. dissertation, University of Oklahoma, 1994.

B300.   Heinemann, Barbara Paula. "Don Quixote and Opera: Libretti and Music." Ph.D. dissertation, State University of New York, Buffalo, 1989.

B301.   Heinrich, Viktor. "Komik und Humor in der Musik." Ph.D. dissertation, University of Vienna, 1931.

B302.   Higgins, Regina Kirby. "Victorian Laughter: The Comic Operas of Gilbert and Sullivan." Ph.D. dissertation, 1985.

B303.   Irvine, Demar B. "The Expression of Ideas and Emotions in Music." Ph.D. dissertation, Harvard University, 1935.

B304.   Jolly, James Lester. "American Operas Based on the Plays of William Shakespeare, 1948–1976." Ph.D. dissertation, Louisiana State University, 1985.

B305.   Kenley, McDowell Eugene. "Sixteenth-Century Matachine Dances: Morescas of Mock Combat and Comic Pantomime." D.M.A. dissertation, Stanford University, 1993.

B306.   Konas, Gary Paul. "From Gershwin to Sondheim: The Pulitzer Prize-Winning Musical." Ph.D. dissertation, University of California, Davis, 1993.

B307.   Kopp, James Butler. "The 'Drame Lyrique': A Study in the Esthetics of *Opéra-Comique*, 1762–1791." Ph.D. dissertation, University of Pennsylvania, 1982.

B308.   Krasner, Orly Leah. "Reginald de Koven (1859–1920) and American Comic Opera at the Turn of the Century." Ph.D. dissertation, City University of New York, 1995.

B309.   Krettenauer, Thomas. "Felix Mendelssohn's *Heimkehr aus der Fremde*: Untersuchungen und Dokumenten zum Liederspiel, Op. 89." Ph.D. dissertation, University of Augsburg, 1993.

B310.   Krott, Rudolfine. "Die Singspiele Schuberts." Ph.D. dissertation, University of Vienna, 1921.

B311.   Krüger, Viktor. "Die Entwicklung Carl Maria von Weber in seiner Jugendopern *Abu Hassan* und *Silvana*." Ph.D. dissertation, University of Vienna, 1907.

B312.   Lafenthaler, Gunter. "Gedanken zum Begriff 'Musikalische Komik' in den Sinfonischen Dichtungen von Richard Strauss." Ph.D. dissertation, University of Vienna, 1980.

B313.   Larderet, Pierre. "Humour, Ironie, Satire, Grotesque: Étude de Quelques Aspects et Procedes du Comique Musical." Ph. D. dissertation, University of Saint-Étienne, 1981.

B314.   Lazarevich, Gordana. "The Role of the Neapolitan Intermezzo in the Evolution of 18th-Century Musical Style: Literary, Symphonic, and Dramatic Aspects, 1685–1735." Ph.D. dissertation, Columbia University, 1970.

B315.   Leveille, Jacques. "Les caricatures musicales dans la vie parisienne de 1863 à 1880." M.A. thesis. University of Laval, 1983.

B316.   Lissa, Zofia. "Über das Komische in der Musik." Ph.D. dissertation, University of Zagreb, 1938. Published in *Aufsätze zur Musik* (Berlin, 1969).

B317.   Loft, Abram. "The Comic Servant on the Lyric Stage of 18th Century Vienna." M.A. thesis, Columbia University, 1944.

B318.   Lowry, Linda Ridge. "Humor in Instrumental Music: A Discussion of Musical Affect, Psychological Concepts of Humor, and Identification of Musical Humor." Ph.D. dissertation, Ohio State University, 1974.

B319.   MacNeil, Anne Elizabeth. "Music and the Life and Work of Isabella Andreini: Humanistic Attitudes toward Music, Poetry, and Theater during the Late Sixteenth and Early Seventeenth Centuries." Ph.D. dissertation, University of Chicago, 1994.

B320.   Marzi, Jean-Denis. "Molière: Structure and Comic Rhythm." Ph.D. dissertation, Fordham University, 1982.

B321.   Maschio, Geraldine Ann. "The Ziegfield Follies: Form, Content, and Significance of an American Revue." Ph.D. dissertation, University of Wisconsin, 1981.

B322.   McKinney, David Conley. "The Influence of Parisian Popular Entertainment on the Piano Works of Erik Satie and Francis Poulenc." D.M.A. dissertation, University of North Carolina, 1994.

B323.   Mendenhall, Christian Dean. "American Musical Comedy from 1943 to 1964: A Theoretical Investigation of Its Racial Function." Ph.D. dissertation, Northwestern University, 1989.

B324.   Moore, Ray W. "A Study of the Renaissance Madrigal Comedy." Ed. D. dissertation, Columbia University, 1964.

B325.   Morales, Donald Maurice. "African American Folk Survivals in Contemporary Black Musical Theater." Ph.D. dissertation, State University of New York at Stony Brook, 1981.

B326.   Musillo, Irene A. "The Rise of Comic Opera." M.A, thesis, Columbia University, 1956.

B327.   Nietan, Hanns. "Die Buffoszenen der spätvenezianischen Oper (1680 bis 1710)." Ph.D. dissertation, University of Halle, 1925.

B328.   Paul, Steven E. "Wit, Comedy, and Humor in the Instrumental Music of Joseph Haydn." Ph.D. dissertation, Cambridge University, 1980.

B329.   Petersen, Karen Elizabeth. "Music of the Chat Noir." Ph.D. dissertation, Northwestern University, 1989.

B330.   Pollack, Howard Joel. "Walter Piston and His Music." Ph.D. dissertation, Cornell University, 1981.

B331.   Powell, John Scott. "Music in the Theater of Molière." Ph.D. dissertation, University of Washington, 1982.

B332.   Rabin, Ronald Jay. "Mozart, Da Ponte and the Dramaturgy of Opera Buffa: Italian Comic Opera in Vienna 1783–1791." Ph.D. dissertation, Cornell University, 1996.

B333.   Richards, Annette. "Fantasy and Fantasía: A Theory of the Musical Pictoresque." Ph.D. dissertation, Stanford University, 1995.

B334.   Ridder, Lisolette de. "Der Anteil der Commedia dell' Arte an der Entstehungs und Entwicklungsgeschichte der Komischen Oper." Ph.D. dissertation, Cologne, 1970.

B335.   Robinson, Carol Jeanne. "One-Act Opéra Comique from 1800 to 1810: Contributions of Henri-Montan Berton and Nicolo Isouard." D.M.A. dissertation, University of Cincinnati, 1986.

B336.   Rubin, Jason. "Lew Fields and the Development of the Broadway Musical." Ph.D. dissertation, New York University, 1991.

B337.   Ruf, Wolfgang. "Die Rezeption von Mozarts *Le Nozze di Figaro* bei den Zeitgenossen." Ph.D. dissertation, University of Freiburg, 1974.

B338.   Russell, Tilden. "Minuet, Scherzando, and Scherzo: The Dance Movement in Transition, 1781–1825." Ph.D. dissertation, University of North Carolina, 1983.

B339.   Schadendorff, Mirjam. "Humor als Formkonzept in der Musik Gustav Mahlers." Ph.D. dissertation, Germany, Metzler, 1995.

B340.   Scheide, Frank Milo. "The History of Low Comedy and Nineteenth- and Early Twentieth-Century English Music Hall as a Basis for Examining the 1914–1917 Films of Charles Spencer Chaplin." Ph.D. dissertation, University of Wisconsin, 1990.

B341.   Schemberg, Ester. "Irony, Satire, Parody, and the Grotesque in the Music of Dmitri Shostakovich." Ph.D. dissertation, University of Edinburgh, 1995.

B342.   B342. Schmitz, Alan William. "Musical Settings of the *Canzoni* from Niccolò Machiavelli's *La Mandragola*: An Original Composition and Essay." Ph.D. dissertation, Rutgers University, 1979.

B343.   Schnoll, Alois. "Erik Satie, Genie oder Scharlatan? Anmerkungen zu den Klavierstücke mit Stories." M.A, thesis, Hochschule für Musik und Darstellende Kunst, Salzburg, 1982.

B344.   Shumway, Jeffrey. "A Comparative Study of Representative Bagatelles for the Piano since Beethoven." D.M. dissertation, Indiana University, 1981.

B345.   Snyder, Linda June. "Leonard Bernstein's Works for the Musical Theatre: How the Music Functions Dramatically." D.M.A. dissertation, University of Illinois at Urbana-Champaign, 1982.

B346.   Snyder, Richard Dale. "The Use of the Comic Idea in Selected Works of Contemporary Opera." Ph.D. dissertation, Indiana University, 1968.

B347.   Soltes, Karla. "Lord Berners: A Survey of His Ballets and an Annotated Bibliography of His Life and Works." M.A. thesis, Kent State University, 1980.

B348.   Spitzer, Michael. "Ambiguity and Paradox in Beethoven's Late Style." Ph.D. dissertation, University of Southampton, 1993.

B349.   Stone, Thomas Joseph. "The Quintessence of Gilbertanism, Directorial Revitilization of Gilbert and Sullivan Operas, and 'Thespis'." Ph.D. dissertation, New York University, 1989.

B350.   Sydow, Brigitte. "Untersuchungen über die Klavierlieder M.P. Musorgskijs." Ph.D. dissertation, University of Göttingen, 1974.

B351.   Thompson, Donald P. "*Dona Francisquita*, a Zarzuela by Amadeo Vives: Translation, Adaptation." Ph.D. dissertation, University of Iowa, 1970.

B352.   Thym, Jurgen. "The Solo Song Settings of Eichendorff's Poems by Schumann and Wolf." Ph.D. dissertation, Case Western Reserve University, 1974.

B353.   Traupman, Carol A. "*I Dimenticati*: Italian Comic Opera in the Mid-Ninetenth Century." Ph.D. dissertation, Cornell University, 1996.

B354.   Tyler-Schmidt, Linda Louis. "Mozart and Operatic Conventions in Austria and Southern Germany, 1760-1800." Ph.D. dissertation, Princeton University, 1988.

B355.   Unruh, Patricia. "'Fumeur' Poetry and Music of the Chantilly Codex: A Study of Its Meaning and Background." M.A. thesis, University of British Columbia, 1983.

B356.   Vallillo, Stephen M. "George M. Cohan, Director." Ph.D. dissertation, New York University, 1987.

B357.   Weaver, Robert L. "Florentine Comic Operas of the Seventeenth Century." Ph.D. dissertation, University of North Carolina, 1958.

B358.   Weintraub, David. "Humor in Song." Ed.D. dissertation, Columbia University, 1974.

B359.   Werner, Klaus-Günter. "Spiele der Kunst: Kompositorische Verfahren in der Oper *Falstaff* von Giuseppe Verdi." Ph.D. dissertation, University of Kiel, 1986.

B360.   White, Richard Kerry. "Historic Festivals and the Nature of American Musical Comedy." Ph.D. dissertation, University of Oregon, 1984.

B361.   Wierzbicki, James Eugene. "Burlesque Opera in London: 1729–1737." Ph.D. dissertation, University of Cincinnati, 1979.

B362.   Wolf, Robert Peter. "Jean-Philippe Rameau's Comedie Lyrique, *Les paladins* (1760): A Critical Edition and Study." Ph.D. dissertation, Yale University, 1977.

B363.   Zach, Miriam Susan. "The Choral Music of Ernst Toch." Ph.D. dissertation, University of Florida, 1993.

B364.   Zauft, Karin. "Möglichkeiten der Wiederbelebung der Komischen Oper des 18. Jahrhunderts: Ein Beitrag zur Untersuchung der Konzeptionell-stilistischen Spezifik der Komischen Oper des 18. Jahrhunderts als Voraussetzung ihrer Werkgetreuen Realisierung für das Heutige Musiktheater." Ph.D. dissertation, University of Halle, 1972.

DICTIONARIES, ENCYCLOPEDIAS, AND REFERENCE WORKS

B365.   *Annals of Opera*. 3d ed. Ed. by A. Lowenberg. Totowa, N.J.:
Rowman & Littlefield, 1978. This source gives performance histo-
ries of each opera listed.

B366.   *Choral Music in Print*. Philadelphia: Music Data, 1974. An important source for the availability of choral music.

B367.   *Cobbett's Cyclopedic Survey of Chamber Music*. Compiled and
edited by W. Cobbett. London: Oxford University Press, 1963. Although this book is dated, this source includes references to rare
humorous chamber works.

B368.   *Commedia dell' Arte: A Guide to the Primary and Secondary Literature*. Ed. by T. Heck. New York: Garland, 1988. This source is
important because of the pervasive impact of the subject.

B369.   *The Complete Encyclopedia of Popular Music and Jazz*. Ed. by B.
Kinkle. New Rochelle, N.Y.: Arlington, 1974. As the title indicates, this source supplements the discussion of these topics in the
final chapter.

B370.   *The Concise Oxford Dictionary of Opera*. 2d ed. Ed. by H. Rosen-
thal and J. Warrack. London: Oxford University Press. This source
can be used in conjunction with B381.

B371.   *The Da Capo Companion to 20th-Century Popular Music*. Ed. by
P. Hardy and D. Laing. New York: Da Capo, 1990. This can be
used in conjunction with B369.

B372.   *Dictionary-Catalogue of Operas and Operettas*. Compiled by J.
Towers. New York: Da Capo, 1967. This can be used in conjunction with B365.

B373.   *Early American Choral Music: An Annotated Guide*. Ed. by D. De
Venney. Berkeley, Calif.: Fallen Leaf Press, 1988. This supplements B365 as well as the discussion of this topic in the chapter on
late 18th-century music.

B374.   *The Encyclopedia of Musical Theater*. Ed. by K. Ganzel. New
York: Schirmer Books, 1994. This is an important source for the
discussion of this topic and can be used with B369.

B375.   *The Encyclopedia of Philosophy*. New York: Macmillan,
1967.This source has an extensive article on humor.

B376.   *The Guinness Encyclopedia of Popular Music*. Ed. by C. Larken.
Guinness: Middlesex, 1992. This relates to B371.

B377.   *Handwörterbuch der musikalischen Terminologie*. Ed. by H. Eggebrecht. Wiesbaden: Franz Stein Verlag, 1972–. This ongoing
source gives the etymologies of the terms for many genres discussed in the narrative.

B378.   *Harvard Dictionary of Music.* 2d ed. Ed. by W. Apel. Cambridge: Harvard University Press, 1969. This edition has an excellent article on satire in music.

B379.   *Index to Opera, Operetta and Musical Comedy: Synopses in Collections and Periodicals.* Ed. by J. Drone. Metuchen, N.J.: Scarecrow Press, 1978. This relates to B372.

B380.   *The International Dictionary of Ballet.* Ed. by M. Bremser. Detroit: St. James Press, 1993. This source gives information on one of the most important comic musical genres.

B381.   *The International Dictionary of Opera.* Ed. by C. Larue. Detroit: St. James Press, 1993. This relates to B370 and B374.

B382.   *Die Musik in Geschichte und Gegenwart.* Ed. by F. Blume. Kassel: Bärenreiter, 1949–51. This source has extensive articles on many genres discussed in the narrative.

B383.   *Die Musik in Geschichte und Gegenwart.* 2d ed. Ed. by L. Finscher. Kassel: Bärenreiter, 1994–. This is the latest edition of B382. The first section is devoted to articles on many comic genres.

B384.   *The New Grove Book of Operas.* Ed. by S. Sadie. New York: St. Martin's Press, 1996. This relates to B387. Only selected operas are included, but with substantially new insights.

B385.   *The New Grove Dictionary.* Ed. by S. Sadie. London: Macmillan, 1980. This relates to B382 and B383. Extensive articles on genres included in the narrative are found.

B386.   *The New Grove Dictionary of American Music.* Ed. by H. Hitchcock and S. Sadie. London: Macmillan, 1986. Articles on composers cited in the final chapter are included.

B387.   *The New Grove Dictionary of Jazz.* Ed. by B. Kernfeld. London: Macmillan, 1986. This relates to B364.

B388.   *The New Grove Dictionary of Opera.* Ed. by S. Sadie. London: Macmillan, 1992. This relates to B384 and B385. Extensive articles on composers and operas appear.

B389.   *The New Harvard Dictionary of Music.* Ed. by D. Randell. Cambridge: Harvard University Press, 1986. This relates to B378. Articles on many genres considered in the narrative are included.

B390.   *The Norton/Grove Concise Encyclopedia of Music.* Ed. by S. Sadie. New York: W.W. Norton, 1988. This relates to B385. Although the articles are short, they offer new insights.

B391.   *Operas in Germany: A Dictionary.* Ed. by M. Griffel. Westport, Conn.: Greenwood Press, 1990. This source has important information on many comic German operas considered in the final three chapters.

B392.   *Reader's Encyclopedia of World Drama.* New York: Crowell, 1969. This source supplements B381.

ARTICLES

The following articles include studies of comedy and humor on individual composers, general studies of comedy in music, and studies that deal with philosophic or psychological issues.

B393. Abraham, Gerald. "The Genesis of *The Bartered Bride.*" *Music and Letters* 28 (1947): 36–49.

B394. Absil, Jean. "L'humour dans la Musique." *Bulletin de la Classe des Beaux-Arts de l'Academie Royale de Belgique* 50 (1968): 226–41.

B395. Ackermann, Peter. "Eine Kapitulation: zum Verhältnis Offenbach—Wagner." *Jacques Offenbach*. Mainz: Schott, 1985, 135–48.

B396. Adorno, Theodore W. "Chaplin Times Two." *The Yale Journal of Criticism* 9 (1996): 57–61.

B397. Allanbrook, Wye Jamison. "Pro Marcellina: The Shape of *Figaro*, Act IV." *Music & Letters* 63 (1982): 69–84.

B398. Allen, Beatrice. "Music with a Sense of Humor." *Clavier* 31 (1992): 21–25.

B399. Altman, Wilhelm. "Lortzing als dramaturgischer Leher." *Die Musik* 8 (1913–14): 154–58.

B400. Anderson, Nicolas. "Rameau's *Platée*: Burlesque or Grotesque?" *Early Music* 11 (1983): 505–9.

B401. Angermüller, Rudolph. "*La finta semplice*: Goldoni/Coltellinis Libretto zu Mozarts ersten Opera buffa (Italienish-Deutsch)." *Mitteilungen der Internationalen Stiftung Mozarteum* 33 (1982): 15–72.

B402. ——. "Haydns *Der Zerstreute* in Salzburg (1776)." *Haydn Studien* 4 (1978): 85–93.

B403. ——. "Mozart und Rousseau: zur Textgrundlage von *Bastien und Bastienne*." Mitteilungen der *Internationalen Stiftung Mozarteum* 30 (1975): 2–37.

B404. ——. "Reformideen von Du Roullet und Beaumarchais als Opernlibrettisten." *Acta Musicologica* 48 (1976): 227–53.

B405. Arias, Enrique Alberto. "Capriccios of the Great Composers." *Clavier* 34 (1995): 13–16.

B406. ——."Cerone and His Enigmas." *Anuario Musical* 44 (1989): 87–114.

B407. Armstead-Johnson, Helen. "Themes and Values in Afro-American Librettos and Book Musicals." *Musical Theatre in America*. Westport, Conn.: Greenwood Press, 1984, 133–42.

B408. Arnheim, Malie. "*Le Devin du village* von Jean-Jacques Rousseau und die Parodie Les amours de *Bastien et Bastienne*." Sammelbände der internationalen *Musikgesellschaft* 4 (1902–3): 686–727.

B409.   Augusto, Sergio. "The *Chanchada* and the Brazilian Musical Comedy: An Overview and Commentary." *Studies in Latin American Popular Culture* 7 (1988): 157–66.

B410.   Auld, Louis E. "Lully's Comic Art." *Jean-Baptiste Lully*. Laaber: Laaber Verlag, 1990, 17–30.

B411.   Austern, Linda Phyllis. "Musical Parody in the Jacobean City Comedy." *Music & Letters* 66 (1985): 255–66.

B412.   Austin, William. "Satie Before and After Cocteau." *The Musical Quarterly* 48 (1962): 216–33.

B413.   Ayre, L. "The Wit of Music." *Opera* 17 (1966): 983.

B414.   Badura-Skoda, Eva. "The Influence of Viennese Popular Comedy on Haydn and Mozart." *Proceedings of the Royal Musical Association* 100 (1973–74): 185–99.

B415.   ——. "'Teutsche Comoedie-Arien' und Joseph Haydn." *Der junge Haydn*. Graz: Akademische Druck- und Verlaganstalt, 1972, 59–73.

B416.   Ballantine, Cristopher. "Social and Philosophic Outlook in Mozart's Operas." *The Musical Quarterly* 67 (1981): 508–26.

B417.   Banccorsi, Alfredo. "La sinfonia del *Barbiere* prima del *Barbiere*." *Rassegna Musicale* 24 (1954): 210–19.

B418.   Banoun, Bernard. "*Arabella*, Realisme 'Noir' et Comedie Forcée." *Austriaca* 37 (1993): 9–18.

B419.   Barassi, Ferrari. "La tradizione della Moresca e uno sconsciuto ballo del cinque-seicento." *Rivista italiana di musicologia* 5 (1970): 37–60.

B420.   Barry, C.A. "Introductory to the Study of Wagner's Comic opera *Die Meistersinger von Nürnberg*." *Proceedings of the Royal Musical Association* 100 (1981): 74–97.

B421.   Baumgartner, Ulrich. "Die Musikalischen Komodianten Europas, oder Wann ist Musik Lustig?" *Österreichische Musikzeitschrift* 23 (1968): 241–43.

B422.   Becker, Daniele. "Allegorie du theatre ou theatre d'allegories? Les ensaladas de Mateo Flecha." *Les premiers operas en Europe et les formes dramatiques apparentées: Actes du 4e-seminaire international de la Societé Internationale d'Histoire Comparée du Theatre, de l'Opéra et du Ballet*. Paris: Klincksieck, 1992, 95–115.

B423.   ——."El teatro lirico en tiempo de Carlos II: Commedia de música y zarzuela." *Dialogos hispanicos de Amsterdam* 8 (1989): 409–34.

B424.   Becker, Friederike. "'Singspielhalle des Humors': Zu den dramatischen Meisterwerken Paul Hindemiths." *Hindemith Jahrbuch* 18 (1989): 7–54.

B425.   Bellaigue, Camille. "Les Epoques de la musique: L'opéra comique." *Revue des deux mondes* 5 (1905): 177–210.

B426.   Benham, Evelyn. "Humor in Music." *Chesterian* 9 (1928): 146–51.

B427.   Berger, Arthur V. "*The Beggar's Opera*, the Burlesque, and Italian Opera." *Music and Letters* 17 (1936): 93–105.

B428.   Bernstein, Lawrence. "*La Courone et fleur des Chansons a troys*: A Mirror of the French Chanson in Italy in the Years Between Ottaviano Petrucci and Antonio Gardano." *Journal of the American Musicological Society* 26 (1973): 1–68.

B429.   Bernstein, Leonard. "Discusses Humor in Music and conducts *Till Eulenspiegel's Merry Pranks*." (record). Columbia Masterworks. #R60–1440. 1962.

B430.   Block, Jeffrey. "The Broadway Canon from *Show Boat* to *West Side Story* and the European Operatic Ideal." *The Journal of Musicology* 11 (1993): 53–45.

B431.   Boer, Bertil van. "Gustaf III's 'Divertissement med sang' Fodelsedagen: A Gustavian Political Satire." *Scandanavian Studies* 61 (1989): 28–40.

B432.   ———. "The Gustavian Pasticcio: Musical Collaborations." Gustav III and the Swedish Stage: Opera, Theatre, and Other Foibles: Essays in Honor of Hans *Astraud*. Lewiston, N.J.: Mellen, 1993: 219–35.

B433.   ———. "Joseph Martin Kraus's *Soliman den Andra*: A Gustavian Turkish Opera." *Svensk Tidskrift for Musikforskning* 70 (1988): 9–30.

B434.   Bohn, Emil. "*Theophilus*: Niederdeutsches Schauspiel aus einer Handschrift des 15. Jahrhunderts." *Monatshefte für Musikgeschichte* 9 (1877): 3–25.

B435.   Bollert, Werner. "Komik und Sentiment in der deutschen Spieloper (1835-1850): *Musik, Libretto, Dramaturgie.*" *Festschrift Arno Forchert zum 60. Geburtstag 29. Dezember 1985.* Kassel: Bärenreiter, 1986, 228–33.

B436.   ———. "Tre opere di Galuppi, Haydn e Paisiello sul' *Mondo della luna* di Goldoni." *Musica d'oggi* 21 (1939): 265–70.

B437.   Bonds, Mark Evan. "Haydn, Laurence Sterne, and the Origins of Musical Irony." *Journal of the American Musicological Society* 44 (1991): 57–91.

B438.   Bonin, Jean M. "Music from 'The Splendidest Sight': The America Circus Songster." *Notes* 45 (1989): 699–713.

B439.   Bordman, Gerald. "Jerome David Kern: Innovator/Traditionalist." *The Musical Quarterly* 71 (1985): 468–73.

B440.   Borris, Siegfried. "Das Lächeln der Melpomene: Betrachtungen über das Komische in der Musik." *Festschrift für einen Verleger Ludwig Strecker zum 90. Geburtstag.* Mainz: Schott, 1973, 111–18.

B441.   ———. "Vier Aspekte zum Musical." *Musik und Bildung* 3 (1971): 171–76.

B442. Bowles, Edmund. "The Role of Musical Instruments in Medieval Sacred Drama." *Musical Quarterly* 49 (1959): 67–84.

B443. Brandstetter, Gabriele. "So Machen Alle: Die Frühen Übersetzungen von Da Pontes und Mozarts *Così fan tutte* für Deutsche Buhnen." *Die Musikforschung* 35 (1982): 27–44.

B444. Branmüller, Robert. "Der Einzige Fremde: Hans Werner Henze Oper *Der junge Lord* and der Tradition der Komodie." *Musica Germany* 50 (1996): 184–88.

B445. Branscombe, Peter. "Music in the Viennese Popular Theatre of the Eighteenth and Nineteenth Centuries." *Proceedings of the Royal Musical Association* 98 (1971–72): 101–12.

B446. Braun, Werner. "Musiksatirische Kriege." *Acta Musicologica* 63 (1991): 168–99.

B447. Bregy, Jean-François. "Ciel! Mes bijoux!" *L'avante-scene Opéra* 110 (1988): 4–5.

B448. Bridges, Thomas W. "Louis XII and Guillaume: One Note, One More Time." *The Creative Process*. New York: Broude Brothers, 1992, 3–16.

B449. Brown, Bruce Alan. "Le Pazzie d'Orlando, *Orlando paladino*, and the Uses of Parody." *Italica* 64 (1987): 583–605.

B450. Brown, Howard Mayer. "The *Chanson Rustique*: Popular Elements in the 15th- and 16th-Century Chanson." *Journal of the American Musicological Society* 12 (1959): 16–26.

B451. Bukofzer, Manfred F. "Allegory in Baroque Music." *Journal of the Warburg Institute* 3 (1939–40): 1–21.

B452. Busoni, Ferruccio. "Beethoven and Musical Humor." *The Essence of Music and Other Papers*. Trans. by R. Ley. New York: Dover Publications, 1965, 134–37.

B453. Caballero, Carlo. "'A Wicked Voice': On Vernon Lee, Wagner, and the Effect of Music." *Victorian Studies* 35 (1992): 385–408.

B454. Cain, Jacques. "Musique et jouissance, ou de l'incompatibilité de la psychanalyse avec la musique." *A la musique: Recontres psychanaltiques d'Aix-en Provence 1991*. Paris: Belles Lettres, 1993, 145–95.

B455. Campbell, Thomas P. "Machaut and Chaucer: *Ars Nova* and the Art of Narrative." *The Chaucer Review* 24 (1990): 275–89.

B456. Cano, Cristiana. "Il Gioco Mozartiano." *Studi Musicali* 11 (1982): 261–76.

B457. Carr, Cassandra. "Charles Ives' Humor As Reflected in His Songs." *American Music* 7 (1989):123–39.

B458. Carter, Tim. "A Florentine Wedding of 1608." *Acta Musicologica* 55 (1983): 89–107.

B459.   Casares Rodicio, Emilio. "El teatro do los bufos o una crisis en el teatro lirico del XIX español." *Anuario musical* 48 (1993): 217–28.

B460.   Castelvecchi, Stefano. "From 'Nina' to 'Nina:' Psychodrama, Absorption, and Sentiment in the 1780s." *Cambridge Opera Journal* 8 (1996): 91–112.

B461.   Cauchie, Daniele. "The Highlights of French *Opéra Comique*." *The Musical Quarterly* 25 (1939): 306–12.

B462.   Cazden, Norman. "Humor in the Music of Stravinsky and Prokofiev." *Science and Society* 18 (1954): 52–74.

B463.   Chater, James. "Castelletti's *Stravaganze d'amore* (1585): A Comedy with Interludes." *Studi Musicali* 8 (1979): 85–148.

B464.   Chenneviere, Rudhyar D. "Erik Satie and the Music of Irony." *The Musical Quarterly* 5 (1919): 469–78.

B465.   Christout, Marie-Francoise. "*Les noces de Pelé et Thetis*, Comedie Italienne en Musique Entremelée d'un Ballet Danse par le Roi." *Baroque: Revue International* 5 (1972): 59–62.

B466.   Clark, Caryl. "Intertextual Play and Haydn's *La fedeltà premiata*." *Current Musicology* 51 (1993): 59–81.

B467.   Cohen, Norm. "Songs of Humor and Hilarity." *Ethnomusicology* 23 (1979): 486–91.

B468.   Comer, Irene Forsyth. "Lotta Crabtree and John Brougham: Collaborating Pioneers in the Development of American Musical Comedy." *Musical Theatre in America*. Westport, Conn.: Greenwood Press, 1984, 99–110.

B469.   Cone, Edward T. "The Uses of Convention: Stravinsky and His Models." *Music: A View from Delft*. Ed. by R. Morgan. Chicago: University of Chicago Press, 1989, 281–92.

B470.   Cooke, Deryck. "*The Rake* and the 18th Century." *The Musical Times* 103 (1962): 20–23.

B471.   Coolidge, Richard A. "The Musical Mask of Comedy." *Southwestern Texas Music Educator* (1973): 2–5.

B472.   Cooper, B. Lee. "Sultry Songs as High Humor." *Popular Music and Society* 17 (1993): 77–85.

B473.   Corwin, George. "The Madrigal Comedy." *CAustriaSM/ACEUMj* 3 (1974): 38–58.

B474.   Covach, John Rudolph. "The Rules and Use of Specific Models in Music Satire." *Indiana Theory Review* 11 (1990): 119–44.

B475.   Craft, Robert. "Reflection on *The Rake's Progress*." *The Score* 9 (1954): 24-30.

B476.   Critchfield, Richard. "Lessing, Diderot, and Theatre." *Eighteenth-Century German Authors and Their Aesthetic Theories; Literature and the Other Arts*. Columbia, S.C.: Camden Press, 1988, 11–28.

B477.   Cronk, Nicholas. "The Play of Words and Music in Molière-Charpentier's *Le malade imaginaire.*" *French Studies* 47 (1993): 6–19.

B478.   Crozier, Eric. "Foreword to *Albert Herring.*" *Tempo* 4 (1947): 10–14.

B479.   Curzon, Henri de. "Les Opéras-comique de Boieldeau." *Revue musicale* 14 (1933): 249–63.

B480.   Cusic, Don. "Comedy and Humor in Country Music." *Journal of American Culture* 16 (1993): 45–50.

B481.   Dahlhaus, Carl. "Komodie mit Musik und musikalische Komodie: Zur Poetik der Komischen Oper." *Neue Zeitschrift für Musik* 157 (1986): 24–27.

B482.   Dahnan, Gilbert. "Une Dramaturgie au Second Degree: La Comedié-Madrigalesque—L'exemple de la *Pazzia Senile.*" *Les Premiers Operas en Europe et les Formes Dramatiques Apparentées: Actes du 4e-Seminaire International de la Societé Internationale d'Histoire Comparée du Theatre, de l'Opéra et du Ballet.* Paris: Klincksieck, 1992, 79–94.

B483.   Dalmonte, Rossana. "Toward a Semiology of Humor." *International Review of the Aesthetics and Sociology of Music* 26 (1995): 167–87.

B484.   Danckwardt, Marianne. "Der Paukenschlag im Andante der Sinfonie Nr. 94: Ein Haydnscher Witz?" *Quaestiones in Musica: Festschrift für Franz Krautwurst.* Tutzing: Hans Schneider, 1989, 61–69.

B485.   Danuser, Hermann. "Zum Stilbegriff bei Sergej Prokofjew." *Bericht über das Internationale Symposium Sergej Prokofjew: Aspekte seines Werkes und der Biographie.*" Regensburg: Bosse, 1992, 75–89.

B486.   Daverio, John. "Brahms's Academic Festival Overture and the Comic Modes." *American Brahms Society Newsletter* 12 (1994): 1–3.

B487.   Davieu, Donald G. "The Final Chapter of the Strauss-Hofmannthal Collaboration on *Ariadne auf Naxos.*" *Music and German Literature: Their Relationships since the Middle Ages.* Columbia, S.C.: Camden, 1992, 242–56.

B488.   Davis, Josephine K. "What Makes Music Funny?" *Music Journal* 15 (1957): 14–18.

B489.   Davison, Nigel. "Continental Cousins of the In Nomine Family." *The Music Review* 52 (1991): 1–11.

B490.   Debly, Patricia Anne. "Social Commentary in the Music of Haydn's Goldoni operas." *Metaphor: A Musical Dimension.* Sydney: Currency, 1991, 51–68.

B491.   Degrada, Francesco. *"Lo fratre'nnamorato e l'estetica della commedia musicale napoletana."* Napoli e il teatro musicale in Europa tra Sette e Ottocento: Studi in onore di Friedrich Lippmann. Florence: Olschki, 1993, 21–35.

B492.   Della Corte, Andrea. "La Comicità e la Musica." *De ratione in musica: Festschrift für Erich Schenk.* Kassel: Bärenreiter, 1975, 105–14.

B493.   ——. "Tragico e comico nell'opera veneziana della seconda parte del Seicento." *Rassegna musicale* 11 (1938): 325–33.

B494.   Dent, Edward J. "Ensembles and Finales in 18th-Century Italian Opera." *Sammelbände der internationalen Musikgesselschaft* 11 (1909–10): 543–69; 12 (1910–11): 112–38.

B495.   Dill, Heinz J. "Romantic Irony in the Works of Robert Schumann." *The Musical Quarterly* 73 (1989): 172–95.

B496.   Dittersdorf, Karl Ditters von. "Über die Grenzen des Komischen und des Heroischen in der Musik." *Allgemeine Musik Zeitung* 9 (1798): cols. 139–41.

B497.   Dona, Mariangela. "Johann Kuhnau e *Der musikalische Quacksalber." Liuteria: Organo uffiziale dell'Associazione Liuteria Italiana* 11 (1991): 34–42.

B498.   Dorfmüller, Kurt. "Das 'Umgekehrte Erhabene' im Schulssatz von Mozarts Streichquartett KV 387." *Festschrift: Rudolf Bockholdt zum 60. Geburtstag.* Pfaffenhofen: Ludwig, 1990, 201–6.

B499.   Downes, Edward. "Music That Laughs and Capers." *Opera News* 31 (1967): 24–25.

B500.   Drew, David. "Brecht Versus Opera." *The Score* 23 (1958): 7–10.

B501.   Duhamal, Raoul. "Quelques Maîtres de l'opéra-comique aux XIXe Siècle." *Revue musicale* 14 (1933): 291–302.

B502.   Eberle, Gottfried. "Der Titularrät and die Generalstochter: von Musikalischer Satire im Russischen Lied." *Musica* 42 (1988): 172–76.

B503.   Eggebrecht, Hans Heinrich. "Der Begriff des Komischen in der Musikästhetick des 18. Jahrhunderts." *Die Musikforschung* 4–5 (1951–52): 144–52.

B504.   Einstein, Alfred. "Die Parodie in der Villanella." *Zeitschrift für Musikwissenschaft* 2 (1920): 212–24.

B505.   ——. "Some Musical Representations of the Temperaments." *Essays on Music.* New York: W.W. Norton, 1962, 121–31.

B506.   Engel, Carl. "A Note on Domenico Cimarosa's *Il matrimonio segreto." The Musical Quarterly* 33 (1947): 201–6.

B507.   Engel, Lehman. "The Condition of the American Musical Today." *Musical Theatre in America.* Westport, Conn.: Greenwood Press, 1984, 13–20.

B508.   Epstein, Peter. "Paul Hindemiths Theatermusik." *Die Musik* 23 (1931): 582–87.

B509.   Evans, Peter. "Britten's *A Midsummer Night's Dream*: A Preview." *Tempo* 53-54 (1960): 34–48.

B510.   Farahat, Martha. "On the Staging of Madrigal Comedies." *Early Music History* 10 (1991): 123–44.

B511.   Farnsworth, Rodney. "*Così fan tutte* as Parody and Burlesque." *The Opera Quarterly* 6 (1988–89): 50–68.

B512.   Felz, Nelly. "*The Rake's Progress*: Masque Elisabethain Sous un Loup Venetien." *Revue de Musicologie* 77 (1991): 59–80.

B513.   Ferlan, Françoise. "Rires et Sourires." *L'avant-scene Opéra* 116–117 (1989): 198-201.

B514.   Ferrari Barassi, Elena. "La Tradizione della Moresca e uno Sconosciuto Ballo del Cinque-seicento." *Rivista Italiana di Musicologia* 5 (1970): 37–60.

B515.   Fifield, Christopher. "Smetana and *The Devil's Wall*." *Musical Times* 128 (1987): 78–80.

B516.   Fischer, Alan. "Gilbert and Donizetti." *The Opera Quarterly* 11 (1995): 29–42.

B517.   Fischer, Fred. "But Is It Funny? Humor at the Keyboard." *Clavier* 7 (1968): 16–24.

B518.   ——. "Humor in the Haydn Sonatas." *Piano Teacher* 7 (1954): 13–17.

B519.   ——. "Musical Humor: A Future as Well as a Past?" *The Journal of Aesthestics and Art Criticism* 32 (1973): 375–83.

B520.   Fischer, Kurt von. "Erik Saties Choralkompositionen." *De musica et cantu: Studien zur Geschichte der Kirchenmusik und der Oper—Helmut Hücke zum 60. Geburtstag*. Hildesheim: Olms, 1993, 693–710.

B521.   Flood, W.H. Grattan. "*The Beggar's Opera* and Its Composers." *Music and Letters* 3 (1922): 402–6.

B522.   Flothius, Marius. "Einige Betrachtungen über den Humor in der Musik." *Österreichische Musikzeitschrift* 38 (1983): 688–95.

B523.   Folstein, Robert L. "A Bibliography on Jacques Offenbach." *Current Musicology* 12 (1971): 116–28.

B524.   Frati, Lodovico. "Satire di musicisti." *Rivista musicali italiani* 22 (1915): 560–6.

B525.   Fricke, Dietmar. "Ein Vorform der Oper: *Le bourgeois gentilhomme* von Molière und Lully." *Neue Zeitschrift für Musik* 148 (1987): 10–13.

B526.   Friedman, Lawrence S. "Words into Power: Renaissance Expression and Thomas Campion." *English Studies* 69 (1988): 130–45.

B527.   Fuller, David R. "Portraits and Characters in Instrumental Music of Seventeenth- and Eighteenth-Century France." *Early Keyboard Music* 8 (1990): 33–59.

B528.   Füller, Klaus. "Das Stilmittel der Parodie in den Bühnenwerken Jacques Offenbachs: ein Beitrag zum Musikunterricht an der Realschule." *Zeitschrift für Musikpädagogik* 13 (1988): 3–12.

B529.   Gaillard, P.A. "L'humour en musique." *Schweizerische Musikzeitung* 112 (1972): 18–20.

B530.   Garn, Maria. "Berliner Operette zwischen 1933 und 1945: Kulturpolitische Vorgaben und Realität." *Nationaler Stil und Europaische Dimension in der Musik derJahrhundertwende.* Darmstadt: Wissenschaftliche Buchgesellschaft, 1991, 147–59.

B531.   Gatti, Guido Maria. "The Stage Works of Ferruccio Busoni" *The Musical Quarterly* 20 (1934): 267–77.

B532.   Gavezzeni, Gianandrea. "Donizetti e *l'Elisir d'amore*." *Rassegna musicale* 6 (1933): 44–50.

B533.   Geck, Martin. "Spuren eines Einzelgangers: vom Unergründlichen Humor in Bachs 'Bauernkantate.'" *Neue Zeitschrift für Musik* 153 (1992): 24–29.

B534.   Geiringer, Karl "Haydn and His Viennese Background" *Haydn Studies.* New York: W.W. Norton, 1981. 3–13.

B535.   Gerboth, Walter. "The Comic Element in Music." Lecture at MLA Conference, USA, 1974.

B536.   Gianturco, Carolyn. "A Possible Date for Stradella's *Il Trespolo Tutore*." *Music & Letters* 54 (1973): 25–37.

B537.   Gilbert, Henry F. "Humor in Music." *The Musical Quarterly* 12 (1926): 40–55.

B538.   Gillmore, Alan M. "Erik Satie and the Concept of the Avant-Garde." *The Musical Quarterly* 59 (1983): 104–19.

B539.   ——. "Musico-Poetic Form in Satie's 'Humoristic' Piano Suite (1913-14)." *Canadian University Music Review* 8 (1987): 1–42.

B540.   Glasow, E. "*Così fan tutte*: Sexual Rhythmics." *The Opera Quarterly* 11 (1995): 17–29.

B541.   Gloede, Wilhelm. "'Ein musikalischer Spass'-ernst genommen: Über spekulative Tendenzen bei Mozart." *Mitteilungen der Internationalen Stiftung Mozarteum* 38 (1987): 56–62.

B542.   Godt, Irving. "Mozart's Real Joke." *The College Music Symposium* 26 (1986): 27–41.

B543.   Godwin, Joscelyn. "Layers of Meaning in The Magic Flute." *The Musical Quarterly* 64 (1979): 471–92.

B544.   Goldschmidt, Harry. "Zitat oder Parodie?" *Beiträge zur Musikwissenschaft* 12 (1970): 171–98.

B545.   Gomez, Maricarmen. "The *Ensalada* and the Origins of Lyric Theater in Spain." *Comparative Drama* 28 (1994): 367–93.

B546. Gossett, Philip. Liner notes for Rossini, *Sins of My Old Age*. None-such D-79027.

B547. Graves, James B. "The American Musical Comedy: A Theoretical Discussion." *Journal of Popular Culture* 19 (1986): 17–26.

B548. ——. "English Comic Opera: 1760–1800." *Monthly Musical Record* 87 (1957): 208–15.

B549. Green, Richard. "*Il Distratto* of Regnard and Haydn: a Re-Examination." *Haydn Jahrbuch* 11 (1980): 183–95.

B550. Green, Susan. "Comedy and Puccini's Operas." *Opera Quarterly* 2 (1984): 102–13.

B551. Griggs, John C. "The Influence of Comedy upon Operatic Form." *The Musical Quarterly* 3 (1917): 552–61.

B552. Grout, Donald J. "Seventeenth-Century Parodies of French Opera." *The Musical Quarterly* 27 (1941): 211–19; 514–26.

B553. Grovlez, Gabriel. "Jacques Offenbach: A Centennial Sketch." *The Musical Quarterly* 5 (1919): 329–37.

B554. Grühn Wilfried. "Wie heiter ist der Kunst?" *Österreichische Musikzeitschrift* 38 (1983): 677.

B555. Guck, Marion A. "Taking Notice: A Response to Kendall Walton." *The Journal of Musicology* 11 (1993): 45–51.

B556. Gui, Vittorio. "*Arlecchino*." *Rassegna musicale* 13 (1940): 30–37.

B557. Guichard, Leon. "A Propos d'Erik Satie: Notules Incoherentes." *Recherches et Travaux: U.E.R. de Lettres* 7 (1973): 63–80.

B558. Gürsching, Albrecht. "Urteil Exklusiv: die Negative Sinfonie. Mozarts 'Musikalischer Spass' KV 522." *Musica* 36 (1982): 246–49.

B559. Haas, Robert. "Die Musik in der Wiener deutscher Stegreifkomödie." *Studien zur Musikwissenschaft* 12 (1925): 1–64.

B560. ——."Teutsche Comodie Arien." *Zeitschrift für Musikwissenschaft* 3 (1920–21): 405–15.

B561. ——."Wiener deutsche Parodieopern um 1730." *Zeitschrift für Musikwissenschaft* 8 (1925–26): 201–25.

B562. Hafner, Ottfried. "Von Krahwinkel nach Nürnberg: Neues zur Vorgeschichte von Wagners Meistersingern." *Österreichische Musikzeitschrift* 49 (1994): 545–50.

B563. Hamann, Heinz Wolfgang. "Eine unbekannte Familien-Reminiszen in Mozarts Serenade KV 522 ('Ein musikalischer Spass')." *Die Musikforschung* 13 (1960): 180–82.

B564. Hancock, Sandra G. "Aaron Curtis' 'Comic Broadsides': The Legacy of an Obscure Black Minstrel Singer." *Tennessee Folklore Society Bulletin* 55 (1992): 89–100.

B565. Harley, Maria. "Technika Komedii w Falstaffie G. Vierdiego." *Muzyka* 36 (1991): 3–25.

B566. Harrison, John. "Comedy in *Don Giovanni*." *The Opera Journal* 4 (1971): 16–18.

B567.   Hasbany, R. "Saturday Night Fever and Nashville: Exploring the Comic Mythos." *Journal of Popular Culture* 12 (1978): 557–71.

B568.   Heartz, Daniel. "The Creation of the Buffo Finale in Italian Opera." *Proceedings of the Royal Musical Association* 104 (1977-78): 67–78.

B569.   ——. "Les Lumineres: Voltaire and Metastasio; Goldoni, Favart and Diderot." *The Report of the International Musicological Conference, Berkeley 1977.* Kassel: Bärenreiter, 1981, 233–38.

B570.   Heldt, Gerhard. "*Der Rosenkavalier*, komödie für Musik." *Hohenpunkte der Dresden Opergeschichte im 20. Jahrhundert.* Dresden: Hochschule C.M. von Weber, 1984, 903–15.

B571.   Helfert, Vladimir. "Zur Gechichte des Wiener Singspiels." *Zeitschrift für Musikwissenschaft* 5 (1922–23): 194–209.

B572.   Helm, Everett. "Virgil Thomson's *Four Saints in Three Acts*." *The Music Review* 15 (1954): 127–32.

B573.   Heuss, Alfred. "Der Humor im letzten Satz von Haydns Oxford-Symphonie." *Die Musik* 12 (1912): 270–86.

B574.   Hoffman, William. "Confessions of a Librettist: How Rossini's *Barbiere* influenced *Ghosts of Versailles*." *Opera News* 59 (1995): 8–10.

B575.   Hoffmann, Niels. "Satirisches Verfahren und Kompositorisches Material." *Oper heute: Formen der Wirklichkeit im Zeitgenossischen Musiktheater.* Vienna: Universal, 1985, 244–57.

B576.   Hohenemser, Richard. "Über Komik und Humor in der Musik." *Jahrbuch der Musikbibliothek Peters* 24 (1917): 65–83.

B577.   Holmes, William Carl. "Comedy-Opera—Comic Opera." *Analecta Musicologica* 5 (1968): 92–103.

B578.   Holzer, Ludmilla. "Die komische Opern Glucks." *Studien zur Musikwissenschaft* 13 (1926): 3–37.

B579.   Hornby, Richard. "The Decline of the American Musical Comedy." *Hudson Review* 41 (1988): 182–88.

B580.   Hücke, Helmut. "Alessandro Scarlatti und die Musikkomödie." *Colloquium Alessandro Scarlatti.* Tutzing: Schneider, 1975, 177–90.

B581.   ——. "Die Szenische Ausprägung des Komischen im Neapolitanischen Intermezzo in in der *Commedia Musicale*." *Bericht über den Internationalen Musikwissenschaftlichen Kongress Bonn 1970.* Kassel: Bärenreiter, 1971, 183–85.

B582.   Hunter, Mary. "Some Representations of Opera Seria in Opera Buffa." *Cambridge Opera Journal* 3 (1991): 89–108.

B583.   Hussey, Dyneley. "Casanova and *Don Giovanni*." *Music & Letters* 8 (1927): 470–72.

B584.   Hyart, Charles. "Gretry et Bouilly: Le Musicien et son Librettiste." *Revue General: Perspectives Européenes des Sciences Humaines* 10 (1984): 21–32.

B585.   Imeson, Sylvia. "Ridentem Dicere Verum: Reflexive Aspects of Haydn's Instrumental Style, c. 1768–72." *Canadian University Music Review* 11 (1991): 50–67.

B586.   Irving, Howard. "Haydn and Laurence Sterne: Similarities in Eighteenth-Century Literary and Musical Wit." *Current Musicology* 40 (1985): 34–49.

B587.   Istel, Edgar. "Mozart's *Magic Flute* and Freemasonry." *The Musical Quarterly* 13 (1927): 510–27.

B588.   Jackson, Gertrude. "*Kiss Me Kate*—ein Musical von Shakespeare." *Contact* 15 (1970): 31–34.

B589.   Jackson, Timothy L. "Mozart's 'Little Gigue' in G major K.574: A Study in Rhythmic Shift—a Reminiscence of the Competition with Hassler." *Mitteilungen der Internationalen Stiftung Mozarteum* 37 (1989): 70–82.

B590.   Jensen, Eric Frederick. "George Horatio Darby's 'Musical Review Extraordinary' or, Felicien David in the New World." *American Music* 8 (1990): 351–58.

B591.   Josephson, David. "The Case for Percy Grainger, Edwardian Musician, on His Centenary." *Music and Civilization: Essays in Honor of Paul Henry Lang.* New York: W.W. Norton, 1984, 350–62.

B592.   Kalisch, Volker. "Von lachenden Musik, vom Lachen in der Musik." *Neue Zeitschrift für Musik* 157 (1996): 6–11.

B593.   Karkoschka, Ehrard. "Auch ein musikalischer Spass?" *Musica Germany* 45 (1991): 68–70.

B594.   Karlinsky, Simon. "Russian Comic Opera in the Age of Catherine the Great." *Nineteenth Century Music* 7 (1984): 318–25.

B595.   Kein, Rudolph. "Gibt es musikalischen Humor?" *Hi Fi Stereophonie* 19 (1980): 790–91.

B596.   Keldys, Jurij. "Die Anfänge der Russische Oper." *Probleme und Konzeptionen: Aktuelle Arbeiten SowjetischeMusikwissenschaftlicher.* Leipzig: VEP Deutscher Verlag für Musik, 1977, 158–81.

B597.   Keller, Hans. "Britten's *Beggar's Opera.*" *Tempo* 10 (1948–49): 7–13.

B598.   ——. "Schoenberg's Comic Opera." *The Score* 21 (1957): 27–36.

B599.   Kentler, J. and Dmitrievski, Vitalij Nikolaevic. "Zum Genre des Musicals." *Gruse* 22 (1974): 756–68.

B600.   Kephart, Carolyn. "An Unnoticed Forerunner of The Beggar's Opera." *Music & Letters* 61 (1980): 266–71.

B601.   Keppler, Philip Jr. "Some Comments on Musical Quotation." *The Musical Quarterly* 42 (1956): 473–85.

B602.   Kerman, Joseph. "Opera à la mode." *The Hudson Review* 6 (1953–54): 560–77.

B603.   ——. "Tandelnde lazzi: On Beethoven's Trio in D major, Opus 70, No. 1." *Abraham Festschrift*. Oxford: Oxford University Press, 1985, 109–22.

B604.   Kidd, James C. "Wit and Humor in a Tonal Syntax." *Current Musicology* 21 (1976): 70–82.

B605.   Kimball, Robert. "The Road to *Oklahoma!*" *Opera News* 58 (1993): 12–16, 18–19.

B606.   King, Ruth. "Victor Borge, Comedy's Music Man." *Music Journal* 35 (1977): 4.

B607.   Kirby, Percival R. "A 13th Century Ballad Opera." *Music & Letters* 11 (1930): 163–71.

B608.   Kirkendale, Warren. "Franceschina, Girometta, and Their Companions in a *Madrigal a Diversi Linguaggi* by Luca Marenzio and Orazio Vecchi." *Acta Musicologica* 44 (1972): 181–235.

B609.   Kling, H. "Caron de Beaumarchais et la musique." *Rivista musicale italiana* 7 (1900): 673–97.

B610.   Klotz, Volker. "Faustchen 1 und 2: Reflexe auf Goethes Tragödie in der Operette-Herves Le petit Faust und Yvains La-haut." *Dahlhaus Festschrift*. Laaber: Laaber Verlag, 1988, 229–40.

B611.   Knapp, Margaret M. "Theatrical Parodies in American Topical Revues." *Journal of Popular Culture* 12 (1978): 482–90.

B612.   Komozynski, Egon von. "*Die Zauberflöte*: Entstehung und Bedeutung des Kunstwerks." *Neue Mozart-Jahrbuch* 1 (1941): 147–74

B613.   Konold, Wulf. "Die Schwierigkeiten mit dem Komischen: Zu *Alexander Zemlinsky's Kleider machen Leute.*" *Alexander Zemlinsky: Aesthetik, Stil und Umfeld*. Vienna: Bohlau, 1995, 117–26.

B614.   Kostelanetz, Richard. "John Cage as Horspielmacher." *Journal of Musicology* 8 (1990): 291–99.

B615.   Krasner, David. "Parody and Double Consciousness in the Language of Early Black Musical Theatre." *African American Review* 29 (1995): 307–17.

B616.   Krones, Hartmut. "Das 'Hohe Komische' bei Joseph Haydn." *Österreichische Musikzeitschrift* 38 (1983): 2–8.

B617.   Kucaba, John. "Beethoven as Buffoon." *The Music Review* 41 (1980): 103–20.

B618.   Kühn, Hellmut. "Charakter und Dramaturgie in Mozarts Musikalischer Komodie." *Gattungen der Musik und ihre Klassiker*. Laaber: Laaber Verlag, 1988, 155–68.

B619.   Kunze, Stefan. "Ironie des Klassizismus: Aspekte des Umbruchsin der musikalischen Komodie um 1800." *Die stilistische Entwicklung der Italienischen Musik*. Laaber: Laaber Verlag, 1982, 72–98.

B620.   Laaff, Ernst. "Der musikalische Humor in Beethovens achter Symphonie." *Archiv für Musikwissenschaft* 20 (1963): 213–29.

B621.   Landon, H.C. Robbins. "Haydn's Marionette Operas." *The Haydn Yearbook* 1 (1962): 111–97.

B622.   Lang, Paul Henry. "Haydn and the Opera." *Musical Quarterly* 18 (1932): 274–81.

B623.   Larderet, Pierre. "Humour, Ironie, Satire, Parodie dans la Musique Francaise des XVIIe et XVIIIe siecles." *Aspects de la Musique Baroque et Classique a Lyon et en France.* Lyon: University of Lyon, 1989, 125–34.

B624.   ——."Roussel et l'humour—Autour du Testament de la tante Caroline." *Albert Roussel: Musique et Esthetique.* Paris: Vrin, 1989, 283–96.

B625.   La Rue, Jan. "A 'Hail and Farewell' Quodlibet Symphony." *Music & Letters* 37 (1956): 250–59.

B626.   Lavauden, Thérèse. "L'humour dans l'oeuvre de Debussy." *Revue Musicale* 11 (1930): 97–105.

B627.   Lawrence, William John. "Early Irish Ballad and Comic Opera." *The Musical Quarterly* 8 (1922): 397–412.

B628.   Lazarevich, Gordana. "Hasse as a Comic Dramatist: The Neapolitan Intermezzi." *Analecta Musicologica* 25 (1987): 287–303.

B629.   ——. "Humor in Music: Literary Features of Early Eighteenth-Century Italian Musical Theatre." *The International Musicological Society Report of the Eleventh Congress Copenhagen 1972.* Vol. II Ed. by H. Glahn, S. Sorens, and P. Ryom. Copenhagen, 1973, 531–38.

B630.   ——. "The Significance of the Italian Comic Intermezzo As an 18th-Century Small Form." *Geschichte und Dramaturgie des Operneinakters.* Laaber: Laaber Verlag, 1991, 85–94.

B631.   LeBlanc, Albert, Sims, Wendy L., Malin, Sue A, and Sherrill, Carolyn. "Relationship between Humor Perceived in Music and Preferences of Different-Age Listeners." *Journal of Research in Music Education* 40 (1992): 269–82.

B632.   Leichtentritt, Hugo. "Schubert's Early Operas." *The Musical Quarterly* 14 (1928): 620–38.

B633.   Leopold, Silke. "Curtio precipitato—Claudio Parodiato." *The Well Enchanting Skill: Music, Poetry, Drama in the Culture of the Renaissance: Essays in Honour of F.W. Sternfeld.* Oxford: Clarendon Press, 1990, 65–76.

B634.   ——. "Einige Gedanken zum Thema: Komische Oper in Venedig vor Goldoni." *Die Musikforschung* 36 (1983): 85–93.

B635.   ——. "Protokoll Vor- und Frühgeschichte der Komische Oper." *Die Musikforschung* 36 (1983): 135–9.

B636. Lesenger, Jay. "*Don Giovanni*, Sozialkomödie oder Moraltragodie? Ansichten eines Regisseurs." *Wege zu Mozart: "Don Giovanni."* Vienna: Holder-Pichler-Tempsky, 1987, 59–66.

B637. Lester, Joel. "Major-Minor Concepts and Modal Theory in Germany 1592-1680." *Journal of the American Musicological Society* 30 (1977): 208–53.

B638. Levy, Herb. "Serious Fun: Music and Humor." *New Music Across America.* Valencia: California Institute of the Arts, 1992, 72–74.

B639. Levy, Janet. "'Something Mechanical Encrusted on the Living': A Source of Musical Wit and Humor." *Convention in Eighteenth- and Nineteenth-Century Music: Essays in Honor of Leonard G. Ratner.* New York: Pendragon Press, 1992, 225–56.

B640. Lewin, David. "Some Musical Jokes in Mozart's *Le Nozze di Figaro.*" *Studies in Music History.* Ed. by H. Powers. Princeton, N.J.: Princeton University Press, 1968, 443–67.

B641. Lichtfuss, Martin. "Wenn man das Leben durch Champagnerglas betrachtet." *Öesterreiche Musikzeitschrift* 51 (1996): 296–99.

B642. Liebscher, Julia. "Biedermeier-Elemente in der Deutschen Spieloper: Zu Otto Nicolais Die Lustigen Weiber von Windsor." *Die Musikforschung* 40 (1987): 229–37.

B643. Linder-Beroud, Waltraud. "O Tante Baum...und Stille Macht...: Themen und Typen der Weinachtsliedparodie." *175 Jahre Stille Nacht! Heilige Nacht!: Symposiumbericht.* Salzburg: Selke, 1994, 101–28.

B644. Linstead, George. "Wit in Music." *Musical Opinion* June, 1945: 262–63.

B645. Lippmann, Friedrich. "Haydn's *La fedeltà premiata* und Cimarosas *L'infedeltà fedele.*" *Haydn-Studien* 5 (1982): 1–15.

B646. ——. "Haydn und die Opera Buffa: Vergleiche mit Italienischen Werken Gleichen Textes." *Joseph Haydn: Tradition und Rezeption.* Cologne: Gesellschaft für Musikforschung, 1982, 113–40.

B647. Lissa, Zofia. "Die Kategorie des Komischen in der Musik." *Report of the International Musicological Congress 1958.* Kassel: Bärenreiter, 1958, 181–83.

B648. Livermore, Ann. "*The Magic Flute* and Calderón." *Music & Letters* 36 (1955): 7–16.

B649. ——."Rousseau, Beaumarchais, and Figaro." *The Musical Quarterly* 57 (1971): 466–90.

B650. Loewenberg, Alfred. "*Bastien and Bastienne* Once More." *Music & Letters* 25 (1924): 176–81.

B651. ——. "Paisiello's and Rossini's *Barbiere di Siviglie.*" *Music & Letters* 20 (1939): 157–62.'

B652. Loft, Abram. "The Comic Servant in Mozart's Operas." *The Musical Quarterly* 32 (1946): 376–89.

B653.   ———. "Musical Comedy." *Reader's Encylopedia of World Drama* . New York: Crowell, 1969, 96.

B654.   Longyear, Katherine Eide. "Henry F. Gilbert's Unfinished 'Uncle Remus' Opera." *Yearbook for Inter-American Musical Research* 10 (1974): 50–67.

B655.   Longyear, Rey M. "Beethoven and Romantic Irony." *The Musical Quarterly* 56 (1970): 647–64.

B656.   Lubin, Ernest. "Alec Templeton—the Pianist and His Music." *The Music Journal* 35 (1977): 22–31.

B657.   Lucas, John. "The Comic Spirit in Jazz." *Second Line* 13 (1962): 3–6.

B658.   Luhning, Helga. "Mozart gegen Da Ponte? Ernst und Komödie in Quintett 'Si scrivermi ogni giorno' in *Così fan tutte.*" *Napoli e il teatro musicale in Europa tra Sette e Ottocento: Studi in onore di Friedrich Lippmann.* Florence: Olschki, 1993, 235–45.

B659.   Maertens, Willi. "Zwischen Patriot und Bass-Geige: Zu Georg Philipp Telemanns Kapitansmusik 1724." *Ars Musica: Festgabe Willi Maertens.* Michaelstein: Institut für Auffuhrung der Musik des 18. Jahrhunderts, 1985, 46–77.

B660.   Mahabir, Cynthia. "Wit and Popular Music: The Calypso and the Blues." *Popular Music* 15 (1996): 55–81.

B661.   Malipiero, G. Francesco. "A Plea for True Comedy." *Modern Music* 6 (1929): 10–13.

B662.   Maniates, Maria Rika. "Combinative Chansons in the Dijon Chansonnier." *Journal of the American Musicological Society* 23 (1970): 228–81.

B663.   Markovich, Tatjana. "W.A. Mozart *Le nozze di Figaro*—J.K. Novak *Figaro*: Uporedna studjia." *XV Sureti Muzickih Akademija-Fakulteta Jugoslavije.* Belgrad: Fakultet Muzicke Umetnosti, 1988.

B664.   Marrocco, W. Thomas. "Music and Dance in Boccaccio's Time." *Dance Research Journal* 10 (1978): 19–22.

B665.   Marsoner, Karin. "Mit diesem Kapriccio schlag ich euch." *Neue Zeitschrift für Musik* 157 (1996): 29–33.

B666.   Mason, Colin. "Stravinsky's Opera." *Music & Letters* 23 (1952): 1–9.

B667.   Maus, Fred Everett. "Introduction: Music Theory and Other Disciplines—Three Views." *The Journal of Musicology* 11 (1993): 7–10.

B668.   Maus, Octave. "L'humour dans la musique." *Revue Musicale* 4 (1904): 81–87.

B669.   Mazouer, Charles. "La comtesse d'Escarbagnas et Le malade imaginaire: Deux comedies-ballets." *Litteratures classiques* 1993: 25–44.

B670.   Mendenhall, Christian. "American Musical Comedy As a Liminal Ritual of Woman as Homemaker." *The Journal of American Culture* 13 (1990): 57–69.

B671.   Messenger, Michael. "Donizetti's Comedy of Sentiment." *Opera* 24 (1973): 108.

B672.   Messmer, Franzpeter. "*Der Rosenkavalier* und die Tradition der musikalischen Komödie um 1911." *Musik und Theater im "Rosenkavalier" von Richard Strauss.* Vienna: Österreichischer Akademie der Wissenschaften, 169–210.

B673.   Meyer, Leonard B. "On Rehearing Music." *Journal of the American Musicological Society* 14 (1961): 257–67.

B674.   Michaelis, Christian Friedrich. "Ueber das Humoristische oder Launige in der musikalsichen Komposition." *Allgemeine musikalische Zeitung* IX/46 (1807): Cols. 725–29.

B675.   Misch, Ludwig. "The Composer Jests." *Musical America* 76 (1956): 20–32.

B676.   ——. "Das Komische in der Musik." *Neue Beethoven-Studien und anderen Themen.* Munich: G. Henle, 1967, 211–22.

B677.   Mitchell, Donald. "Prokofiev's *Three Oranges*: A Note on Its Musical-Dramatic Organisation." *Tempo* 4 (1956): 20–24.

B678.   ——. "The Serious Comedy of *Albert Herring*." *The Opera Quarterly* 4 (1986): 45–59.

B679.   Mohr, Wilhelm. "*Der Papst, der Will, der Kaiser muss*: Anmerkung zum Thema 'Humor in der Musik'." *Mitteilungen der Hans-Pfitzner Gesellschaft* 32 (1974): 39–41.

B680.   Molinari, Cesare. "L'altra Faccia del 1589: Isabella Andreinie la sua 'Pazzia'." *Firenze e la Toscana dei Medici.* Florence: Olschki, 1983, 565–73.

B681.   Monson, Ingrid Tolia. "Doubleness and Jazz Improvisation: Irony, Parody, and Ethnomusicology." *Critical Inquiry* 20 (1994): 283–313.

B682.   Montagu, Nathan. "The Origins of The Golden Cockerel." *The Musical Quarterly* 15 (1954): 33–38.

B683.   Montiero, George. "Parodies of Scripture, Prayer and Hymns."*Journal of American Folklore* 77 (1964): 45–52.

B684.   Mull, Helen K. "A Study of Humor in Music." *American Journal of Psychology* 62 (1949): 560–66.

B685.   Müller, Ulrich. "Donna Giovanni und *Der Ring des Liebesjungen*: Anmerkungen zur Alternativen Oper." *Opern und Opernfiguren: Festschrift für Joachim Herz.* Salzburg: Müller-Speiser, 1989: 411–26.

B686.   Murphy, Edward W. "A Programme for the First Movement of Shostakovich's Fifteenth Symphony: 'A Debate About Four Musical Styles.'" *The Music Review* 53 (1992): 47–62.

B687.   Murrill, Herbert. "*The Rake's Progress.*" *The Score* 6 (1952): 55–58.

B688.   Nagy, Michael. "*Ein musikalischer Spass*? Bemerkungen zu Mozarts Divertimento KV 522." *Musikwissenschaftliche Perspektiven aus Wien* 1 (1993): 23–27.

B689.   Naylor, Bernard. "Albert Lortzing." *Proceedings of the Royal Musical Association.* 58 (1931–32): 1–13.

B690.   Neill, Edward D. "Eric Satie." *Musicalia* 1 (1970): 4–11.

B691.   Nettl, Paul. "Mozart, Casanova, Don Giovanni." *Schweizerische Musikzeitung* 96 (1956): 60–65.

B692.   Nick, Edmund. "Divertimento von heiteren Musik." *Musica* 11 (1948): 174–76.

B693.   Noe, Gunther von. "Der musikalische Witz: Über die Freude der Kompositionen am musikalischen Spass." *Das Orchester* 40 (1992): 730–35.

B694.   Noiray, Michel. "Ariettes et vaudevilles dans les anées de formation de l'opéra comique." *Die Musikforschung* 36 (1983): 117–20.

B695.   Noske, Frits. "*Don Giovanni*: An Interpretation." *Theater Research* 13 (1973): 60–74.

B696.   ——. "Index to Opera, Operetta and Musical Comedy Synopses in Collections and Periodicals." *Fontes Artis Musicae* 26 (1979): 244.

B697.   Oliver, A. Richard. "Molière's Contributions to the Lyric Stage." *The Musical Quarterly* 33 (1947): 350–64.

B698.   Ollone, Max d'. "Gounod et l'opéra-comique." *Revue musicale* 14 (1933): 303–8.

B699.   ——. "L'Opéra-comique aux XIXe siècle." *Revue musicale* 14 (1933): 241–312.

B700.   Ossberger, Harold. "Musikalischer Humor an Beispielen der Klaviermusik." *Österreichische Musikzeitschrift* 38 (1983): 696–701.

B701.   Packer, Dorothy S. "François Rabelais, Vaudevilliste." *The Musical Quarterly* 57 (1971): 107–28.

B702.   Partsch, Erich Wolfgang. "Scherz, Parodie und tiefere Bedeutung: die Gesangsszene in Richard Strauss' Oper *Die schweigsame Frau.*" *Neue Zeitschrift für Musik* 153 (1992): 50–51.

B703.   Pasler, Jann. "New Music as Confrontation: The Musical Sources of Jean Cocteau's Identity." *The Musical Quarterly* 75 (1991): 255–78.

B704.   Paul, Steven E. "Comedy, Wit, and Humor in Haydn's Instrumental Music." *Haydn Studies:Proceedings of the International Haydn Conference* Washington, D.C., 1975. Ed. by J. Larson, H. Serwer, J. Webster. New York: W.W. Norton, 1981, 386–402

B705.   ——. "Wit and Humor in the Operas of Haydn." *Bericht über den Internationalen Joseph Haydn Kongress* Wien, *Hofburg, 5–12 September 1982.* Munich: Henle, 1986, 386–402.

B706.   Pauly, Reinhard G. "Benedetto Marcello's Satire on Early 18th Century Opera." *The Musical Quarterly* 34 (1948): 222–33.

B707.   Pearson, Arthur A. "Comedy and Drama in Folksong." *Proceedings of the Royal Musical Association* 50 (1923–24): 118.

B708.   Peckman, Rudolf. "Zur Typologie der Operngestalten Telemanns und ihre Beziehung zur Italienischen Librettistik." *Telemann und seine Dichter*. Magdeburg: Rat der Stadt, 1978, 52–57.

B709.   Pendle, Karin. "A bas les convents: Anticlerical Sentiment in French Opera of the 1790s." *The Music Review* 42 (1981): 22–45.

B710.   ——."A Working Friendship: Marsollier and Dalayrac." *Music & Letters* 64 (1983): 44–57.

B711.   Perry-Camp, Jane. "A Laugh a Minuet: Humor in Late Eighteenth-Century Music." *College Music Symposium* 19 (1979): 19–29.

B712.   Phyllis Austern, Linda. "Musical Parody in the Jacobean City Comedy." *Music & Letters* 66 (1985): 355–66.

B713.   Pigman, G.W. III. "Versions of Imitation in the Renaissance," *Renaissance Quarterly* 33 (1980): 1–32.

B714.   Piontek, Steffen. "'Strahlt auf mich der Glanz des Goldes'—oder der glückliche Ausgang einer missglückten Entführung. Gedanken zu Rossinis *Barbier von Sevilla." Opern und Opernfiguren: Festschrift für Joachim Herz. Salzburg:* Müller-Speiser, 1989, 427–32.

B715.   Pirrotta, Nino. "The Tradition of Don Juan Plays and Comic Opera." *Proceedings of the Royal Musical Association* 107 (1981): 60–70.

B716.   ——. *"Commedia dell' arte* and Opera." *The Musical Quarterly* 41 (1955): 305–24.

B717.   Pistone, Danièle. "Emmanuel Chabrier: Opera Composer." *The Opera Quarterly* 12 (1996): 17–25.

B718.   Pix, Gunther. "Die Operndramaturgie des *Rosenkavalier* zwischen Hoffmansthals Libretto und Strauss' musikalischer Komposition." *Sprache im Technischen Zeitalter* 3 (1984): 179–97.

B719.   Porter, William V. "Lamenti recitativi da camera." *Con che soavità: Studies in Italian Opera, Song, Dance 1580–1640.* Ed. by I. Fenlon and T. Carter. Oxford: Clarendon Press, 1995, 73–110.

B720.   Powell, John S. "Music, Fantasy, and Illusion in Molière's *Le Malade Imaginaire." Music & Letters* 73 (1992): 222–44.

B721.   ——. "Music and the Self-Fulfilling Prophecy in Molière's *Le Mariage Forcé." Early Music* 21 (1993): 213–30.

B722.   Preibisch, Walter. "Quellenstudien zu Mozarts *Entführung aus dem Serail*: ein Beitrag zur Geschichte der Türkenoper." *Sammelbände der internationalen Musikgesellschaft* 10 (1908–9): 430–76.

B723.   Prizer, William F. "Games of Venus: Secular Vocal Music in the Late Quattrocento and Early Cinquecento." *Journal of Musicology* 9 (1991): 3–56.

B724.   Proute, Henri. "La Musique et les Musiciens dans la Caricature." *Bulletin de la Societé Archeologique, Historique et Artistique du Vieux Papier* 30 (1983): 97–102.

B725.   Prunières, Henry. "Défense et illustration de l'Opéra-comique." *Revue musicale* 14 (1933): 243–47.

B726.   Puttman, Max. "Zur Geschichte der deutschen Komischen Oper von ihren Anfänge bis Dittersdorf." *Die Musik* 3 (1903–4): 334–49; 416–28.

B727.   Radiciotti, Giuseppe. "Il Signor Bruschino ed il Tancredi di G. Rossini." *Rivista musicale italiana* 27 (1920): 231–66.

B728.   Ramacci, Cherubina. "Il periodo umoristico nella produzione di Erik Satie: Le opere per pianoforte del 1912 al 1915." *Nuova rivista italiana* 28 (1994): 664–82.

B729.   Rastall, Richard. "Humor in Music." BBC program, no date available.

B730.   Ratner, Leonard. "Topical Content in Mozart's Keyboard Sonatas." *Early Music* 19 (1991): 615–19.

B731.   Ravizza, Victor. "Möglichkeiten des Komischen in der Musik." *Archiv für Musikwissenschaft* 31 (1974): 137–50.

B732.   Rehin, George. "Blackface Street Minstrels in Victorian London and Its Resorts: Popular Culture and Its Racial Connotations as Revealed in Polite Opinion." *Journal of Popular Culture* 15 (1981): 19–38.

B733.   Reich, Willi. "Humor in der Musik." *Musica Aeterna*. Zürich: Max Metz, 1948, 179–87.

B734.   Reinaecker, Gerd. "Lachende Opernfiguren." *Neue Zeitschrift für Musik* 157 (1996): 18–23.

B735.   Reiss, Gunter. "Schumacher und Poet dazu: Anmerkung zur Kunst der Meister in Richard Wagner's Meistersingerkomödie." *Das Drama Richard Wagners als Musikalische Kunstwerk*. Laaber: Laaber Verlag, 1988, 277–98.

B736.   ——. "das Verweigerte Einverstandnis: Versuch zur Geschichte der Musikkomödie von Mozart bis Brecht." *Oper und Operntext*. Heidelberg: Winter Verlag, 1980, 11–43.

B737.   Rendall, E.D. "Some Notes on Purcell's Dramatic Music, with Especial Reference to the *Fairy Queen*." *Music & Letters* 1 (1920): 135–44.

B738.   Riedinger, Lothar. "Karl von Dittersdorf als Opernkomponist."*Studien zur Musikwissenschaft* 2 (1940): 212–349.

B739.   Riehle, Wolfgang. "Hundert Jahre Boitos und Verdis *Falstaff*." *Shakespeare-Jahrbuch* 129 (1993): 99–117.

B740.   Riethmüller, Albrecht. "Busoni-Studien." *Archiv für Musikwissenschaft* 42 (1985): 263–86.

B741.   Rosset, Clement. "Le Rire en Musique." *Critique* 407 (1981): 390–96.

B742.   Ruhnke, Michael. "Komische Elemente in Telemanns Opern und Intermezzi." *Die Musikforschung* 36 (1983): 94–107.

B743.   Rushton, Julian Gordon. "Berlioz's Swan-Song: Towards a Criticism of *Beatrice and Benedict.*" *Proceedings of the Royal Musical Association* 109 (1982–83): 105–18.

B744.   Russell, Ian. "Parody and Performance." *Everyday Culture: Popular Song and the Vernacular Milieu.* Milton Keynes: Open University, 1987, 70–104.

B745.   Russell, Tilden A. "'Über das Komische in der Musik': The Schütze-Stein Controversy." *The Journal of Musicology* 4 (1985–86): 70–90.

B746.   Rutherford, Lois. "'Harmless Nonsense': The Comic Sketch and the Development of Music-Hall Entertainment." *Music Hall: Performance and Style.* Milton Keynes: Open University, 1986, 131–51.

B747.   Sabbeth, Daniel. "Dramatic and Musical Organization in *Falstaff.*" *Atti dei IIIo Congresso Internazionale di Studi Verdiani.* Milan: Piccola Scala, 1972, 415–42.

B748.   ———. "Freud's Theory of Jokes and the Linear-Analytic Approach to Music: a Few Points in Common." *Psychoanalytic Explorations in Music.* Madison, Wisc.: International Universities, 1990, 49–59.

B749.   Saint-Foix, Georges de. "Les Maîtres de l'opéra buffe dans la musique de chambre à Londres." *Rivista musicale italiana* 31 (1924): 507–26.

B750.   Salmon, Gregory. "Tutti accusan le donne: Schools of Reason and Folly in *Così fan tutte.*" *Repercussions* 1 (1992): 81–102.

B751.   Sanders, Ernst. "*Oberon* and *Zar und Zimmermann.*" *The Musical Quarterly* 40 (1954): 521–32.

B752.   B752. Savage, Roger. "The Shakespeare-Purcell Fairy Queen: A Defense and Recommendation." *Early Music* 1 (1973): 200–21.

B753.   Scheel, Hans Ludwig. "*Le Mariage de Figaro* von Beaumarchais und das Libretto der *Nozze di Figaro* von Lorenzo da Ponte." *Die Musikforschung* 27 (1975): 156–73.

B754.   Scheit, Gerhard. "Mozart und Hans Wurst: Bemerkungen zur Dramaturgie der Aufklärung." *Festschrift Georg Knepler.* Hamburg: Bockel, 1993, 69–82.

B755.   Schlötterer, Reinhard. "Ironic Allusions to Italian Opera in the Musical Comedies of *Richard Strauss.*" *Richard Strauss: New Perspectives on the Composer and His Work.* Durham, N.C.: Duke University, 1992, 173–96.

B756.   ———. "Musik und Theater im *Rosenkavalier* von Richard Strauss." *Musik und Theater im "Rosenkavalier" von Richard Strauss.* Vienna: Verlag der Österreichischen Akademie der Wissenschaften, 1985, 9–60.

B757. Schlundt, Christena. "Jerome Robbins and His Contributions to the Theatre of Musical Comedy." *Musical Theatre in America.* Westport, Conn.: Greenwood Press, 1984, 331–38.

B758. Schmitz, Eugen. "Formgesetze in Mozarts *Zauberflöte.*" *Festschrift Max Schneider.* Leipzig: Deutscher Verlag für Musik, 1955, 209–14.

B759. Schneider, Hans. "Zur Gattungsgeschichte der frühen Opéra-comique." *Die Musikforschung* 36 (1983): 107–16.

B760. Schulte, Michael. "Hatte Schönberg Humor, Herr Cage?" *DU* 5 (1991): 40–41.

B761. Schumann, Carl. Liner notes for the recording: *The Comic Mozart,* Seraphim 60050.

B762. Schumann, Robert. "Das Komische in der Musik." *Gesammelte Schriften über Musik und Musiker.* Leipzig: Breitkopf und Härtel, 1914, 108–9.

B763. Schünemann, George. "Mendelssohns Jugendopern." *Zeitschrift für Musikwissenschaft* 5 (1922–23): 506–45.

B764. Schwarz-Danuser, Monika. "Melodram und Sprechstimme bei Ferruccio Busoni." *Gesellschaft für Musikforschung.* Kassel: Bärenreiter, 1984, 449–54.

B765. Seebass, Tilman. "The Use of Folk Music for Satirical Purposes in the *Roman de Fauvel.*" *Folklor i njegova umetnicka transpozicija. II.* Belgrade: Fakultet Muzicke Unetnosti, 1989, 331–36.

B766. Seidel, Wilhelm "Figaro's Cavatina 'Se vuol ballare Signor Contino': ein Gegen oder Fintenstück?" *Neue Musik und Tradition: Festschrift Rudolf Stephan zum 65. Geburtstag.* Laaber: Laaber Verlag, 1990, 149–70.

B767. ——. "Streit und Versohnung: Zu Cimarosas *Il matrimonio segreto* und ihre Vorlage." *De musica et cantu: Studien zur Geschichte der Kirchenmusik und der Oper—Helmut Hücke zum 60. Geburtstag.* Hildesheim: Olms, 1993, 527–41.

B768. Seipt, Angelus. "Gesagt, gesungen, gemeint: Über Ironie in der Oper." *Kunst—Kommunikation—Kultur: Festschrift zum 80. Geburtstag von Adolph Silbermann.* Frankfurt am Main: Lang Verlag, 1989, 267–77.

B769. Serper, Arie. "Amour courtois et amour divin chez Raimbaut d'Orange." *Studia Occitanica in Memoriam Paul Remy.* Kalamazoo: Western Michigan University, 1986, 279–89.

B770. Shaw-Taylor, Desmond. "The Operas of Leoš Janácek." *Proceedings of the Royal Music Association* 85 (1958–59): 49–64.

B771.   Silver, Kenneth. "Jean Cocteau and the *Image d'Épinal*: An Essay on Realism and Naiveté." *Jean Cocteau and the French Scene.* New York: Abbeville, 1984, 81–105.

B772.   Sisman, Elaine R. "Haydn's Theater Symphonies." *Journal of the American Musicological Society* 43 (1990): 292–352.

B773.   Smaczny, Jan. "Smetana's Romantic Comedy." *Opera* 38 (1987): 34.

B774.   Snow, Joseph. "The Satirical Poetry of Alfonso X: A Look at Its Relationship to the *Cantigas de Santa Maria.*" *Alfonso X of Castille: The Learned King (1221–1284).* Cambridge: Harvard University Press, 1990, 110–31.

B775.   Sopart, Andreas. "Claudio Monteverdis 'Scherzi musicali' (1607) und ihre Beziehung zum Scherzo-Begriff in der italienische Barocklyric." *Archiv für Musikwissenschaft* 38 (1981): 227–34.

B776.   Springfelds, Mary. "Paris from Villon to Rabelais: Music of the Streets, Theater, and Courts." Program Notes for the Newberry Consort Concerts, Fall 1996.

B777.   Squire, William Barcley."An Index of Tunes in the Ballad-Operas." *Musical Antiquary* 2 (1910–11): 1–17.

B778.   Stedman, Jane W. "Wagner in Travesty." *Opera News* 27 (1963): 24–27.

B779.   Stein, Karl. "Versuch über das Komik Musik." *Caecilia* 15 (1833): 221–66.

B780.   Steinbeck, Wolfram. "'Ein Wahres Spiel mit Musikalischen Formen' zum Scherzo Ludwig van Beethoven." *Archiv für Musikwissenschaft* 38 (1981): 194–226.

B781.   Stempel, Larry. "The Musical Play Expands." *American Music* (1992): 136–69.

B782.   Steptoe, Andrew. "Mozart, Mesmer and *Così fan tutte*." *Music & Letters* 67 (1986): 248–55.

B783.   Stevenson, Robert. "Espectaculos Musicales en la España del Siglo XVII." *Revista Musical Chilena* 27 (1973): 3–44.

B784.   Sturm, George. "Convention in Opera." *The Opera Journal* 15 (1982): 25–42.

B785.   Taruskin, Richard. "Handel, Shakespeare, and Musorgsky: The Source and Limits of Russian Musical Realism." *Music and Language.* New York: Broude, 1983, 247–68.

B786.   Tcherepnin, Ivan. Liner notes for Ivan Tcherepnin Flores Musicales, Five Songs, Santur Live! CRI CD 684.

B787.   Teachout, Terry. "A Little Night Music: Britten's *A Midsummer Night's Dream* Marked a Rare Departure into Comedy for This Composer." *Opera News* 61 (1996): 20–22.

B788.   Teidemann, Hans-Joachim. "Scherz und Spott in der absoluten Musik: Versuch einer Auseinandersetzung mit musikalischer Satire und Parodie." *Musik Unterricht* 58 (1967): 322–29.

B789.   Tenes, Martial. "Jacques Offenbach: His Centennary." *The Musical Quarterly* 6 (1920): 98–117.

B790.   Torrefranca, Fausto. "*Il Rosencavalier* di R. Strauss." *Rivista musicale italiana* 18 (1911): 147–79.

B791.   ——."Strumentalità della commedia musicale A: Buona figliuola, Barbiere, Falstaff." *Nuova Rivista Musicale Italiana* 18 (1984): 1–9.

B792.   Toscani, Bernard. "*La serva padrona*: Variations on a Theme." *Studi Pergolesiani* Florence: Nuova Italia, 1988, 185–94.

B793.   Tutenberg, Fritz. "Die *opera-buffa* Sinfonie und ihre Beziehung zur Klassichen Sinfonie." *Archiv für Musikwissenschaft* 8 (1926–27): 452–72.

B794.   Tyler, Linda L. "*Bastien und Bastienne* and the Viennese Volkskomödie." *Mozart-Jahrbuch* (1991): 576–79.

B795.   Tyson, Alan. "Notes on the Genesis of Mozart's 'Ein musikalisher Spass,' KV 522." *Mozart: Studies of the Autograph Scores*. Cambridge: Harvard University Press, 1987, 234–45.

B796.   Van Dam, Theodore. "The Influence of West African Songs of Derision in the New World." *African Music* 7 (1954): 53–56.

B797.   Van Vechten, Carl. "The Cat in Music." *The Musical Quarterly* 6 (1920): 573–85.

B798.   Vené, Ruggero. "The Origins of *Opera Buffa*." *The Musical Quarterly* 21 (1935): 33–38.

B799.   Voss, Egon. "Der *Barbier von Bagdad* als Komische Oper." *Peter Cornelius als Komponist*. Regensburg: Bosse, 1977, 129–38.

B800.   Walker, Frank. "*Orazio*: The History of a Pasticcio." *The Musical Quarterly* 38 (1952): 369–83.

B801.   Walter, Horst. "On the History of the Composition and Performance of *La vera costanza*." *Haydn Studies*. New York: W.W. Norton, 1981, 154–57.

B802.   Walton, Kendall L. "Understanding Humor and Understanding Music." *The Journal of Musicology* 11 (1993): 32–51.

B803.   Wandermee, Robert. "Le Ballet de Cour." *Gattungen der Musik in Einzeldarstellungen: Gedenkschrift Leo Schrade. Bern: Francke,* 1973, 621–54.

B804.   Wapnewski, Peter. "*Così fan tutte*: Die sehr ernsten Scherze eines Dramma Giocoso." *Mozarts Opernfiguren: Grosse Herren, rasende Weiber, gefährliche Liebschaften*. Bern: Haupt Verlag, 1991, 115–34.

B805.   Ward, John. "Apropos the British Broadside Ballad." *Journal of the American Musicological Society* 20 (1967): 28–86.

B806.   Warning, Rainer. "Von der Revolutionskomodie zur Opera Buffa: *Le nozze di Figaro* und die Erotik der Empfindsamkeit." *Mozarts Opernfiguren: Grosse Herren, rasende Weiber, gefährliche Liebschaften.* Bern: Haupt Verlag, 1991, 49–70.

B807.   Weaver, William. "Hints of Humor: Verdi's Forays into Comedy." *Opera News* 54 (1990): 26–29.

B808.   Weber, Daniel. "Ueber komische Charakteristik und Karrikatur in praktischen Musikwerken." *Allgemeine musikalische Zeitung* 9-10 (1800): Cols. 137–43, 157–62.

B809.   Weber, Horst. "Der *Serva-padrona* Topos in der Oper: Komik als Spiel mit Musikalischen und sozialischen Normen." *Archiv für Musikwissenschaft* 45 (1988): 87–110.

B810.   Wegerer, Kurt. "Musik und Komödie um 1500." *Österreichische Musikzeitschrift* 23 (1968): 269–74.

B811.   Weichert, Gisela. "Die Stellung des Heiteren Innerhalb der Musik des 18. Jahrhunderts." *Wissenschaftliche Zeitschrift der Pedagogische Hochschule "Ernst Schneller"* Zwickau, Germany 14 (1978): 46–53.

B812.   Weiss, Piero. "Venetian commedia dell arte 'operas' in the age of Vivaldi." *The Musical Quarterly* 70 (1984): 195–217.

B813.   ——. "Verdi and the Fusion of Genres." *Journal of the American Musicological Society* 35 (1982): 138–56.

B814.   Weisstein, Ulrich. "Benedetto Marcellos *Il teatro all moda*: Scherz, Satire, Parodie oder tiefere Bedeutung?" *Opern und Opernfiguren: Festschrift für Joachim Herz.* Salzburg: Müller-Speiser, 1989, 31–57.

B815.   Wellesz, Egon. "*Don Giovanni* and the 'dramma giocoso.'" *The Musical Quarterly* 4 (1943): 21–26.

B816.   Werner, Eric."Leading or Symbolic Formulas in *The Magic Flute*." *The Music Review* 18 (1957): 286–93.

B817.   Wesseley, Othmar. "Bruckner, Wagner und die Neudeutschen in Linzer Parodie des 19. Jahrhunderts." *Bruckner-Jahrbuch* (1987-88): 93–94.

B818.   Wheelock, Gretchen. "Engaging Strategies in Haydn's Op 33." *Eighteenth Century Studies* 25 (1991): 1–30.

B819.   White, Eric Walter. "*The Rake's Progress*." *Tempo* 20 (1951): 10–18.

B820.   Whiting, Steven Moore. "Erik Satie and Vincent Hyspa." *Music & Letters* 77 (1996): 64–91.

B821.   Winesanker, Michael. "Musico-Dramatic Criticism of English Comic Opera." *The Journal of the American Musicological Society* 2 (1949): 87–96.

B822.   Winkler, Gerhard J. "Opernparodie in der Oper: Zur Arie des Musikmeisters in Haydns *La Canterina*." *Joseph Haydn und die*

Oper seiner Zeit. Eisenstadt: Burgenlandisches Landesmuseum, 1992, 131–51.

B823. Wirth, Helmut. "The Operas of Haydn before *Orfeo.*" Recording of *Orfeo.* Boston: Haydn Society, 1951, 12–48.

B824. Wittke, Paul. "The American Music Theatre (Coverage in *The New Grove Dictionary*)." *The Musical Quarterly* 68 (1982): 274–82.

B825. Wolff, Hellmuth Christian. "Die Buffoszenen in den Opern Alessandro Scarlattis." *Scarlatti Symposium.* Tutzing: Hans Schneider, 1975, 191–200.

B826. ———."Die Komödie *Les opera* (1677) des Saint-Evremond und ihre deutsche Fassung von Gottsched (1741)." *Festschrift Heinz Becker zum 60. Geburtstag am 26. Juni 1982.* Laaber: Laaber Verlag, 1982, 26–37.

B827. Wollenberg, Susan. "A New Look at C.P.E. Bach's Musical Jokes." *C.P.E. Bach Studies.* Oxford: Clarendon Press, 1988, 295–314.

B828. Wynne, Peter. "Zanies, Lovers, Fools." *Opera News* 57 (1992): 18–20.

B829. Yellin, Victor Fell. "Sullivan and Thomson, Gilbert and Stein." *The Journal of Musicology* 11 (1993): 478–98.

B830. Young, Percy. "Emancipation Through Satire: Political Content of Comic English Opera of the 19th Century." *Festschrift für Ernst Hermann Meyer zum sechstigen Geburtstag.* Leipzig, Deutscher Verlag für Musik, 1973, 583–90.

B831. Zekulin, Nicholas G. "Tourgueniev et Mozart." *Cahiers Ivan Tourgueniev, Pauline Viardot, Maria Malibran* 15 (1991): 63–78.

B832. Zimmermann, Michael. "'laissons a l'Italie. De tous ces faux brillans ces faux brillans l'eclatante folie'—Rameau und die 'Narrische' Musik Italiens." *Gesellschaft für Musikforschung.* Kassel: Bärenreiter, 1984, 532–36.

Musical Works Cited
and Discography

The following are the abbreviations for series, anthologies, or periodicals used in this section of the book:

AM   *Anthology of Music* (Köln: Arno Volk Verlag, 1959–).

AMI   L. Torchi, ed. *L'Arte musicale in Italia* (1897–1908).

ARM   *Anthology of Renaissance Music*, ed. A. Atlas (New York: W.W. Norton, 1997).

Bernst   J. Bernstein, ed. *French Chansons of the Sixteenth Century* (University Park: The Pennsylvania State University, 1985).

CDMI   *I Classici della Musica Italiana* (Milan: Istituto Editoriale Italiano, 1918–20).

CM   *Collegium Musicum* (Madison, Wisc.: A-R Editions, 1969–).

CMBM   R.M. Stevenson, ed. *Christmas Music from Baroque Mexico* (Berkeley: University of California Press, 1974).

CMI   *I Classici Musicali Italiani* (Milan: I classici musicali italiani, 1941–43, 1956).

CMM   *Corpus mensurabilis musicae* (Rome: American Institute of Musicology, 1948–).

CW   *Das Chorwerk* (Wolfenbüttel: Möseler Verlag, 1929–).

Cykler   E. Cykler and E. Kraus, eds. *121 Canons for Singing and Playing on Various Instruments* (Zürich: Musikverlag zum Pelikan, 1965).

DdT   *Denkmäler deutscher Tonkunst* (Leipzig: Breitkopf und Härtel, 1892–1931; repr. Wiesbaden, 1957–61).

DTÖ   *Denkmäler der Tonkunst in Österreich* (Graz: Akademische Druck- und Verlaganstalt, 1966–).

EDM   *Das Erbe deutscher Musik* (Kassel: Nagel, 1935–).

EIG   A. Einstein, ed. *The Golden Age of the Madrigal* (New York: G. Schirmer, 1942).

EIM   A. Einstein. *The Italian Madrigal* (Princeton, N.J.: Princeton University Press, 1949).

ELS   E. Fellowes, ed. *The English Lute School* (London: Stainer & Bell, 1920–32).

EMS   E. Fellowes, ed. *English Madrigal School* (London: Stainer & Bell, 1914–24).

FIM   J. Roche, ed. *The Flower of the Italian Madrigal* (New York: Galaxy Music Corporation, 1988).

Fitz   J.A. Fuller Maitland and W. Barclay Squire, eds. *The Fitzwilliam Virginal Book* (New York: Dover, 1963).

GAS   B. Taylor, ed. *Great Art Songs of Three Centuries* (New York: G. Schirmer, 1990).

Glory   *The Glory Days of Rock and Roll* (Hollywood: Warner Bros., 1993).

GMB   A. Schering, ed. *Geschichte der Musik in Beispielen* (Leipzig: Breitkopf & Härtel, 1931).

Gold H. Goldschmidt. *Studien zur Geschichte der italienischen Oper im 17. Jahrhundert* (Leipzig: Breitkopf & Härtel, 1901–4).

Green1   *An Anthology of Elizabethan Lute songs, Madrigals, and Rounds* (New York: W.W. Norton, 1970).

Green2   N. Greenberg, ed. *An Anthology of English Medieval and Renaissance Vocal Music* (New York: W.W. Norton, 1961).

Green3   N. Greenberg, ed. *An Anthology of Early Renaissance Music* (New York: W.W. Norton, 1975).

GRP   J. Blezzard, ed. *German Romantic Partsongs* (London: Oxford University Press, 1993).

HAM   A. Davison and W. Apel, eds. *Historical Anthology of Music* (Cambridge: Harvard University Press, 1950).

Hoppin   R. Hoppin, ed. *Anthology of Medieval Music* (New York: W.W. Norton, 1978).

LACMA   Stevenson, ed. *Latin American Colonial Music Anthology* (Washington, D.C.: Organization of American States, 1975).

Laur   L. Laurencie, *L'École française de violon de Lully a Viotti* (Paris: Delagrave, 1922-24).

MA   G. Reese, *Music in the Middle Ages* (New York: W.W. Norton, 1940).

MB   *Musica Britannica* (London: Stainer & Bell, 1951–).

MiA   W. Marrocco and H. Gleason, eds. *Music in America: An Anthology from the Landing of the Pilgrims to the Close of the Civil War 1620–1865* (New York: W.W. Norton, 1964).

MM   C. Parrish and J. F. Ohl, eds. *Masterpieces of Music Before 1750* (New York: W.W.Norton, 1951).

MME   *Monumentos de la Música Española* (Barcelona: CSIC, 1941–).

MR   G. Reese, *Music in the Renaissance,* 2d ed. (New York: Norton, 1959).

MRM   E. Lowinsky, ed. *Monuments of Renaissance Music* (Chicago: University of Chicago Press, 1964–).

NAWM   C. Palisca, ed. *Norton Anthology of Western Music,* 2nd ed. (New York: W.W. Norton, 1988).

NMA   *Nagels Musik-Archiv* (Hannover: Adolf Nagel, 1927–).

OEM   *The Oxford Book of English Madrigals* (London: Oxford, 1978).

OFC   F. Dobbins, ed. *The Oxford Book of French Chansons* (London: Oxford, 1987).

OIM   *The Oxford Book of Italian Madrigals* (London: Exford, 1983).

OMM   W. Marrocco and N. Sandon, eds. *Oxford Anthology of Medieval Music* (New York: Oxford University Press, 1977).

PM   L. Schrade, ed. *Polyphonic Music of the Fourteenth Century* (Monaco: Oiseau-Lyre, 1956–).

Scores   R. Johnson, ed. *Scores: An Anthology of New Music* (New York: Schirmer Books, 1981).

SS   J. Godwin, ed. *Schirmer Scores: A Repertory of Western Music* (New York: G. Schirmer, 1975).

Stev   D. Stevens, ed. *The Penguin Book of English Madrigals* (Baltimore: Penguin, 1967).

TEM   C. Parrish, ed. *A Treasury of Early Music* (New York: W.W. Norton, 1958).

TGG   D. Johnson, ed. *Ten Georgian Glees* (London: Oxford University Press, 1981).

WA   J. Wasielewski. *Instrumentalsätze vom Ende des XVI. bis Ende des XVII.Jahrhundert* (Bonn: Max Cohen, 1874).

For further information: *Collected Editions, Historical Series and Sets*, ed. G. Hill and N. Stephens (Berkeley: Fallen Leaf Press, 1997). The composer's name is followed by the title of the composition and publication information. Easily accessible editions are cited. Many examples, especially from the earlier chapters, are found in anthologies. These are indicated with the preceding system of abbreviation. Collected editions and thematic catalogues are cited at the end of entries. Further necessary information, references to related works, and bibliography (using the designation B) are presented at the end of the entry. In instances of composers who wrote both vocal and instrumental works, vocal works are cited first, followed by the instrumental. Large-scale orchestral genres (symphony, concerto, suite) are presented first, followed by small-scale genres (overture, tone poem). Chamber music genres are then presented followed by music for solo keyboard.

THE MEDIEVAL PERIOD

General Studies: B113, B663.
Secular Song: B65, B170, B248, B251, B723.

W1.   **Adam de la Halle:** *Le jeu de Robin et Marion* (Bloomington, Ind.: Early Music Institute,1991). B607.
W2.   **Cordier, Baude:** "Belle bonne" in CMM, v. 11.
W3.   **Grimace:** "Alarme, alarme" in CMM, v. 53.
W4.   **Guillaume de Machaut:** "Ma fin est ma commencement" in PM, v. 3; MA, 351-52. B455.
W5.   **Marcabru:** "L'autrier jost'una sebissa" Hoppin 43. See also B769, B774 for related repertory.
W6.   **Massini, Lorenzo:** "Dolgomi a voi" cited by Willi Apel in "Satire" in B378.
W7.   **Neidhart von Reuental:** "Maienzit" in *The Songs of Neidhart von Reuental* (Manchester: Manchester University Press, 1958).
W8.   **Nicolò da Perugia:** "Dappoi che'l sole" in *Fourteenth-Century Italian Caccie* (Cambridge: Medieval Academy of America, 1961). Hoppin 65, OMM 80. See HAM 52 for another example.
W9.   **Oswald von Wolkenstein:** "Der May" HAM 60.
W10. **Solage:** "Fumeux fume" in CMM, v.53; NAWM 26. See HAM 47–48 for similar examples. B355.

The following are anonymous compositions listed in alphabetical order according to title:
W11. "Ad mortem festinamus" from the *Llibre Vermell* MA, 375.
W12. *Carmina Burana in Publications of Medieval Manuscripts* (Brooklyn: Institute of Medieval Music, 1957–), v. 9; *Harmoniae Musarum* (Macomb: Dean, 1975), v. 5 includes 20 songs for voices and instruments from this manuscript.
W13. "Danse macabre" discussed and exemplified in B99, B100, and B161. See HAM 40–41 and R1 for examples of medieval dances.
W14. *Le Fils de Gédron* in *Drames liturgiques du moyen age*, ed. E. de Coussemaker, reprint (New York: Broude, 1964).
W15. "Hare, hare-Balaam-Balaam" in Edith Borroff, *Music in Europe and the United States* (Englewood Cliffs, N.J.: Prentice-Hall, 1971), Ex. 23b.
W16. "On parole-A Paris-Frèse nouvelle" HAM 33b.
W17. "Orientis partibus" HAM 17a.

W18.   *The Play of Daniel* (New York: Oxford University Press, 1959); *Medieval Church Music-Dramas: A Repertory of Complete Plays* (Charlottesville: University Press of Virginia, 1976). B217. See also B193, B440.

W19.   *Robin and Marion Motets* (North Arston: Antico Editions, 1985).

W20.   *Le Roman de Fauvel*, PM, v. 1.

W21.   "Se je chant" Hoppin 60.

W22.   "Sumer is Icumen In" HAM 42.

For further reference:

R1.   *Medieval Instrumental Dances* (Bloomington: Indiana University Press, 1989).

THE RENAISSANCE PERIOD

General Studies: B7, B42, B153, B158, B195, B701, B713, B776, B810.
Chanson and Madrigal: B69, B95, B428, B450, D1.
Keyboard Music: B5.
Madrigal Comedy: B177, B608.
Theater: B35, B47, B177, B220, B319. B434, B458, B463, B465, B473.
Theory: B637.
Symbolism: B70.

W23.   **Azzaiolo, Filippo:** *Villotte* in *Thesaurus Musicus* No. 56 (London: Pro Musica, 1986).

Banchieri, Adriano: B177, B473.

W24.   *Festino nella sera del giovedi grasso; Opera omnia* (Rome: de Santis, 1960).

W25.   *La Pazzia senile* AMI, v. 4; Excerpts in CDMI, v .2 ; excerpts from a similar work, *Il zabaione musicale,* HAM 186. B482.

W26.   *La Battaglia* (Macomb: R. Dean, 1974); *Canzoni alla Francese* (Madison, Wisc.: A-R Editions, 1975); *Opera omnia* (Bologna: Forni, 1963-).

W27.   **Bataille, Gabriel:** "Qui veut chasse une migraine" *Airs de cour pour voix et luth.* (Paris: Heugel, 1961).

W28.   **Bateson, Thomas:** "Those Sweet Delightful Lilies" OEM 51.

W29.   **Beaujoyeux, Balthazar de:** *Balet comique de la royne* (Rome: American Institute of Musicology, 1971). B803.

W30.   **Bernhard the Elder:** *Ein Guter Dantz* AM, v. 1.

W31.   **Binchois, Gilles:** "Files à marier" *Die Chansons von Gilles Binchois* (Mainz: Schott, 1957); HAM 70.

W32.   **Bossinensis, Franciscus:** Intabulations of *frottole, Le frottole per canto e liuto intabulate de Franciscus Bossinensis* (Milan: Ricordi, 1961). B205.

Bull, John:

W33.   *Les Buffons* MB, v. 14.
W34.   *The King's Hunt* Fitz, v. 2.

W35.   **Busnois, Antoine:** "Amours nous traitte" in *The Combinative Chanson: An Anthology* (Madison, Wisc.: A-R Editions, 1989). B662.

W36.   **Caimo, Gioseppe:** "Mentre il Cuculo" in *Introduction to the Italian Madrigal* (New York: Galaxy, 1989).

W37.   **Campion, Thomas:** Lute songs as a group, ELS, Series 1, vols. 4 and 13. B206, B411, B526.

W38.   **Cara, Marchetto:** "A la absentia" O. Petrucci, *Frottole, Buch I und IV* (Leipzig: Breitkopf und Härtel, 1935). CM 2nd series, v. 8, ARM 51.

W39.   **Compère, Loyset:** "Che fa la ramacina" *Opera omnia* CMM, v. 15.

W40.   **Cornago, Johannes:** *Missa Mappa Mundi* (Madison, Wisc.: A-R Editions, 1984).

W41.   **Crecquillon, Thomas:** "Ung gay bergier" *Opera omnia* CMM, v. 63.

W42.   **Croce, Giovanni:** *Triaca Musicale* AMI, v. 2. B298.

Deering, Richard:

W43.   "Country Cries."
W44.   "Street Cries."
MB, v. 25.

W45.   **Demantius, Christoph:** *Conviviorum deliciae* (Zürich: Musikverlag zum Pelikan, 1973). EDMR Series 2, v. 1.

Desprez, Josquin (see Josquin):

Dowland, John:

W46.   "Fine Knacks for Ladies."
W47.   "Say, Love, If Ever Thou Didst Find."
W48.   "Up, merry mates!"
MB, v. 6.

Du Fay, Guillaume:

W49.   "Bon jour, bon mois."
W50.   "Ce jour de l'an."
W51.   "Ce jour le doibt."
W52.   "Donnez l'assault."
W53.   *Missa L'homme armé* HAM 66c. *Opera Omnia* CMM, v. 3.

W54.   **Encina, Juan del:** Theatrical pieces as a group in MME, v. 2; HAM 98 presents three short examples; see also ARM 55.

W55.   **Farnaby, Giles:** *His Humor* in MB, v. 24: Fitz, v. 2.

W56.   **Fernández, Gaspar:** "Tantarrantan, a la Guerra van" LACMA, 120. LACMA contains other *villancicos,* which are likewise humorous.

W57.   **Flecha, Mateo (the Elder):** "La Bomba" in *Las Ensaladas* (Barcelona: Bibliotec Central Barcelona, 1954). B422, B545.

Gabrieli, Andrea:

W58.   *Aria battaglia in Canzoni alla francese für Orgel oder Cembalo*, ed. P. Pidoux (Kassel: Bärenreiter, 1953). Green3 37 presents Isaak's "A la bataglia." B5.
W59.   Canzona on "Un gay bergier" MM 20, 21. B108.

Gastoldi, Giovanni:

W60.   "L'Ardito." FIM, 16
W61.   "Viver lieto voglio."
Balletti a Cinque voci (Paris: Heugel, 1968); further examples in OIM; HAM 158 is another example.

Gibbons, Orlando:

W62.   "Street Cries." EM, v. 5.
W63.   "Toy." MB, v. 20.

W64.   **Greiter, Matthias:** "Elselein/Es taget..." in AM, v. 28.

W65.   **Hassler, Hans Leo:** "Tanzen und Springen," in *Lustgarten* in *Sämtliche Werke* (Wiesbaden: Breitkopf und Härtel, 1961–); other examples in GMB 155; HAM 165.

W66.   **Henry VIII:** "Pastyme with Good Company" MB, v. 18. For William Cornysh's "Hey, Robin," see Resse, *MR,* 770; Cooper's "I Have Been a Foster" is HAM 86b.

W67.   **Hove, Joachim van den:** *Delitiae Musicae,* excerpts in Bruger, H.D., ed., *Schule des Lautenspiels* (Wolfenbüttel: Moseler, 1926).

W68.   **Hume, Tobias:** *Poeticall Musicke* (Menston: Scolar, 1969).

Isaak, Heinrich:

W69.   "Donna di dentro" in MRM, v. 7 ; Green3 37; HAM 82 presents a quodlibet from the *Glogauer Liederbuch.*
W70.   *Missa Carminum* in *Opera Omnia* CMM; CW, v. 7; Kalmus Study Score No. 703 is a reprint of this edition (New York: Edwin F. Kalmus, 1968).
W71.   *A la bataglia* in Green3 38 ; *The Art of the Netherlands* v. 1 (London: Pro Musica, n.d.).

Janequin, Clément:

W72.   "L'alouette." HAM 107.
W73.   "La bataille" (note that this is the work that spawned many battle pieces).
W74.   "Le caquet des femmes."
W75.   "Le chant des oiseaux."
W76.   "Les cris de Paris" ARM 65.
Chansons polyphoniques: oeuvres complètes (Monaco: l'Oiseau-Lyre, 1965–71).

W77.   **Jones, Robert:** Lute songs in ELS, vols. 5–6.

Josquin Desprez: B448.

W78.   "Basiez-moy" SS 49.
W79.   "Faute d'argent" OFC 4; in MRM, v. 2; HAM 91 (HAM 118 is an instrumental arrangement by Girolamo Cavazzoni.); ARM 50.
W80.   "El grillo è buon cantore" in Green 3, ARM 53.
W81.   "Une musque de Biscaye."
W82.   "Petite Camusette" OFC 3; Green 3 22.
W83.   "Scaramella" Another setting of this tune by Compère exists and can be found in *Opera Omnia* (Rome: American Institute of Musicology, 1958–).
Werken van Josquin des Prés: Wereldijke Werken II (Amsterdam: Vereniging voor Nederlanse Muziskgeschiedenis, 1965–68). *Sixteen Secular Pieces* (London: Pro Musica, 1994) contains some of Josquin's most popular chansons; *Par-*

ody Chansons, ed. M. Picker (Hackensack: Jerona, 1980) contains settings based on popular songs. Each three-voice chanson is paired with one for more than three voices, thus demonstrating parody technique.

W84.   **La Grotte, Nicolas de:** "Quand ce beau printemps" in *Chansons au luth et airs de cour français* (Paris: E. Droz, 1934).

W85.   **Landi, Antonio:** *Il commodo* excerpts in *Feste musicali della Firenze Medicea (1480–1589)* (Bologna: Forni, 1969), 49.

Lassus, Orlande:

W86.   "Bon jour, mon coeur" HAM 145. A keyboard arrangement by Peter Philips exists in Fitz, v. 2.
W87.   "Ich weiss mir ein meidlein."
W88.   "Matona mia cara" SS 50.
W89.   "O la, o che bon eccho."
W90.   *Missa Doulce memoire.*
W91.   *Missa Entre vous filles.*

W92.   *Villanesche, moresche* in *Canzoni Villanesche and Villanelle* (Madison, Wisc.: A-R Editions, 1991). B272.

Sämtliche Werke (Leipzig: Breitkopf und Härtel, 1894–1927); *New Series* (Kassel: Bärenreiter,1956–); *Complete Chansons* (Hamden: Garland, 1997).

W93.   **Mainerio, Giorgio:** *Ballo Ungarescha* in *Musikalische Denkmäler* (Mainz: Schott, 1961). B305, B419, B504, B514.

Marenzio, Luca: B608.

W94.   "Cedan l'antiche tue chiare vittorie."
W95.   "Già torna."
W96.   "Mi fa lasso languire."
W97.   "O tu che fra le selve."
The Secular Works (New York: Broude Bros., 1977–). See EIG and EIM for many related examples.

W98.   **Matthias (Werrecore):** *Battaglia taliana* DTÖ vols. 147–48.

W99.   **Medici, Lorenzo de':** *Canzoni a ballo* in EIM.

Morley, Thomas: B163.

W100.   "It Was a Lover and His Lass."
W101.   "Now Is the Month of Maying."
W102.   "Phillis I Fain Would Die Now."

W103.   "Shoote False Love."
W104.   "Sing We and Chant It."
EMS 4; see HAM 159 for another example.
W105.   *Il Grillo* in *Hortus Musicus* No. 136 (Kassel: Bärenreiter, 1956).

W106.   **Narváez, Luys de:** *Guárdame las vacas* MME, v. 3; HAM 122. See W128 for another setting.

Neusidler, Hans:

W107.   *Hoftanz* HAM 105a.
W108.   *Ein Judentanz* HAM 105b (incorrect transcription creating dissonance not found in the original notation).

Obrecht, Jacob:

W109.   "T'Andernacken."
W110.   "T'saat een meskin" HAM 78.
New Obrecht Edition (Amsterdam: Vereniging voor Nederlandse Muziekgeschiedenis, 1983–).

W111.   **Othmayr, Caspar:** "Octo sunt passiones" *Ausgewählte Werke* (Leipzig: Peters, 1941–56).

W112.   **Padilla, Juan Gutíerrez:** "A la Xacara, Xacara, Xacarilla" in CMBM, 113.

W113.   **Palestrina, Pierluigi:** "Vestiva i colli" in *Le opere complete* (New York: Kalmus, n.d.).

W114.   **Passereau, Pierre:** "Il est bel et bon" *Opera omnia* CMM, 45; OFC 22, ARM 64. See Bernst for many related examples.

W115.   **Ponce, Juan:** "Ave, color vini clari" Green 3 40. See HAM 85 for an English drinking song of the same period.

W116.   **Praetorius, Michael:** *Terpsichore* in *Gesamtausgabe der musikalischen Werken* (London: Schott, 1989); see HAM 167b for an excerpt.

W117.   **Ruffo, Vincenzo:** *Il Capriciosso* in B108.

W118.   **Sannazaro, Iacopo:** *Il Trionfo di Fama* cited in B106.

W119.   **Schmid, Bernhard, the Elder:** *Ein Guter Dantz* AM, v. 1.

Senfl, Ludwig:

W120. "Das G'laut zu Speier" ARM 68.
W121. "Ein Maidlein zu den Brunnen ging."
W122. "Oho! So Geb Der Mann In'n Pfenning."
Sämtliche Werke (Wolfenbüttel: Möseler, 1937–61).

Sermisy, Claudin de:

W123. "Dont Vient Cela" CMM, v. 52; dance based on this chanson arranged
by Susato (1551) AM, v. 27.
W124. "Tant que vivray" NAWM 53. There is a duo by Gero on this chanson
in ARM 69. See HAM 147 for Guillaume Costeley's "Allons, gay,
gay," a chanson that is similar in style.
Opera omnia, CMM, v. 52.

W125. **Striggio, Alessandro:** *Il Ciclamento delle donne al bucato* AMI, v. 1.

W126. **Tomkins, Thomas:** *A Toy: Made at Poole Court* MB, v. 5.

W127. **Tye, Christopher:** *In Nomine Crye* NAWM 65; *The Instrumental Music of Chrisopher Tye* (Madison, Wisc.: A-R Editions, 1967); see HAM
176 for an example by Thomas Tomkins. B489.

W128. **Valderrábano, Enriquez de:** *Guárdame las vacas* MME, v. 31; HAM
124. See W106 for another setting. See ARM 70 for a setting by Cabezón.

W129. **Vásquez, Juan:** "¿De Donde Venis, Amores?" MME, v. 4; *Songs from
the Spanish Cancioneros*, ed. C. Poutain (Kikenny: Boethius Editions,
1988).

W130. **Vautor, Thomas:** "Shepherds and Nymphs" EMS, v. 34.

Vecchi, Orazio: B112, B177, B324, B473, B608.

W131. *L'Amfiparnaso* (Chapel Hill, N.C.: University of North Carolina Press,
1977). B510.
W132. "Fa una Canzona" in *Balletti* (Madison, Wisc.: A-R Editions, 1993).

Verdelot, Philippe: B177.

W133. "O dolce notte."
W134. "Quanto sia liet'd giorno."
Opera omnia CMM, v. 28.

W135.   **Victoria, Tomás Luis de:** *Missa pro Victoria* in *Opera omnia* MME, v. 30.

W136.   **Ward, John:** "Hope of My Heart" EMS, v. 19.

W137.   **Weck, Hans:** *Hopper dancz* HAM 102b.

Weelkes, Thomas:

W138.   "As Vesta Was from Latmos Hill Descending" EMS, v. 13; ARM 98.
W139.   "O Care, Thou Wilt Dispatch Me" MB, v. 22, NAWM 61. See HAM 170 for a similar example.
W140.   "Street Cries" MB, v. 22; see W44.
W141.   "Thule, the Period of Cosmography" EMS, v. 12; OEM 52.

W142.   **Wilbye, John:** "Thus Saith My Cloris Bright" Stev 29.

The following compositions either are anonymous or represent a type. These are listed in alphabetical order according to title:

W143.   "A la absentia" *Frottola* from Petrucci in EIM.
W144.   *Callino Casturame* Fitzwilliam, v. 1.
W145.   *Canzona Allegre* as a type, see B108.
W146.   *The Carman's Whistle* Fitz, v. 1.
W147.   "C'est Grand Plaisir" "Tourdion" AM, v. 27.
W148.   "Dale si la das" MME, v. 2.
W149.   "Es gingen drei Baur'n" GMB 886.
W150.   "Es ist ein Schloss in Österreich" MR, 637.
W151.   "Fricassée" TEM 31.
W152.   "Orsu, car' Signori" HAM 96, NAWM 51.
W153.   *Der ratten Schwantz* from *Glogauer Liederbuch*, EDMR, v. 4. See Ham 83b for a similar example.
W154.   "Riu riu chiu" *Cancionero de Upsala*, ed. J. Bal y Gay (Mexico City: El Colegio de México, 1944).
W155.   "Rodrigo Martínez" MME, v. 2.
W156.   "Rusticus ut asinum" MR, 159.

The following are some collections of chansons from the various publications of Attaingnant, Petrucci, and other Renaissance publishers:

Attaingnant: B104.

R2.   *Anthologie de la chanson parisienne au xvie siècle* (Monaco: Editions de L'Oiseau-Lyre, 1953).
R3.   *French Chansons of the Sixteenth Century* (University Park: Pennsylvania State University, 1985).

R4. *French Chansons for Three Voices (ca. 1550)* (Madison, Wisc.: A-R Editions, 1982).

R5. *Six Comical Chansons of the Sixteenth Century* (London: Pro Musica Editions, 1986).

R6. *Thirty Chansons for Three and Four Voices from Attaingnant's Collections* in CM (1960).

R7. *Thirty-Six Chansons by French Provincial Composers (1529–1550)* (Madison, Wisc.: A-R Editions, 1981). B594.

Petrucci:

R8.   *Harmonice Musices Odhecaton A* (Cambridge: Medieval Academy of America, 1946).

R9.   *Canti B* (Chicago: University of Chicago Press, 1967).

R10.   *Canti C* repr. (New York: Broude Bros., 1978).

Other sources:

R11.   **Le Roy and Ballard,** *Livre d'Airs de Cour* (1571) in *Le Choeur des Muses,* series 2 (Paris: Éditions du Centre National de la Recherche Scientifique, 1975).

R12.   **Simpson, Christopher.** *A Compendium of Practical Musick* (London: H. Brome, 1667).

Collections alphabetical by title:

R13.   *Cancionero de Palacio* MME, vols. 2–3.

R14.   *Das Glogauer Liederbuch* EDMR, v. 4. "O rosa bella quodlibet" HAM 61.

R15.   *Das Locheimer Liederbuch* (Wiesbaden: M. Sändig, 1976).

R16.   *Musica Transalpina* (Farnborough: Gregg, 1972).

R17.   *Il Trionfo di Dori* (New York: GAUDIA, 1990).

R18.   *The Triumphes of Oriana* in EMS.

For further reference:

R19.   *I canti carnascialeschi nelle fonti musicali del xv e xvi secolo* (Florence: Olschki, 1937).

R20.   *Gesellschaftslied in Austria, 1480–1550* (DTÖ, v. 72).

R21.   *Libro Primo de la Croce* (Rome, 1526) in CM, 2nd series, v. 8.

R22.   *300 Years of English Partsongs* (London: Faber & Faber, 1983).

THE BAROQUE PERIOD

General Studies: B37, B178, B451.
Baroque (French): B3, B527, B623.
Baroque (Spanish): B783.

Comic Opera (General): B64, B88, B167, B226.
Comic Opera (French): B41, B51, B78, B267, B297, B465, B552.
Comic Opera (German): B559, B560, B561, B825.
Comic Opera (Italian): B35, B706.
Instrumental Music: B114.
Keyboard Music: B5.
Quodlibet: B164
Song (Jacobean): B712.

W157. **Abel, Heinrich:** *Sonate-Bataillen in Die mehrstimmige Spielmusik des 17. Jahrhunderts in Nord- und Miteleuropa* (Kassel: Bärenreiter, 1934), 176. B171.

W158. **Aubert, Jacques:** Sonata No. 10 in Laur, v. 1, 219ff. B171.

Bach, Johann Sebastian:

(These secular cantatas are listed in numeric order.)

W159. No. 201, *Der Streit zwischen Phoebus und Pan* BWV.201, BG 11/2, 3;NBA 1/40, 119.
W160. No. 202, *Weichet nur, betrübte Schatten* ("Wedding Cantata") BWV.202, BG 11/2, 75; BGA 1/12, 3.
W161. No. 205, *Der Zufriedengestellte Aeolus* BWV.205 BG 11/2, BGA 1/38, 3.
W162. No. 208, *Was mir behagt, ist nur die muntre Jagdl* ("Hunting Cantata") BWV.208a, BG 29, 3; NBA 1/35, 3.
W163. No. 211, *Schweigt stille, plaudert nicht* ("Coffee Cantata") BWV.211, BG 11/2, 3; NBA 1/60, 195.
W164. No. 212, *Mer hahn en neue Oberkeet* ("Peasant Cantata") BWV.212, BG 29, 175; BGA 1/39, 155; see B533.

Brandenburg Concerti:
W165. No. 1, BWV.1046, BG 19, 3; NBA 7, 2, 3.
W166. No. 2, BWV.1047, BG 19, 33; NBA 7, 2, 43.
W167. No. 5, BWV.1050, BG 19, 127; NBA 7, 2, 145.
W168. *Capriccio on the Departure of a Brother*, BWV.992, BG 36, 190;NBA 5/10.
W169. *Goldberg Variations*, BWV.988, BG 3, 263; NBA 5/2.
W170. Keyboard Partita No.2, BWV.836, BG 3, 15; NBA 5/2.
W171. Sonata in D for Solo Keyboard BWV.963, BG 26, 19: NBA 5/10.

Werke (Leipzig: Bach-Gesellschaft, 1851–99); *Neue Ausgabe sämtliche Werke*

(Kassel: Bärenreiter, 1954–); W. Schmieder, *Thematisch-systematisches Verzeichnis der musikalischen Werken von Johann Sebastian Bach* (Wiesbaden:

Breitkopf und Härtel, 1977). Reprint of the cantatas from the Bach Gesellschaft edition in *Kalmus Study Scores* (New York: Edwin F. Kalmus, 1961).

W172.   **Barton, Andrew:** *The Disappointment, or the Force of Credulity* (Madison, Wisc.: A-R Editions, 1977).

W173.   **Bassani, Giovanni:** *Il Musico Svogliato*. Manuscript in Bologna, Liceo Musicale.

W174.   **Besson, Michel-Gabriel:** Sonatas for Violin and Basso Continuo in Laur, v. 1, 230ff. B171.

W175.   **Biber, Heinrich:** *La Battaglia* in DTÖ, v. 15.

W176.   **Cabanilles, Juan:** Battle pieces for organ in *Opera Omnia* (Barcelona: Diputación provincial de Barcelona, Biblioteca Central, 1927–56).

Caldara, Antonio:

W177.   *Il Giuoco del Quadriglio*. Manuscript in the Austrian National Library; Vienna. Recorded on Nonesuch H 71103.
W178.   "Questi son canoni" CW 25.

W179.   **Campion, Thomas:** *The Masque of Lord Hayes* (Providence: Brown University Press, 1991). The first two songs are by Campion; the others are by Thomas Lupo and Thomas Giles.

W180.   **Campra, André:** B265. *Les fêtes vénetiennes* in *Le Pupitre* No. 19 (Paris: Heugel, 1972); excerpts in GMB 261; TEM 45. Arias from other works of this type in *The Baroque Operatic Arias* (London: Oxford University Press, 1973).

W181.   **Carissimi, Giacomo:** "Venerabilis barba Capucinorum" B164, 60.

W182.   **Cavalli, Francesco:** *Giasone*, Prologue and Act 1 in *Publikationen älterer praktischer und theoretischer Musikwerke* (Leipzig: Breitkopf und Härtel, 1873–1905), v. 12; excerpts in GMB 201; AM, v. 38.

Charpentier, Marc-Antoine: B265.

W183.   *Ad beatam Virginem Canticum*.
W184.   *Epitaphium Carpentarii*.

W185.   *Airs Serieux et a Boire* (Paris: Heugel, 1968).

W186. *Le Màlade imaginaire.* B182, B477, B720.

W187. *Le Marriage Forcé.*

Music for Molière's Comedies (Madison, Wisc.: A-R Editions, 1990). *Oeuvres* (Paris: Minkoff, 1990). B285, B290, B320 for all the theater music.

W188. **Chédeville, Nicolas:** *Les Galanteries amusantes* Nos. 3 and 6 in NMA, v. 26.

W189. **Coppola, Filippo:** *El Robo de Proserpina y Sentencia de Jupiter* MME, v. 50.

Couperin, François:

W190. *L'apothéose de Corelli.*

W191. *L'apothéose de Lully.*

W192. *Le bandoline.*

W193. *Les baricades mistérieuses.*

W194. *La distrait.*

W195. *Les fastes de la grande et ancienne Mynxstrxndxs.*

W196. *Le Gaillard-boiteux.*

W197. *La harpée.*

W198. *Les Satires chavre-pieds.*

W199. *Soeur Monique* HAM 265.

W200. *Le tic-toc-choc ou les maillotins.*

Oeuvres complètes (Paris: L'oiseau-Lyre, 1932–33).

Complete Keyboard Music (New York: Dover, 1988); *Pièces de clavecin*, ed. K. Gilbert in Le Pupitre (Paris: Heugel, 1970).

Dagincourt, François:

W201. *Le Moulin a vent.*

W202. *Les Tourterelles.*

Pièces de clavecin (Paris: Heugel, 1969).

W203. **Daquin, Claude:** *Le Coucou. Pièces de clavecin* (Geneva: Minkoff, 1982).

Dornel, Louis-Antoine:

W204. *La Couperin.* Cited in B171.

W205. *La Marais.* Cited in B171.

W206. **Dowland, Robert:** *A Musicall Banquet* (Menston: Scolar, 1969); EL, Ser 1, v. 14.

W207. **Draghi, Antonio:** *Il Carneval.* Manuscript in the Austrian National Library, Vienna.

W208. **Farina, Carlo:** *Capriccio Stravagante* incomplete in WA 11.

W209. **Frescobaldi, Girolamo:** *Capriccio on the Call of a Cuckoo* in *Orgel-und Klavierwerke. Gesamtausgabe nach dem Urtext* (Kassel: Bärenreiter, 1949–54). B5.

W210. **Gay, John:** *The Beggar's Opera.* Facsimile of 1729 edition (Larchmont: Argonaut, 1961); complete edition (London: Boosey, 1920); in *The Ballad Opera* (New York: Garland, 1974); excerpts in Norton 81, HAM 264; B81, B126, B212, B237, B361, B427, B521, B600, B777.

W211. **Geminiani, Francesco:** *The Inchanted Forest* (London: J. Johnson, 1775).

W212. **Giramo, Pietro:** *Il Pazzo.* Manuscript at Northwestern University in Evanston, Illinois.

W213. **Gletle, Johann Melchior:** *Vorlesung über die Gesundheit* B164, 127.

Handel, George Frideric:

W214. *Acis and Galatea* in HG 3, 53; HHA 1/9.
W215. *Semele* in HG 7; HAA i/19. *Werke* (Ridgewood: Gregg International, 1965–66); HHA=*Hallische Händel Ausgabe* (Kassel: Bärenreiter, 1955–).

W216. **Hidalgo, Juan:** Songs for the Plays of Calderón in *Spanish Art Songs in the Seventeenth Century* (Madison, Wisc.: A-R Editions, 1985). B180.

Kerll, Johann Kaspar: B5.

W217. *Battaglia.*
W218. *Capriccio Cücu.*
Ausgewählte Werke DTB, v. 2.

Krieger, Adam:

W219. "Aechen."
W220. "Amanda" from *Clodius Liederbuch* DdT, v. 19.

W221. **Lambardi, Francesco and others:** *Festa a Ballo "Delizie di Posilipo Boscaresce a Maritime"* (Madison, Wisc.: A-R Editions, 1978).

Lampe, John Frederick: B12, B361.

W222. *The Dragon of Wantley* (London: Shoestring, 1960).

W223.   *Margery* (London: J. Wilcox, 1738).

W224.   *Pyramus and Thisbe* (London: Stainer & Bell, 1988).

Landi, Stefano:

W225.   *La morte d'Orfeo* excerpts in Gold, v. 1, 188–201.

W226.   *Il Sant' Alessio* facs. ed. (Bologna: Forni, 1967); excerpts in Gold, v. 1, 202–57; HAM 208, 209. B278.

W227.   **Leopold I, Kaiser:** "Amor Care" in *Musikalische Werke* (Farnborough: Gregg, 1972).

W228.   **Le Sage, de Richée, P.F.:** *Télémaque* (Berlin: Liepmannsohn, 1912).

W229.   **Locke, Matthew:** *Masque of Cupid and Death* in MB, v. 2.

Lully, François: B30, B270, B410, B697, B721.

W230.   *Alceste* excerpts in HAM 224, 225.

W231.   *Les amants magnifiques.*

W232.   *Amore malato.*

W233.   *L'amour médecin.*

W234.   *Ballet de L'Impatience.*

W235.   *Ballet de la Raillerie.*

W236.   *Le bourgeois gentilhomme* B525.

Oeuvres complètes de J.B. Lully (New York: Broude, 1966).

See the following for the comic works: B182, B285, B290, B295, B320.

W237.   **Marais, Marin:** *Gallstone Sonata* (New York: Broude, 1980–).

W238.   **Marazzoli, Marco:** *Dal mal il bene* excerpts in Gold, v. 1, 325–48.

W239.   **Marcello, Benedetto:** *Stravaganze d'Amore* excerpts in TEM 49.

W240.   **Mazzocchi, Vergilio:** *Chi soffre speri* excerpts in Gold, v. 1, 312–24.

W241.   **Merula, Tarquinio:** "Nominativo Hic Haec Hoc; Nominativo Quis vel qui" B164, 43.

W242.   **Moniglia, Andrea:** *La Tancia*. Cited with examples in B202. See B536 for a comic opera by Antonio Stradella produced in Rome at the same period.

Monteverdi, Claudio:

W243. *Il Ballo delle Ingrate.*
W244. "Dialogo di ninfa e pastore."
W245. "Io mi son giovinetta" in FIM, v. 2.
W246. *Scherzi musicali.* B775.
Tutte le opere (Bryn Mawr: Universal, 1966–).

W247. **Naudot, Jean-Jacques:** Music for vielle, hurdy-gurdy, and musette. Cited in B171.

W248. **Pergolesi, Luigi:** *La Serva Padrona* in *Opera omnia* (Rome: Gli mici della Musica da Camera, 1943); ed. K. Geiringer (Vienna: Universal, 1953); excerpts in HAM 287.

W249. **Playford, John:** *The English Dancing Master* (New York: Dance Horizons, 1975).

Poglietti, Alessandro:

W250. *Capriccio über dass Hennergeschrey* TEM 40; AM, v. 1.
W251. *Rossignolo* DTÖ, v. 27.

Excerpts from the descriptive *Aria allemagna con alcuni variazioni* in HAM 236.

Purcell, Henry:

W252. *Diocletian* B737.
W253. *The Fairy-Queen* B752.
W254. *King Arthur.*
W255. *The Tempest.*

Orpheus Britannicus:
W256. "Hence with Your Trifling Deity!"
W257. "I'll Sail upon the Dog Star."
W258. "Man Is for the Woman Made."
W259. "Nymphs and Shepherds." GAS, 60. (Ridgewood: Gregg Press, 1965).

Canons as a group: See D24.
W260. *The Catch Club* (1733) facs. (New York: Da Capo Press, 1965). W261 *The Catch Club* (1762) facs. (Farnborough: Gregg, 1965).
Complete Works (London: Novello, 1957–).

Rameau, Jean-Philippe: B832.

W261. *Les fêtes d'Hébé.*
W262. *Les Indes galantes.*
W263. *Platée* B400.

W264.   *Les Cyclops.*
W265.   *L'egiptienne.*
W266.   *La Poule.*
W267.   *Le rappel des oiseaux.*
Pièces de clavecin (Kassel: Bärenreiter, 1958). *Oeuvres complètes*, ed. C. Saint-Saëns (Paris: Durand, 1896–1924).

Rathgeber, Valentin:

W268.   *Die Bettelzech* B164, 144.
W269.   "Gioviale Consolante-Melancholico Lamente."
W270.   "Quodlibeticum."
W271.   "Von Allerhand Nasen."
*Ohrenvergnügendes und gemütergötzenden Tafelk*onfekt (Mainz: Schott, 1942).

W272.   **Rousseau, Jean Jacques:** *Le devin du village* (Madison, Wisc.: A-R Editions, 1998); excerpts in HAM 291.

W273.   **Sartorio, Antonio:** *Seleuco.* Cited with excerpts in B202.

W274.   **Savioni, Mario:** *Dido.* Cantata cited with excerpts in B719.

Scarlatti, Alessandro: B4, B199, B209, B327, B825.

W275.   *La caduta dei decemviri.*
W276.   *Eraclea .*
W277.   *Gl'Inganni felici* excerpt in GMB 258.
W278.   *Il prigionerio fortunato.*
W279.   *Il Trionfo dell'onore* (Milan: Carisch, 1941). See also B491, B493.
The Operas of Alessandro Scarlatti (Cambridge: Harvard University Press, 1974–83).

Telemann, Georg Philipp: B708.

W280.   *Der geduldige Socrates* (Kassel: Bärenreiter, 1967).
W281.   *Pimpinone* (Kassel: Bärenreiter, 1950); EDM, v. 6; excerpt in GMB 266. *Pimpinone* by Tomaso Albinoni (Madison, Wisc.: A-R Editions, 1983).
W282.   *Der Schulmeister* (Mainz: Schott, 1955).
W283.   *Burlesque de Quixotte*, ed. G. Lenzewski in *Musikschätze der Vergangenheit* (Berlin: F. Schroeder, 1963). Telemann also wrote a one-act opera, *Don Quichotte* (Madison, Wisc.: A-R Editions, 1991). B286, B300.
W284.   *Musique de Table* (Mainz: Schott, 1970).
Musikalische Werke (Kassel: Bärenreiter, 1950–).

Vivaldi, Antonio: B473.

W285.   *The Four Seasons* (London: Eulenburg, 1982). RV.269, 293, 297, 315.
W286.   *La tempesta di mare* Op. 8 No. 5 RV.253.
The Four Seasons and Other Concerti (New York: Dover, 1995); *Concerti*, ed.
W. Fortner (New York: Schott, 1960); P. Ryom, *Verzeichnis der Werke Antonio Vivaldis* (Leipzig: VEB Deutscher Verlag für Musik, 1977).

W287.   **Walther, Johann Jacob:** *Scherzi da violino solo* in EDMR,   Series 1,
        v. 17. B171.

Webbe, Samuel:

W288.   "Glorious Apollo" HAM 309a.
W289.   "Hot Cross Buns" HAM 309b.
W290.   "Now I'm Prepar'd" TGG 1.

The following are collections from the period in modern editions listed alphabetically according to title:

R23.   **Hilton, John:** *Catch That Catch can* (New York: Da Capo Press,
       1970). D14.
R24.   **Ravenscroft, Thomas:** *Deuteromelia*; *Melismata*; *Pammelia* in *Thomas Ravenscroft: Pammelia and Other Rounds and Catches* (Philadelphia: American Folklore Society, 1961).

For further reference:

R25.   *Elizabeth Rogers Hir Virginall Booke* (New York: Dover, 1975).
R26.   *English Pastime Music, 1630–60* (Madison, Wisc.: A-R Editions,
       1974).
R27.   *Music for London Entertainment 1660–1800* (London: Stainer & Bell,
       1989). This collection was intended for amateur musicians who wanted
       to sing songs heard at the court or theater.
R28.   *Wiener Tanzmusik in der Zweiten Hälfte des Siebzehnten Jahrhunderts.*
       ed. P. Nettl (Graz: Akademische Druck, 1960). This is a collection of
       dances from late 17th-century Vienna. Many have humorous titles.

THE CLASSIC PERIOD

General Studies: B1, B194, B203, B712, B811.
Aesthetics: B222, B503.
Bach, C.P.E.: B827.
Comic Opera (General): B61, B246, B288, B317, B326, B334, B443, B475, B494, B568, B569, B622, B627 (Irish Ballad's impact), B634, B749.
Comic Opera (French): B307, B709, B759.
Comic Opera (German): B196, B726.

Comic Opera (Russian): B594, B596.
Comic Opera (Swedish): B156, B430, B431, B432.
Fantasía: B33.
Minuet: B711.
Satire: B705, B814,
Symphony: B142.
Theater Music (English): B77.
Theory: B674.
Unless otherwise indicated, the citations for orchestral works are for miniature score, and those for vocal works are piano-vocal scores.

W291. **Antoš, Jan:** *Operetta o sedlekej svoboda*. Cited with examples in B131.

Arne, Thomas: B131.

W292. *Comus* in MB, v. 3.
W293. *Thomas and Sally* (London: Eulenburg, 1977).
W294. *Love in a Village* (Washington, D.C.: C.T. Wagner, 1979).

Billings William:

W295. "Jargon."
W296. "Modern Music" MIA 44.
Complete Works (Charlottesville: University Press of Virginia, 1978-).

W297. **Boccherini, Luigi:** Symphony No. 23 in d minor, *Dalla Casa del Diavolo,* in *Diletto Musicale* No. 623 (Vienna: Doblinger, 1988).

W298. Broadside Ballads as a group: *16th Century Broadsides* (Hamden: Garland, 1997). B216, B805.

W299. **Burns, Robert:** *The Scots Musical Museum* (Edinbugh: Blackwood, 1853).

Cimarosa, Antonio: B233, B242, B506.

W300. *L'italiana in Londra* (Milan: Ricordi, 1986).
W301. *Il maestro di cappella* (Milan: Ricordi, 1963).
W302. *Il matrimonio segreto* (Leipzig: Peters, 1871); (Mainz: Schott, n.d); (Milan: G. Ricordi, 1944). B46, B767.

W303. **Clementi, Muzio:** Capricci as a group in *The London Pianoforte School* (New York: Garland, 1985).

W304. **Cooke, Benjamin:** "Hark, Hark the Lark!" TGG 4, 3.

W305.   **Czerny, Carl:** Capricci as a group in *Systematische Anleitung zur Fantasierung auf dem Pianoforte* (New York: Longman, 1981).

W306.   **Dibdin, Charles:** *The Padlock* (London: Davidson, 1849). B548.

Dittersdorf, Carl Ditters von:

W307.   *Doktor und Apotheker* in Senfl's *Opernbibliotek* (Berlin: R. Birnbach, 1943); excerpt in the style of a sleeping song in HAM 305. B738.

W308.   *Ovid* Symphonies as a group (Vienna, 1785).

W309.   **Fomin, Yestigney Ipat'yevich:** *Jamciki, na podstawe* (Moscow: Muzyka, 1977). B131.

W310.   **Galuppi, Baldassare:** *Il filosofo di campagne* (Milan: Carisch, 1938); excerpt HAM 285.

W311.   **Gassmann, Florian:** *La contessa* (Vienna: Artaria, 1959).

W312.   **Gluck, Christoph Willibald:** *La rencontre imprévue* B578. *Sämtliche Werke* (Kassel: Bärenreiter, 1951–).

W313.   **Grétry, André Ernest:** *La Rosière Republicaine ou La Fête de la vertue*, in *Collection complète des oeuvres de Grétry* (New York: University Music, 1974). B584.

W314.   **Hafner, Philipp:** *Megära, die förterliche Hexe.* Hafner is the author of the text, but the composer is unknown.

Haydn, Franz Josef: B203, B249, B414, B415, B437, B464, B490, B534, B586, B616, B646, B823.

Operas: B279, B400, B402, B622, B705.
W315.   *La cantarina* HW 25/2, 28:2. B822.
W316.   *Die Feuerbrunst* HW 24/3 29b:A. B621.
W317.   *L'incontro improvviso* HW 25/6 28:6. B14.
W318.   *Il mondo della luna* HW 25/ 7 28:7. B.278, B436.
W319.   *Orlando paladino* HW 25/2 28: 2. B448.
W320.   *Lo speziale* HW 25/ 3 28:3. B278.
W321.   *La vera costanza* HW 25/8, 356 28:8. B801.

Oratorios:
W322.   *The Creation* H 21:2.

W323.   *The Seasons* H 21:3.

Canons: HW 31.
W324.   "Auf einen Adeligen Dummkopf" H 27b2.
W325.   "Aus nichts wird nichts" H 27b15.

Songs: HW 29/1.
W326.   "Lob der Faulheit" H 26a 22.
W327.   "The Mermaid's Song" H 26a 25.
W328.   "Sailor's Song" H 26a 31.
W329.   "Ein sehr gewöhnliche Geschichte" H 26a 4.

Symphonies (Ww.330–44): See B328, B573, B585, B704 for all the instrumental music.

W330.   No. 6.
W331.   No. 7.
W332.   No. 8.
W333.   No. 31.
W334.   No. 45. B625.
W335.   No. 60. B549, B772.
W336.   No. 73.
W337.   No. 82.
W338.   No. 83.
W339.   No. 90.
W340.   No. 93.
W341.   No. 94. B484.
W342.   No. 100.
W343.   No. 101.
W344.   No. 104.

Critical Edition of the Complete Symphonies (Vienna: Universal, 1967–).
W345.   Notturni and Scherzandi as a group HW 40 B338.
W346.   Keyboard Concerto in D HW 18:11 B15.

String Quartets: H 3.
W347.   *Joke* (Op. 33 No. 2). B818.
W348.   *Frog* (Op. 50 No. 6).
W349.   *Rider* (Op. 74 No. 3).
30 Celebrated String-Quartets (Melville, N.Y.: Belwin Mills, n.d.).

Piano Works: H 3; B518.
W350.   Sonata No. 29
W351.   Sonata No. 51
Sämtliche Klaviersonaten (Vienna: Universal, 1963).

W352.   Capriccio in G HW 17:1, HU, 5; WU, 1. B405, B664.

H=*Werke* (Munich: G. Henle, 1958–); *Thematic Catalogue*, ed. A. van Hoboken (Mainz: B. Schott's Söhne, 1957–78).

W353.   **Haydn, Michael**: Music to *Zaire* (Vienna: Doblinger, 1981).

W354.   **Hewitt, James:** *Battle of Trenton* (Miami: Belwin, 1989).

W355.   **Hiller, Johann Adam:** *Lisuart und Dariolette* Excerpts in HAM 301.

W356.   **Hopkinson, Francis:** "The Battle of the Kegs" in A. Loesser, *Humor in American Song* (Detroit: Gale Research Co., 1974).

W357.   **Koczwara, František:** *The Battle of Prague* (Dublin, 1788).

W358.   **Martín y Soler, Vicente:** *Una cosa rara* (Munich: G. Henle, 1990).

W359.   **Moore, Thomas:** *Irish Melodies* (Boston: Ditson, 1852). See B283.

W360.   **Moral, Pablo del:** *La opera casera* in José Subirá, *Tonadilla escenica* (Madrid: Union Musical Española, 1970), v. 3. B52, B89, B180, B228, B229, B261, B423.

Mozart, Leopold:

W361.   *Sinfonia burlesca* in *Diletto Musicale* No. 83 (Vienna: Doblinger, 1970).
W362.   *Sinfonia da caccia* in *Diletto Musicale* No. 83 (Vienna: Doblinger, 1970).
W363.   *Toy* Symphony. This has been ascribed to Haydn and Leopold Mozart. *Ausgewählte Werke* (Leipzig: Breitkopf und Härtel, 1908).

Mozart, Wolfgang Amadeus: B27, B203, B218, B456, B830.

Operas: B27, B103, B268, B282, B332, B354, B416, B618, B652.
W364.   *Bastien und Bastienne* K.50 MW 5/4; NMA 2:5/3. B403, B650, B794.
W365.   *Così fan tutte* K.558 MW 5/19; NMA 5/3; full score (New York: Dover, 1983). B34, B294, B443, B511, B540, B658, B782, B804.
W366.   *Don Giovanni* K.527 MW 5/28; NMA 5/17; full score (New York: Dover, 1974). B260, B583, B691, B695.
W367.   *Die Entführung aus dem Serail* K.384 MW 5/13; NMA 5/11; full score (New York: Dover, 1989). B14, B722.
W368.   *La finta semplice* K.51 MW 5/4; NMA 2: 5/2. B401.

W369.   *Le nozze di Figaro* K.492 MW 5/17; NMA 2: 5/16; full score (New York: Dover, 1989). B144, B337, B397, B404, B609, B649, B753, B766, B806.

W370.   *Der Schauspieldirektor* K.486 MW 5/16; NMA 5/15.

W371.   *Die Zauberflöte* K.620 MW 5/20; NMA 2: 5/19; miniature score (Kassel: Bärenreiter, 1970). B31, B223, B543, B587, B612, B648, B758, B816.

Canons: See D13.

W372.   "Difficile lectu mihi Mars" K.559 MW 7/2, 29; NMA 3:10, 47.

W373.   "Leck mich im Arsch" K.231 (a6), K.233 (a3).

W374.   "Lieber Freistädtler" K.232 MW 7/2, 8; NMA 3:10, 27; (a6) MW 7/2, 5; NMA 3:10, 11; (a3) MW V7/2, 11; NMA 3:10, 17. D11.

Songs:

W375.   "Ich möchte wohl der Kaiser sein" K.539 MW 6/2, 177; NMA 2: 7/4, 79.

W376.   "Das Veilchen" K.476 MW 7/1, 42; NMA 3:8, 26.

Symphonies:

W377.   No. 33 K.319 MW VIII/ii, 213; NMA IV:11/vi, 23.

W378.   No. 35 K.385 MW 8/3, 1; NMA 4:11/6, 113.

W379.   No. 38 K.504 MW VIII/iii, 97; NMA IV:II/viii, 63.

W380.   No. 39 K.543 MW 8/ 3, 137; NMA 11/9, 1.

W381.   No. 40 K.550 MW VIII/iii, 181; NMA IV:11/ix, 63.

W382.   No. 41 K.551 MW 8/3, 230; NMA 4:11/9, 187.

Divertimenti:

W383.   *Galimathias Musicum* K.32 MW 25, No. 12; NMA 4:12/i, 3.

W384.   *Ein musikalischer Spass* K.522 MW 10, 58; NMA 8:18, 223. *Complete Serenades* (New York: Dover, 1989). B147, B541, B542, B558, B563, B593, B688, B693, B795.

Concerti:

W385.   No. 9 K.271 MW 16/2, 1; NMA 5:15/11, 65.

W386.   No. 17 K.453 MW 16/3, 22; NMA 5:15/v, 3.

W387.   No. 18 K.456 MW 16/3, 55; NMA 5:15/v, 71.

W388.   No. 19 K.459 MW 16/3, 119; NMA 5:15/5, 151.

Piano Concertos Nos.11–16 and Piano Concertos Nos.17–22 (New York: Dover, 1987).

W389.   *Turkish* Violin Concerto K.219 MW 12/1, 113; NMA 5:14/1.

String Quartets:

W390.   *The Hunt* K.458 MW 14, 152; NMA 8:20/1/2, 57.

The Ten Celebrated String Quartets (Kassel: Bärenreiter, 1990).

W391. Variations on "Unser dummer Pöbel meint" for Piano K.455 MW 21, 74; NMA 9:26, 98. Tchaikovsky used this set of variations for the finale of his Orchestral Suite No. 4 (*Mozartiana*). *Variations for Piano* (New York: Kalmus, 1942).

Piano Sonatas: B730.
W392. No. 8 in a K.310 MW 20, 78; NMA 9:25.
W393. No. 11 in A K.331 MW 20, 118; NMA 9:25.
W394. No. 17 in D K.576 MW 20, 194; NMA 9:25.
Sonatas and Fantasies for the Piano (Bryn Mawr, Penn.: Theodore Presser, 1960). B.589.

MW=*W.A. Mozarts sämtliche Werke* (Ann Arbor, Mich.: Edwards, 1951–56);

NMA=*Neue Ausgabe sämtliche Werke* (Kassel: Bärenreiter, 1955–);

K=L.Köchel, *Chronologisch-thematisches Verzeichnis* (Wiesbaden: Breitkopf und Härtel, 1964).

Paisiello, Giovanni:

W395. *Il barbiere di Siviglia* (Milan: Ricordi, 1868); piano-vocal score (Milan: Ricordi, 1903); CDMI, v. 20. B651
W396. *Nina* (Milan: Ricordi, 1987). B460.
W397. *Socrate immaginario* (Mainz: Schott, 1986).

Pergolesi, Giovanni:

W398. *Il Maestro di Musica* (Rome: Amici della musica da camera, 1956); excerpt in HAM 286. B628, B630.
W399. *La Serva Padrona* Miniature Score (Vienna: Universal, nd); piano-vocal: (New York: G. Schirmer, 1972); excerpt in HAM 287. B314, B630, B809.

W400. **Philidor, François:** *Tom Jones* (London: Boosey & Hawkes, 1978).

W401. **Piccini, Niccolò:** *La buona figliuola* in CDMI, v. 7.

W402. **Rodríguez de Hita, Antonio:** *Las Labradoras de Murcia* (Madrid, 1769). B229.

Scarlatti, Domenico:

W403. *Cat* Fugue, K.30, L.499

W404.   Sonatas as a group: *Opere complete per clavicembalo* (New York: Ricordi, 1947–51); *Sixty Sonatas* (New York: G. Schirmer, 1953).

W405.   **Schulz, Johann:** *Lieder in Volkston bey dem Klavier zu singen* (Mainz: Schott, 1930).

W406.   **Standfuss, Johann C.:** *Der Teufel ist los* (Leipzig: Junius, 1770).

W407.   **Umlauf, Ignaz:** *Der Dorfbarbier*, DTÖ, v. 48.

W408.   **Vanhal, Johann:** *Sinfonia comista* (New York: Garland, 1981).

W409.   **Werner, Gregor Joseph:** *Musikalischer Instrumental-Calender* EDMR, v. 31.

Wranitzky, Pavel:

W410.   *Oberon, König der Elfen.* Text alone remains. Excerpt from *Die Gutte Mutter* in the anthology of B131.

W411.   *Sinfonia Quodlibet.* Cited in B328.

For further reference:

R29.   *Das deutsche Lied im.18 Jahrhundert.* Ed. M. Friedländer (Stuttgart: J.G. Cotta, 1902). This collection demonstrates the wide range of 18th-century song.

R30.   *Die Singende Muse an der Pleisse* DdT, vols. 35–36. This is a collection of early 18th-century songs.

THE ROMANTIC PERIOD

General Studies: B1, B131.
Ballet: B11.
Caricature: B258.
Comic Opera (General): B25, B246, B445, B696, D17.
Comic Opera (English): B830.
Comic Opera (French): B50, B335, B460, B501, B610, B694, B699, B709, B710, B725.
Comic Opera (German): B435, B816.
Comic Opera (Italian): B353.
Comic Opera (Spanish): B457.
Folk Song (American): B145, B149.
Minstrels: B732.
Operetta: B94, B96, B115, B125, B479, B611 (Parody of *Faust*), B696.
Song (French): B174.

Symphony: B142.
Unless otherwise indicated, miniature scores for orchestral and piano-vocal scores for operas are cited.

W412.   **Albéniz, Isaac:** *Pepita Jiménez* (Madrid: ICCMU, 1996). B275, B351.

Alkan, Charles-Valentin:

W413.   *Le festin d'Estope.*
W414.   *Scherzo diabolico.*
The Piano Music of Alkan (New York: G. Schirmer, 1964).

W415.   **Auber, Daniel:** *Fra Diavolo* (Melville: Belwin Mills, n.d.).

W416.   **Balfe, Michael:** *The Bohemian Girl* (Boston: Birchard, 1914).

W417.   **Barbieri, Francisco:** *El Barberillo de Lavapiés* (Madrid: Union Musical Española, 1971).

W418.   **Beach, Amy Marcy Cheneys:** *Children's Carnival* (Bryn Mawr, Penn.: Hildegard, 1990).

Beethoven Ludwig van: B203, B210, B348, B452, B603, B617, B655, B780.

Canons:
W419.   "Ich bitt' dich" WoO 172 GA 23/256/13.
W420.   "Schuppanzigh ist ein Lump" WoO 100 HS 5.
W421.   "Signor Abate" WoO 178.
W422.   "Ta. Ta. Ta. lieber Mäzel" WoO 162 HS 9.

Songs:
W423.   "L'amante Impaziante."
W424.   "Elegie auf ein Tod eines Pudels."
W425.   "Das Flohlied aus *Faust*."
Sämtliche Lieder (Munich: G. Henle, 1992).

Symphonies:
W426.   No. 1.
W427.   No. 2.
W428.   No. 3.
W429.   No. 4.
W430.   No. 5.
W431.   No. 6.
W432.   No. 7.
W433.   No. 8 B620.
W434.   No. 9.

All symphonies in v. 9 of the Collected Edition; *Symphonies* (New York: Dover, 1989–).

W435.   *Wellington's Sieg oder Die Schlacht bei Vittoria* Op. 91 GA 2/10; NA 2/1.

Piano Concerti:
W436.   No. 1 9/65.
W437.   No. 2 9/66.
W438.   No. 3 9/67. B15.

W439.   Overture to *The Ruins of Athens* 20/207.

W440.   Serenade in D 7/5 8; NA 6/6.
The Chamber Music of Beethoven (Melville: Belwin Mills, 1973).

W441.   Piano Trios, Op. 1

Piano Sonatas: B39, B273, B761.
W442.   Op. 31 No. 3 16/141.

Variations:
W443.   *Diabelli* Op. 120 GA 17/165; NA 7/5.
W444.   "Ich bin der Schneider Kakadu" Op. 121a GA 11 187; NA 4/3.

W445.   Bagatelles, Op. 126 18/190 B344.
W446.   Capriccio in G "The Rage over a Lost penny in the Form of a Caprice" B405.

Another work that has a humorous title is *Duett mit zwei obligaten Augengläsern*, or *Duet with the Accompaniment of Two Eyeglasses* GA 6, NA 6/6.

GA=*Ludwig van Beethovens Werke* (Ann Arbor, Mich.: Edwards, 1949); in miniature scores (New York: Kalmus, 1971); NA=*Neue Sämtliche Werke* (Munich: G. Henle, 1961–); Georg Kinsky and Hans Halm, *Das Werke Beethovens: Thematisch-bibliographisches Verzeichnis seiner sämtlichen vollendenten Kompositionen* (Munich: Henle, 1955).

Berlioz, Hector:

W447.   *Beatrice et Benedict* (New York: Kalmus, n.d.). B743.
W448.   *La damnation de Faust* (New York: Kalmus, 1969); miniature score (London: Ernst Eulenburg, n.d.).

W449.   *Symphonie fantastique* (London: Ernst Eulenburg, n.d.).

W450.   Overture to *Le carnaval romain* (London: Ernst Eulenburg, n.d.).
Werke (New York: Kalmus, 1971).

W451.   **Berwald, Franz:** Symphony No. 2 *Capricieuse* (Kassel: Bärenreiter, 1971). *Sämtliche Werke* (Kassel: Bärenreiter, 1966–).

Bizet, Georges:

W452.   "La coccinelle." The manuscript is at Stiftelsen Musikkulturens Fräjande, Stockholm, Sweden. B174.

W453.   Symphony in C (New York: Associated, n.d.).

W454.   *Jeux d'enfants* (Paris: Editions Musicales du Marais, 1990).

W455.   *The Black Crook* (anonymous musical comedy). Songs in *Showsongs from The Black Crook to The Red Mill* (New York: Dover, 1974). A waltz composed by V.B. Aubert also exists (Chicago: Lyon & Healy, 1918). B49, B237, B277, B564, B590, B615.

W456.   **Boieldieu, François-Adrien:** *Le dame blanche* (Paris: Launer, n.d.). B131, B479.

W457.   **Borodin, Alexander:** *Prince Igor* (New York: Edition Musicus, 1943).

Brahms, Johannes:

Canons:
W458.   "Ein Gems auf dem Stein."
W459.   "Sitzt a shön's Vögelrn auf'm Dannabaum." BW 21,179; *121 Canons for Singing and Playing on Various Instruments* (Zürich: Musikverlag zum Pelican, 1965) Nos. 15 and 73.

Part-songs:
W460.   "Da unter im Tale."
W461.   "Erlaube mir, feins Mädchen." BW 20,165.

Songs:
W462.   "Blinde Kuh."
W463.   "Den Wirbel schlag ich."
W464.   "Der Schmied."
W465.   "Unüberwindlich."
W466.   "Vergebliches Ständchen."
70 Songs (New York: International Music, 1954).

W467.   Symphony No. 4 (Melvill N.J.: Belwin Mills, n.d.).

W468.   Serenade No. 1 (London: Eulenburg, n.d.).

W469.   Serenade No. 2 (London: Eulenburg, n.d.).

W470.   *Academic Festival Overture* (Melville: Belwin Mills, n.d.). B486.

W471.   String Quartet No. 3 *Complete Chamber Music for Strings and Clarinet Quintet* (New York: Dover, 1988).
Sämtliche Werke (Ann Arbor, Mich.: J.W. Edwards, 1949); as miniature scores (New York: Kalmus, 1970).

W472.   **Bruckner, Anton:** Symphony No. 4 *Romantic* (New York: Dover, 1990). B817. *Sämtliche Werke, kritische Gesamtausgabe* (Vienna: Musikwissenschaftlicher Verlag, 1951–).

Cervantes, Ignacio:

W473.   *La Carcajada.*

W474.   *Pst!*

W475.   *Zigs-zags.*
Ignacio Cervantes: A Highlight Collection of His Best-Loved Original Works (New York: Shattinger, 1976).

Chabrier, Emmanuel:

W476.   *L'Etoile* (Paris: Enoch, 1947). B717.

W477.   "Ballade du gros dindons" (New York: A. Fassio, 1935). B174.

W478.   *Bourrée Fantasque* (Miami Lakes, Fla.: Masters, 1980).

W479.   Impromptu in C in *Piano Music* (Miami Lakes, Fla.: Masters, 1980).

W480.   *Joyeuse Marche* (Paris: Enoch, 1900).

W481.   *Pièces pittoresques* (New York: International, 1962). B287.

Cherubini, Luigi:

W482.   *Anacréon* (Paris: Cherubini, 1803).

W483.   *Le Crescendo* manuscript in the Deutsche Staatsbibliothek, overture (Rome: Boccaccini & Spada, 1988).

W484.   **Chopin, Fryderyk:** Variations on "La ci darem la mano" *Werke* (Leipzig: Breitkopf und Härtel, 1878–80).

Cornelius, Peter:

W485.   *Der Barbier von Bagdad* (Leipzig: Universal, 1910). B102, B174, B799.

W486.   "Nichts ohne Liebe" GRP 22.
Musikalische Werke (Farnborough: Gregg, 1971).

Délibes, Leo:

W487. "Les animaux de Granville."
W488. "Le code fashionable."
W489. "Chanson espagnole."
W490. "Les filles de Cadiz."
W491. "La taxe sur la viande."
Chansons (Paris: Heugel, 1894). See B174.

W492. *Coppélia* (Melville, N.J.: Belwyn Mills, n.d.).

Donizetti, Gaetano: B516, B671.

W493. *Don Pasquale* full score (Milan: Ricordi 1961); piano-vocal score (New York: Franco Colombo, 1963).
W494. *L'elisir d'amore* full score (Milan: Ricordi, 1916); piano-vocal score (Huntington: Kalmus, 1968). B159, B317.
W495. *La fille du regiment* (New York: International, 1972).

W496. "La Connochia."
W497. "A mezzanotte."
Composizioni da camera (Milan: Ricordi, 1961).

Dvořák, Antonin:

W498. *Carnival Overture* (London: Ernst Eulenburg, n.d.).
W499. *Scherzo capriccioso* (London: Ernst Eulenburg, n.d.).

W500. Piano Quintet in A (London: Ernst Eulenburg, n.d.).

W501. *Humoresken* (Prague: Supraphon, 1984).
Complete Works (Prague: Supraphon, 1955–).

Emmett, Dan:

W502. "Dixie" arranged for piano by W.L. Hobbs (New York: Firth, Bond, 1860).
W503. "Turkey in the Straw" in *The Dance Music of Ireland* (Chicago, 1907). See B654 for a related work.

W504. **Fauré, Gabriel:** *Dolly* (London: Peters, 1995).

W505. **Fry, William Henry:** *Santa Claus Symphony.* Score in the Free Library of Philadelphia. B142.

Gilbert and Sullivan: See Sir Arthur Sullivan.

Glinka, Mikhail: B174.

W506.   *A Life for the Czar* (Moscow: Muzyka, 1964).
W507.   *Ruslan and Ludmila* (Milan: Suvini Zerboni, 1943).

W508.   *Jota aragonesa* (Leipzig: Eulenburg, 1924).

W509.   **Goldmark, Karl:** *A Rustic Wedding Symphony.* This work is also known as *Ländliche Hochzeit* (Mainz: Schott, n.d.).

Gottschalk, Louis Moreau: B281.

W510.   *The Banjo.*
W511.   *Souvenir do Porto Rico.*
Piano Music of Louis Moreau Gottschalk (New York: Dover, 1973).

Gounod, Charles: B698.

W512.   *Le Medicín Malgré Lui* (Paris: Colombier, 1858); (Private publication Mark Herman and Ronnie Apter, with an English translation: 1970).

W513.   *Funeral March of a Marionette* (New York: Carl Fischer, 1911).

W514.   **Graf, C.D.:** *Economical Duet.* B367.

W515.   **Heinrich, Anthony Philip**: *Pushmataha.* Score in the Library of Congress.

Herbert, Victor:

W516.   *Babes in Toyland* (New York: Witmark, 1974).
W517.   *Naughty Marietta* (New York: Witmark, 1910).

W518.   **Holbrooke, J.:** *Pickwich Quartet.* B367.

W519.   **Humperdinck, Engelbert:** *Hänsel und Gretel* (London: Schott, 1970).

W520.   **Lalo, Edouard:** "Ballade à la lune" *Chansons* (Paris: Heugel, 1988). B174.

W521.   **Lehár, Franz:** *Die lustige Witwe* (New York: Dover, 1983). B52.

Liszt, Franz:

W522.   *Dante* Symphony (London: Ernst Eulenburg, n.d.).
W523.   *Faust-Symphonie* (London: Ernst Eulenburg, n.d.).

W524.   *Dante* Sonata.
W525.   Sonata in B minor (Munich: Henle, 1973).

W526.   *Mephisto* Waltz. *Mephisto Waltz and Other Works for Solo Piano* (New York: Dover, 1994).

W527.   *Totentanz* (London: Ernst Eulenburg, n.d.).

Arrangements:

W528.   *Grande Fantasie sur La Fiancée.*

W529.   *Reminiscences de Don Juan. Piano Transcriptions from French and Italian Operas* (New York: Dover, 1982).

W530.   *Soirée musicales* (based on Rossini).

W531.   *Wedding March and Dance from A Midsummer's Night Dream.*

Musikalische Werke (Leipzig: Breitkopf und Härtel, 1967).

Loewe, Carl:

W532.   "Hochzeitslied."

W533.   "Die Katzenkönigin."

W534.   "Die Wandelnde Glocke."

Twelve Songs and Ballads (New York: G. Schirmer, 1903).

W535.   **Lortzing, Albert:** *Zar und Zimmermann* (New York: C.F. Peters, 1952). B399, B689, B751.

Mehul, Etienne:

W536.   *Burlesque grotesque.* Recorded on Angel S 36080 with other examples of burlesques. B142.

W537.   Overture to *La chasse de jeune Henri*, recorded on Nimbus NI- 584/85. *Le Jeune Henri* (Paris, 1797).

Mendelssohn, Felix:

W538.   *Die Hochzeit des Camacho.* B309, B763.

W539.   Canon: "Freund Felix ist ein Guter mann." Cykler 50.

W540.   *A Midsummer Night's Dream* Overture, Incidental Music. *Major Orchestral Works* (New York: Dover, n.d.).

W541.   Octet (London: Ernst Eulenburg, n.d.).

Kritisch durchgesehene Ausgabe (Farnborough: Gregg, 1967); as minature scores (New York: Kalmus, 1971).

Mussorgsky, Modeste: B785.

W542.   *Sorochintsy Fair* (Moscow: Muzyka, 1970).

Songs: B350, B358.

W543.   *The Nursery.*

W544.   "The Musician's Peep Show."

W545.   "The Puppet Show."

W546.   "The Seminarian." GAS, 245
W547.   "Song of the Flea."
Complete Songs (New York: Schirmer, 1995).

W548.   *Night on Bald Mountain* (Melville, N.J.: Belwin Mills, n.d.).
W549.   *Pictures at an Exhibition* (Munich: Henle, 1992). B350.
Polnoe sobranie sochinenii (New York: Kalmus, 1969).

W550.   **Nicolai, Otto:** *Lustige Weiber von Windsor* (New York: G. Schirmer, 1958). B642.

Offenbach, Jacques: B36, B137, B198, B239, B395, B523, B528, B789.

W551.   *La belle Hélène* (Paris: Heugel, 1969).
W552.   *Les contes d'Hoffmann* (New York: G. Schirmer, 1959).
W553.   *Orphée aux enfers* full score: (Paris: Heugel & Cie, 1986).
W554.   *La Périchole* (Paris: Joubert, 1874).

W555.   **Paganini, Nicolò:** Caprices for Solo Violin (New York: International, 1973).

Puccini, Giacomo:

W556.   *Gianni Schicchi* (Milan: Ricordi, 1918).

W557.   "Avanti Urania."
W558.   "E l'ucellino."
Tutte le composizione per voce e pianoforte (Milan: Ricordi, 1918).

W559.   **Reichardt, Johann Friedrich:** *Lieb und Treue* (Berlin, 1800).

W560.   **Rice, Edward E.:** *Evangeline* in *Nineteenth-Century American Musical Theater*, v. 13: *Early Burlesque in America* (New York: Garland, 1994).

Rimsky-Korsakov, Nikolai:

W561.   *Le Coq d'Or* (New York: G. Schirmer, 1900). B682.

W562.   *Capriccio Español* (London: Ernst Eulenburg, n.d.).

Rossini, Gioachino: B26, B727.

W563.   *Il Barbiere di Siviglia* (New York: G. Schirmer, 1962); full score (New York Dover, 1989); *Il barbiere di Siviglia* Overture (London: Eulenburg, n.d.). B84, B417, B577, B651, B714, B719.
W564.   *La Cenerentola* (New York: Kalmus, 1969).

W565. *Le Comte Ory* (Milan: Ricordi, 1973).

W566. *La gazza ladra* (New York: Garland, 1978); overture in *William Tell and Other Overtures* (New York: Dover, 1994).

W567. *L'italiana in Algeri* (New York: G. Schirmer, 1966).

Early Romantic Opera (New York: Garland, 1977).

Part-songs: B47.

W568. "Duetto buffo di due gatti" (ascribed to Rossini) (Tustin: National, 1974). B654.

W569. "'Toast pour le nouvel an."

W570. *Album for Adolescent Children* (Boca Raton, Fla.: Master Music Publications, 1990).

Edizione critica (Pesaro: Fondazione Rossini, 1979–).

Saint-Saëns, Camille:

W571. *Phryné* (Paris: Durand, 1893).

W572. *La princesse jaune* (Paris: Durand, 1872).

W573. *Le carnaval des animaux* (Paris: Durand, 1922).

W574. *Danse Macabre* (Paris: Durand, n.d.).

Schubert, Franz:

W575. *Die Verschworren* D.787. B274, B310, B632.

Canons:

W576. "Der Schnee zerrint" D.130.

W577. "Willkommen, lieber schöner Mai" D.244. Cykler Nos. 32 and 33.

Part-songs:

W578. "Die Advokaten" D.37.

W579. "Edit nonus, edit clerus" D.847.

W580. "Trinklied im Mai" D.426.

Songs:

W581. *Die schöne Müllerin* D.795.

W582. "Die Forelle" D.550.

W583. "Heidenröslein" D.257.

Lieder (Leipzig: C.F. Peters, 1885).

Symphonies:

W584. No. 6 D.589 (New York: Eulenburg, n.d.).

W585. No. 9 D.944 (New York: Eulenburg, n.d.).

W586. Italian Overtures, D.590, D.591 (New York: Eulenburg, n.d.).

W587.   Octet in F D.803.

W588.   Quintet for Piano and Strings *Die Forelle* D.667 (New York: Lea, 1959).

W589.   Impromptus D.899, D.935 (New York: Lea Pocket Scores, 1954).

Kritisch durchgesehene Gesamtausgabe (New York: Dover, 1965); as miniature scores (New York: Kalmus, 1971); D=O.E. Deutsch, Franz Schubert: *Thematische Verzeichnis seiner Werke in Chronologischer Folge* (Kassel: Bärenreiter, 1978).

Schumann, Robert: B495.

Canons:

W590.   "Gebt mir zu trinken" Cykler No. 71.

Part-songs:

W591.   "Der Rekrut" GRP 13.

Songs: B352.

W592.   "Die beide Grenadiere."

W593.   "Der Contrabandiste."

W594.   "Der Hidalgo."

W595.   "Jemand" and "Niemand."

W596.   "Ein Jüngling liebt ein Mädchen."

W597.   "Räthsel."

W598.   "Schlusslied des Narren."

Selected Songs for Solo Voice and Piano, ed. C. Schumann (New York: Dover, 1981).

W599.   *Overture, Scherzo, Finale* (London: Ernst Eulenburg, n.d.).

Piano Works:

W600.   *Carnaval*

W601.   *Davidsbündlertänze.*

W602.   *Faschingsschwank aus Wien.*

W603.   *Humoreske.* B263.

W604.   *Kinderscenen.*

W605.   *Papillons.*

W606.   *Phantasiestücke.*

Piano Music of Robert Schumann (New York: Dover, 1972). *Werke* (Leipzig: Breitkopf und Härtel, 1881–93).

Smetana, Bedřich: B515.

W607.   *The Bartered Bride* (New York: G. Schirmer, 1978). B393, B773.

W608.   *The Kiss* overture (Vienna: Wiener Philharmonischer, 1900).

W609.   **Sousa, John Philip:** *El capitan* (Hamden: Garland, 1997).

Spohr, Louis:

W610. Symphony No. 6 (Vienna: P. Mechetti, 1840).
W611. Symphony No. 9 (Leipzig: Schuberth, 1850).

Strauss, Johann: B59, B120.

W612. *Die Fledermaus* piano-vocal score: (New York: Edwin F. Kalmus, 1968); miniature score (Mainz: Eulenburg, 1968).
W613. *Indigo und die vierzig Raüber* (Vienna: Spina, 1871).

Strauss II, Johann: B131.

W614. *Freut euch des Leben.*
W615. *Die Jovialen.*
W616. *Kuss-walzer.*
W617. *Motor-Quadrille.*
W618. *Tik-Tak Polka.*
W619. *Tritsch-Tratsch Polka.*
W620. *Wiener Bonbons. Gesamtausgabe* (Vienna: Doblinger, 1967–72).

Sullivan, Sir Arthur (Gilbert and Sullivan): B9, B10, B53, B252, B253, B302, B349, B516, B829.

W621. *Cox and Box* (Melville: Belwyn Mills, 1970).
W622. *H.M.S. Pinafore* (New York: G. Schirmer, n.d.).
W623. *The Mikado* (New York: G. Schirmer, n.d.).
W624. *Patience* (New York: G. Schirmer, 1950).
W625. *The Pirates of Penzance* (New York: G. Schirmer, n.d.).
W626. *The Sorcerer* (New York: Belwin Mills, n.d.).
W627. *Trial by Jury* (New York: G. Schirmer, 1941).
Excerpts from these in *A Treasury of Gilbert and Sullivan* (New York: Simon & Schuster, 1941).

W628. **Suppé, Franz von:** *Boccaccio* (Leipzig: Vranz, 1910).

Tchaikovsky, Piotr Ilyich:

W629. Symphony No. 6 (London: Ernst Eulenburg, 1986).
W630. *The Nutcracker* (Melville: Belwyn Mills, n.d.). B11.
W631. *Capriccio italien* (London: Ernst Eulenburg, n.d.).
Polnoe sibranie sochinenii (New York: Kalmus, 1974–).

Verdi, Giuseppe: B807, B813.

W632. *Falstaff* (Milan: Ricordi, 1980); full score (New York: Dover, 1980).
B80, B105, B359, B565, B739, B742, B747, B791.
W633. *Un giorno di regno* (Milan: Ricordi, 1950).

W634. "Lo spazzacamino."
W635. "Stornello."
Composizioni da Camera (Milan: Ricordi, 1968). *Works* (Chicago: University of Chicago Press, 1983-).

Wagner, Richard: B453, B778, B816.

W636. *Das Liebesverbot* (Wiesbaden: Breitkopf und Härtel, 1900).
W637. *Die Meistersinger von Nürnberg* (New York: G. Schirmer, 1932). B68, B244, B420, B562, B735.
W638. *Siegfried* (New York: Dover, 1983).
W639. "Les deux grenadieres"
Sämtliche Lieder (Mainz: Schott, 1982). B174. *Musikalische Werke* (New York: Da Capo Press, 1971).

Weber, Carl Maria von: B311.

W640. *Die drei Pintos* (Madison, Wisc.: A-R Editions, forthcoming). This opera was completed by Mahler.
W641. *Der Freischütz* (New York: G. Schirmer, n.d.).
W642. *Oberon* (Melville: Belwin Mills, n.d.).
W643. *Peter Schmoll und seine Nachbaren* (New York: C.F. Peters, 1963).
W644. *Abu Hassan* overture (Melville: Belwin Mills, n.d.).

Wolf, Hugo:

W645. *Der Corregidor* (Vienna: Musikwissenschftlicher Verlag, 1995).

Songs: B352.
W646. *Italienisches Liederbuch*: "Mein Liebster ist so Klein."
W647. *Spanisches Liederbuch*: "Mausfallen Sprüchlein."

Mörike Liederbuch:
W648. "Abschied."
W649. "Auf dem Grünen Balkon" GAS, 140.
W650. "Elfenlied."
W651. "Nimmersatte Liebe" GAS, 136.
W652. "Der Tambour."
65 Songs for Voice and Piano (New York: International Music, 1961).

W653. *Italienische Serenade* (New York: International, 1942).
Sämtliche Werke (Vienna: Musikwissenschaftliche Verlag, 1960–).

British music hall songs as a group:
R31.   "Bacon & Beans" in *Sixty Years of British Music Hall* (London: Chappell & Co., 1976). See B57.

R32.   "Champagne Charlie" in *Songs of the British Music Hall* (New York: Oak Publications, 1971). See B746 for both. See B432 for a related subject.

For further reference:

R33.   *Democratic Souvenirs: An Historical Anthology of 19th-Century American Music* (New York: Peters, 1988). This anthology includes songs, piano pieces, and excerpts from operas by such composers as Gottschalk, Fry, and Chadwick.

R34.   *The Spirit of the Sixties: A History of the Civil War Song* (St Louis: Educational Publishers, 1964). Some songs of the era are humorous, such as "The Abe-iad, " a political lampoon of Lincoln.

R35.   *Zwanzig schöne alte Volkslieder* (Graz: Doblinger, 1985). Many of these are four-part settings of 19th-century German folksongs.

THE CONTEMPORARY PERIOD

General Studies: B7, B8.

Ballet: B11, B245.

Comic Opera (American): B304.

Comic opera (French): B255.

Film: B150, B245.

Film (Musical Comedy): B2, B138, B235.

Film Music: B39, B54, B245, D5, D14.

Folk Song: B149, B179, B502 (parody in Russian song), B706.

Humor and Performance: B656, Dd2–4, D6, D7, D8, D9, D10, D11, D12, Dd19–23, Dd26–27.

Jazz: B245, B657, B681.

Musical Theater: B21, B22, B23, B33, B56, B65, B74, B75, B83, B91, B152, B155, B197, B243, B256 (Black), B257, B296, B306, B308, B336, B356, B360, B407, B409, B507, B547, B579, B599, B605, B611 (Parody), B653, B696, B757, B829.

Neoclassicism: B157, B245.

Operetta: B530, D25.

Popular Song: B48, B73, B67, B86, B97, B169, B221, B243, B245, B250, B465 (Comparative cultures), B479 (Country music), B567, B660, B744.

Postmodernism: B245.

Satire in Music: B271, B575.

Symphony: B142.

Unless otherwise noted, citations are given for miniature scores for orchestral works and piano-vocal scores for operas. Information for film scores includes year of production, country, and, in some instances, composer or composers. Popular films are cited alphabetically according to title.

W654. **Adams, John:** *The Chairman Dances: Foxtrot for Orchestra* from *Nixon in China* (Milwaukee: Hal Leonard, 1989).

Albright, William:

W655. *Enigma Syncopations* (New York: C.F. Peters, 1987).
W656. *The King of Instruments* (New York: C.F. Peters, 1979).

W657. **Anderson, Laurie:** *Duet for Violin and Door Jamb* Scores 209.

Anderson, Leroy:

W658. *Syncopated Clock* (New York: Mills, 1950).
W659. *The Typewriter* (New York: Mills, 1953).

Antheil, George: B245.

W660. *Airplane Sonata* (New York: New Music, 1931).
W661. *Ballet mécanique* (Delaware Water Gap: Shawnee, 1959).

W662. **Argento, Domenic:** *Casanova's Homecoming* (New York: Boosey & Hawkes, 1985).

W663. *Babe* (1995, American). A sequel appeared in 1999.

W664. **Balakauskas, Osvaldas:** *Alla Turca Once More* (Warsaw: Polish Musical Editions, 1988).

Barber, Samuel:

W665. *Hermit Songs* (New York: G. Schirmer, 1980).
W666. Overture to *The School for Scandal* (New York: G. Schirmer, 1941).
W667. *Excursions* in *Samuel Barber: Complete Piano Music* (New York: G. Schirmer, 1984).

Bartók, Béla:

W668. *Four Slovak Folksongs* (New York: Boosey & Hawkes, 1950).
W669. *Ungarische Volkslieder* (New York: Boosey & Hawkes, 1939).
W670. *Concerto for Orchestra* Sz.116 (New York: Boosey & Hawkes, 1946).

String Quartets:
W671. No. 5 Sz.102.
W672. No. 6 Sz.114.
The String Quartets of Béla Bartók (New York: Boosey & Hawkes, 1945).

W673. *Contrasts for Violin, Clarinet, Piano* Sz.111 (New York: Boosey & Hawkes, 1942).

W674. *Burleskes* Sz.47 (New York: Boosey & Hawkes, 1950).
W675. *Mikrokosmos* Sz.107 (New York: Boosey & Hawkes, 1967).
W676. *Out of Doors Suite* Sz.81 (New York: Boosey & Hawkes, 1954).

Sz.=B. Szabolcsi, *Béla Bartók: Weg und Werke* (Kassel: Bárenreiter, 1972).

The Beatles:

W677. *A Hard Day's Night.*
W678. *Sergeant Pepper's Lonely Heart's Club Band.*

Examples in Glory.

Berg, Alban:

W679. *Lulu* (Vienna: Universal, 1936).
W680. *Wozzeck* (Vienna: Universal, 1952).

Berio, Luciano: B245.

W681. *Un Re en Ascolto* (Milan: Universal, 1983).
W682. *Sinfonia* (London: Universal, 1972).

W683. **Berlin, Irving:** "Alexander's Ragtime Band" *Early Songs, 1907–1914* (Madison, Wisc.: A-R Editions, 1994). B588.

Berners, Lord (Gerald Hugh Tyrwhitt-Wilson): B347.

W684. *Fragments psychologiques.*
W685. *Trois petites marches funèbres.*
W686. *Valses Bourgeoises. The Collected Music for Solo Piano* (London: Chester, 1982).

Bernstein, Leonard:

W687. *Chichester Psalms* (New York: Boosey & Hawkes, 1965).
W688. *Candide* (New York: G. Schirmer, 1959).
W689. *On the Town: Three Dance Episodes* (New York: Boosey & Hawkes, 1968).
W690. *West Side Story* (New York: G. Schirmer, 1959). B430.
W691. *A Musical Toast* (New York: Boosey & Hawkes, 1980).

Blacher, Boris:

W692. *Abstrakte Oper No. 1* (Berlin: Bote & Bock, 1953).
W693. *Variationen über ein Thema von Muzio Clementi* for Piano and Orchestra (Berlin: Bote & Bock, 1962).

W694. **Blitzstein, Marc:** *The Cradle Will Rock* (New York: Random House, 1938).

W695. **Bolcom, William:** *Cabaret Songs* (New York: Edward B. Marks, 1979).

Bowles, Paul:

W696. *Blue Mountain Ballads* (New York: G. Schirmer, 1946).

W697. *Music for a Farce* (New York: Weintraub, 1953).

Britten, Benjamin:

W698. "Wagtail and Baby" in *A Heritage of 20th Century British Song* (London: Boosey & Hawkes, 1977), v. 2.

W699. *Albert Herring* (London: Boosey & Hawkes, 1969). B346, B479, B597, B678.

W700. *Gloriana* (London: Boosey & Hawkes, 1953).

W701. *The Little Sweep* (London: Boosey & Hawkes, 1967).

W702. *A Midsummer Night's Dream* (London: Boosey & Hawkes, 1958). B293, B509, B787.

W703. *Noye's Fludd* (London: Boosey & Hawkes, 1958).

W704. *Simple Symphony* (London: Oxford University Press, 1934).

W705. *The Young Person's Guide to the Orchestra* (New York: Boosey & Hawkes, 1947).

W706. *Diversions* for piano left hand and orchestra (London: Boosey & Hawkes, 1988).

Busoni, Ferruccio: B531, B740, B764.

W707. *Arlecchino* (Wiesbaden: Breitkopf und Härtel, 1968). B191.

W708. *Der Brautwahl* (Berlin: Harmonie, 1914).

W709. *Turandot* (Wiesbaden: Breitkopf & Härtel, 1946).

W710. *Rondo Arlecchino* (Vienna: Wiener Philharmonischer, 1917).

W711. **Butch Cassidy and the Sundance Kid** (1969, American). The score is by Burt Bacharach.

Cage, John: B136, B245, B614.

W712. *String Quartet in Four Parts* (New York: Peters, 1960).

W713. *Aleatoric Music of Unfixed Medium 4'33"* (New York: Peters, 1960).

W714. *Bacchanale* (New York: Peters, 1960).

W715. *Cheap Imitation* (New York: Peters, 1977).

W716. *Fontana Mix* (New York: Peters, 1965).

W717. *Sonatas and Interludes* (New York: Peters, 1965).

W718. *Water Music* (New York: Henmar, 1960).

W719. *Winter Music* (New York: Henmar, 1961).

W720. **Cardew, Cornelius:** *Activities from Scratch Music* SS 70.

W721. **Carpenter, John Alden:** *Krazy Kat* (New York: G. Schirmer, 1948).

Casella, Alfredo:

W722. *Paganiniana* (Vienna: Universal, 1944).
W723. *Pupazetti* (London: Chester, 1921).
W724. *Scarlattiana* for piano and orchestra (Vienna: Universal, 1928).
W725. *A la maniere de* (Paris: Salabert, 1911).

W726. **Chanler, Theodore:** *Eight Epitaphs* (New York: Arrow, 1939).

Copland, Aaron:

W727. *Appalachian Spring* (New York: Boosey & Hawkes, 1945).
W728. *Danzón Cubano* (New York: Boosey & Hawkes, 1949).
W729. *El Salon México* (New York: Boosey & Hawkes, 1939).
W730. *Our Town* (New York: Boosey & Hawkes, 1945).
W731. Clarinet Concerto (New York: Boosey & Hawkes, 1952).
W732. Piano Concerto (New York: Cos Cob Press, 1929).
W733. *The Cat and the Mouse* (New York: Boosey & Hawkes, 1950).

Corigliano, John:

W734. *The Ghosts of Versailles* (New York: G. Schirmer, 1991). B574.

W735. *Gazebo Dances* (New York: G. Schirmer, 1978).

W736. *Pied Piper Fantasy* (New York: G. Schirmer, 1991).

Cowell, Henry:

W737. *Saturday Night at the Firehouse* (New York: Associated, 1949).
W738. Symphony No. 11 *Seven Rituals of Music* (New York: Associated, 1955).
W739. *The Advertisement*.
W740. *The Aeolian Harp* .
W741. *The Bandshee* SS 71.
Piano Music (New York: Associated, 1950–82).

Davies, Peter Maxwell: B245.

W742. *Eight Songs for a Mad King* (London: Boosey & Hawkes, 1971).
W743. *St. Thomas Wake* (London: Boosey & Hawkes, 1972).

Debussy, Claude: B245, B626.

W744. *Fêtes galantes* (New York: International, 1961).

W745.   *La boîte à jouxjoux*   (Boca Raton, Fla.: Master Music Publications, 1991).

W746.   *Jeux* (Paris: Durand, 1914).

W747.   Sonata for Cello and Piano (Paris: Durand, 1915).

W748.   *Children's Corner Suite.*

W749.   Etudes. *Etudes, Children's Corner, Images Book II, and Other Works for Piano* (New York: Dover, 1992).

W750.   Préludes (New York: G. Schirmer, 1991).

W751.   **Del Tredici, David:** *Alice in Wonderland Cycle* (New York: Boosey & Hawkes, 1992).

Disney, Walt (Productions): B150, D5.

W752.   *Fantasia* (1940, U.S.A.) Leopold Stokowski with the Philadelphia Orchestra, narrated by Deems Taylor. A sequel entitled *Fantasia 2000* has appeared.

W753.   *Silly Symphonies* (1929–) This series includes *The Three Little Pigs* (1933), which features the song "Who's Afraid of the Big Bad Wolf?"

W754.   *Snow White and the Seven Dwarfs* (1937, U.S.A.). Songs include "Whistle While You Work" and "Some Day My Prince Will Come."

W755.   *Steamboat Willy* (1927).

W756.   **Dohnányi, Erno:** *Variations on a Nursery Song* for piano and orchestra (London: Simrock, 1922).

W757.   **Duchamp, Marcel**: "Musical compositions" in the library at the Philadelphia Museum. B245.

W758.   **Dukas, Paul:** *The Sorcerer's Apprentice* (New York: International, n.d.).

W759.   *Easter Parade* (1948, U.S.A.). Songs by Irving Berlin are featured.

Egk, Werner:

W760.   *Der Revisor* (Mainz: Schott, 1957).

W761.   *Die Zaubergeige* (Mainz: Schott, 1954).

W762.   **Elgar, Edward:** *Falstaff* (Sevenoaks: Novello, 1981).

Falla, Manuel de:

W763.   *El retablo de maese Pedro* (London: Chester, 1924).

W764.   *El sombrero de tres picos* (London: Chester, 1925).

W765.   *Siete Canciones Populares* (New York: Associated, 1949).

W766. **42nd Street** (1933, U.S.A.). A Warner Brothers production, with choreography by Busby Berkeley, which includes the song "Shuffle off to Buffalo."

W767. **Foss, Lukas:** *Time Cycle* (New York: Fischer, 1960).

W768. **Françaix, Jean:** Concertino for Piano and Orchestra (Paris: Eschig, 1935).

W769. **Friml, Rudolf:** *Rose Marie* (New York: Harms, 1925).

W770. **Ganz, Rudolph:** Piano Concerto (New York: Fischer, 1945).

Gershwin, George: B245.

W771. *Lady Be Good!* (Secaucus, N.J.: Warner, 1988).
W772. *An American in Paris* (New York: New World, 1929).
W773. *Cuban Overture* (Secaucus, N.J.: Warner, 1987).

Ginastera, Alberto:

W774. *Cinco Canciones Populares Argentinas* (Buenos Aires: Ricordi, 1943).
W775. *Overture to the Creole Faust* (Buenos Aires: Barry, 1951).

W776. **Glass, Philip:** *Glassworks* opening section for solo piano (Bryn Mawr, Penn.: Presser, 1984).

W777. **Goossens, Eugene:** *Two Sketches* for string quartet (London: Chester, 1916).

Grainger, Percy: B228.

W778. *Handel in the Strand* (London: Schott, 1912).
W779. *Molly on the Shore* BFMS (New York: Fischer, c. 1962).

W780. **Granados, Enrique:** *Tonadillas* (New York: International, 1952).

W781. **Haley, Bill:** "Rock Around the Clock" in Glory.

Henze, Hans Werner:

W782. *Fragmente aus einer Show* for Brass Ensemble (Mainz: Schott, 1971).
W783. *Voices* (Mainz: Schott, 1973). See also B444 on the opera *Der junge Lord*.

Hindemith Paul: B666.

W784. *Hin und Zurück* (Mainz: Schott, 1927).

W785.   *Neues vom Tage* (Mainz: Schott, 1929).

Both works are discussed in B424, B508.

W786.   *Plöner Musiktage* (Mainz: Schott, 1932).
W787.   *Felix the Cat* (film music, 1920). This is the first example of a sound cartoon.
W788.   *Lustige Sinfonietta* (Mainz: Schott, 1908).
W789.   *Ragtime* for orchestra, also for piano, four hands (Mainz: Schott, 1986).
W790.   *Symphonic Metamorphosis on Themes of Carl Maria von Weber* (New York: Associated, 1945).
W791.   *The Four Temperaments* for piano and strings (New York: Associated, 1948).
W792.   *Kammermusik* No. 4 (Violinkonzert) (New York: Schott, 1953).
W793.   *Der Schwanendreher* for Viola and Orchestra (Mainz: Schott, 1936).
W794.   String Quartet in E-flat (New York: Associated, 1944).
W795.   *Ludus Tonalis* (London: Schott, 1943).
W796.   Piano Sonata No. 3 (London: Schott, 1936).
W797.   *Suite 1922* (Mainz: Schott, 1950). B245.
Sämtliche Werke (Mainz: Schott, 1975–86).

W798.   **Hoiby, Lee:** *Songs for Leontyne* (New York: Southern, 1985).

Holst, Gustav:

W799.   *At the Boar's Head.*
W800.   *The Perfect Fool.*
Collected Facsimile Edition (London: Faber, 1974).

W801.   **Honegger, Arthur:** Concertino for piano and orchestra (Paris: Salabert, 1926).

W802.   **Horovitz, Joseph:** *Horrortorio* (Sevenoaks: Novello, 1974).

Ibert, Jacques:

W803.   *Angélique* (Paris: Heugel, 1926).
W804.   *Don Quichotte à Dulcinée* (Paris: Leduc, 1933). B299.
W805.   *Divertissement* (Paris: Durand, 1952).

Ives, Charles:

W806.   *114 Songs* (Bryn Mawr, Penn.: Merion Music, 1935). B266, B291, B292, B457.
W807.   *Holidays: Decoration Day* (New York: Southern, 1989); *Fourth of July* (New York: Associated, 1932).

W808.   *Halloween* (Hillsdale, N.J.: Boelke-Bomart, 1949).
W809.   Scherzo for String Quartet (New York: Southern, 1958).
W810.   *Concord Sonata* (New York: Associated, 1970).
W811.   *Three-Page Sonata* (New York: Mercury, 1949).

W812.   **Jacob, Gordon:** *The Barber of Seville Goes to the Devil Overture* (London: Oxford, 1960).

W813.   **Janáček, Leoš:** *The Cunning Little Vixen* (Vienna: Universal, 1927).

W814.   **Johnson, Tom:** *Transitory Circumlocutions for Solo Trombone* (New York: Two-Eighteen Press, 1973).

Joplin, Scott:

W815.   *The Entertainer.*
W816.   *Mapleleaf Rag.* This was used in the film *The Sting* with Paul Newman and Robert Redford.
At the Piano with Scott Joplin (New York: Alfred, 1990).

W817.   **Kabalevsky, Dmitry:** *The Comedians* (New York: Leeds, 1948).

W818.   **Kern, Jerome:** *Show Boat* (Santa Monica, Calif.: Welk Music Group, 1980). B430, B439.

W819.   *Kiss of the Spider Woman* (1993, U.S.A.).

Kodály. Zoltan:

W820.   *Háry János* (London: Universal, 1962).
W821.   Suite from the opera (Vienna: Universal, n.d.).

W822.   **Krenek, Ernst:** *Jonny Spielt auf* (Vienna: Universal, 1926).

Liadov, Anatol:

W823.   *Baba Yaga* (London: Boosey & Hawkes, n.d.).
W824.   *The Musical Snuffbox* in *Russian Piano Music* (Boston: Ditson, 1898).

W825.   **Ligeti, György:** *Night/Morning* (Mainz: Edition Schott, 1973).

W826.   *Like Water for Chocolate* (1992, Mexican). This film, based on a novel by Laura Esquivel, has a score by Leo Brower.

W827.   *Lisztomania* (1976, U.S.A.).

W828.   **Loewe, Frederick:** *My Fair Lady* (New York: Chappell, n.d.).

W829.   **Ludwig, Claus Dieter:** *Humoristische variationen über ein Geburtstaglied* (Mainz: Schott, 1987).

Lutosławski, Witold:

W830.   Cello Concerto (London: Chester, 1971).
W831.   *Concerto for Orchestra* (London: Chester, 1982).

Mahler, Gustav: B165, B339.

Songs from *Des Knaben Wunderhorn*:
W832.   "Des Antonius von Padua Fischpredigt."
W833.   "Lob des hohen Verstands."
W834.   "Rheinlegendschen."
W835.   "Wer hat dies Liedlein erdacht."
Funfzehn Lieder, Humoresken und Balladen aus Des Knaben Wunderhorn (Vienna: Universal, 1995).
W836.   *Die Drei Pintos* (completion of an opera by Carl Maria von Weber). (Madison, Wisc.: A-R Editions, forthcoming). See W640.

Symphonies:
W837.   No. 1
W838.   No. 2 (New York: Dover, 1987).
W839.   No. 4 (New York: Dover, 1989).
W840.   No. 5 (New York: C.F. Peters, n.d.).
W841.   No. 9 (London: Universal, n.d.). B4.
Sämtliche Werke (Vienna: Universal, 1960–).

W842.   **Mascagni, Pietro:** *L'amico Fritz* (Milan: Edoardo Sonzogno, 1891).

Menotti, Gian Carlo:

W843.   *The Old Maid and the Thief* (New York: Franco Colombo, 1954).
W844.   *The Telephone* (New York: G. Schirmer, 1947).
W845.   *Moans, Groans, Cries, and Sighs* (New York: G. Schirmer, 1981).
W846.   *The Unicorn, The Gorgon, The Manticore* (New York: G. Ricordi, 1956). B269.

W847.   *A **Midsummer Night's Dream*** (1935, U.S.A.). This famous version by Max Reinhardt introduced Mickey Rooney playing the role of Puck. The score is by Erich Korngold after Felix Mendelssohn.

Milhaud, Darius: B183.

W848.   *Le boeuf sur le toit* (Paris: Eschig, 1969).
W849.   *La création du monde* (Paris: Eschig, 1923). B245.

W850. *Modern Times* (1936, U.S.A.). The music is by Charles Spencer Chaplin. Included are "Smile" and a gibberish song. B340, B396.

W851. **Monk, Meredith:** *Our Lady of Late* for soprano and wine glass filled with water, excerpts in Scores 79.

W852. *Monkey Business* (1931, U.S.A.). This Marx Brothers film has a script written by S.J. Perelman.

W853. **Montsalvatge, Xavier:** *El Gato con Botas* (New York: Southern, 1974).

W854. **Morton, Jelly Roll:** *Jelly Roll Blues. The Collected Piano Works* (Washington, D.C.: The Smithsonian Institution, 1982).

W855. **Musgrave Thea:** *Masko the Miser* (Copenhagen: Hansen, 1964).

Nielsen, Carl:

W856. Clarinet Concerto (Copenhagen: Fog, 1931).
W857. Flute Concerto (New York: Peters, 1952).
W858. Symphony No. 2 *The Four Temperaments* (New York: Belwin Mills, n.d.).
W859. Symphony No. 6 *Sinfonia semplice* (Copenhagen: Samfundet, 1957).

Orff, Carl:

W860. *Die Kluge* (Mainz: Schott, 1942).
W861. *Der Mond* (New York: Schott, 1973).
W862. *Carmina Burana* (New York: Schott, 1965).
W863. *Music for Children* (New York: Schott, 1991).

W864. **Penderecki, Krzysztof:** *Ubu Rex* (London: Schott, 1991).

Piston, Walter: B330.

W865. Suite from the Ballet *The Incredible Flutist* (New York: Associated, 1938).
W866. Concertino for piano and orchestra (New York: Arrow, 1939).

W867. **Porter, Cole:** *Kiss Me Kate* (New York: Harms, 1967).

Poulenc, Francis: B183, B245.

W868. *Les Biches* (Paris: Heugel, 1947).
W869. *L'histoire de Babar* (London: Chester, 1974).
W870. *Les mamelles des Tirésias* (Paris: Au Menestrel, 1970).

W871.   *Le bestiare* (Paris: Sirène, 1920).

W872.   *Chansons Cocardes* (Paris: Heugel, 1925).

W873.   *Chansons Françaises* (Paris: Eschig, 1920).

W874.   **Presley, Elvis:** "You Ain't Nothing but a Hound Dog." In Glory. B213.

W875.   ***The Producers*** (1968, U.S.A.). This score by John Morris includes a takeoff on the production of a musical, which features the famous production number "Springtime for Hitler."

Prokofiev, Serge: B462, B485.

W876.   *The Ugly Duckling* (New York: Boosey & Hawkes, 1955).

W877.   *Peter and the Wolf.*

Four Orchestral Scores (New York: Dover, 1974).

W878.   *The Duenna* (Moscow: Muzyka, 1967).

W879.   *The Gambler* (Melville: Belwyn Mills, 1981).

W880.   *The Love for Three Oranges* (New York: Boosey & Hawkes, 1947). B677.

W881.   *Chout* (New York: Boosey & Hawkes, 1981).

W882.   *Cinderella* (Moscow: Muzyka, 1974).

W883.   Symphony No. 1 *Classical.*

W884.   Symphony No. 7 (New York: Leeds, 1960).

W885.   Piano Concerto No. 2 (Miami: Kalmus, 1987).

W886.   Piano Concerto No. 5 (New York: Boosey & Hawkes, 1947).

W887.   Violin Concerto No. 1 (New York: Boosey & Hawkes, 1947).

W888.   *Lieutenant Kijé Suite* (Boca Raton, Fla.: Kalmus, 1980).

W889.   Piano Sonata No. 6.

W890.   Piano Sonata No. 7 (New York: Leeds, 1957).

W891.   *Sarcasms* (New York: Leeds, 1960).

W892.   *Suggestion diabolique* (Leipzig: Jurgenson, 1912).

Sobranie sochinenii (Melville: Belwyn Mills, 1979–).

W893.   **Rachmaninov, Sergei:** *Rhapsody on a Theme of Paganini* (New York: Charles Foley, 1934).

Ravel, Maurice: B286, B299.

W894.   *Deux Épigrammes* (Paris: Durand, 1980)

W895.   *Don Quichotte à Dulcinée* (Paris: Durand, 1954).

W896.   *Histoires naturelles* (Melville: Belwin Mills, 1932).

W897.   *L'enfant et les sortilèges* (Paris: Durand, 1932).

W898.   *L'heure espagnole* (New York: Dover, 1996). B276.

W899.   *Ma mère l'oye. Four Orchestral Scores* (New York: Dover, 1989).

W900.   *La Valse* (Paris: Durand, n.d.).

W901.   Piano Concerto No. 2 (Bryn Mawr, Penn.: Presser, 1932).
W902.   Sonata for Violin and Cello (Bryn Mawr, Penn.: Presser, 1922).

Reger, Max:

W903.   *Variations and Fugue on a Merry Theme of Johann Adam Hiller* (Berlin: Bote & Bock, 1904).
W904.   *Fünf Humoresken* (Vienna: Universal, 1927).
W905.   *Sechs Burlesken* (Leipzig: Peters, 1900).
Sämtliche Werke (Wiesbaden: Breitkopf und Härtel, 1954–70).

W906.   **Respighi, Ottorino:** *Gli Uccelli* (Milan: Ricordi, 1928).

W907.   **Revueltas, Silvestre:** *Ocho por Radio* (New York: Peer Southern, 1951).

W908.   **Riegger, Wallingford:** *Dance Rhythms* (New York: Associated, 1956).

W909.   **Riley, Terry:** In C. SS 68.

Rochberg, George:

W910.   String Quartet No. 3 (New York: Galaxy, 1976).
W911.   *Carnival Music for Piano* (Bryn Mawr, Penn.: Presser, 1975).

W912.   *Rocky Horror Picture Show* (1976, U.S.A.). This has become a cult classic.

Rodgers and Hammerstein: B90.

W913.   *Oklahoma!* (New York: Williamson, 1943).
W914.   *South Pacific* (New York: Williamson, 1949).

W915.   **Rorem, Ned:** *Four Dialogues for Two Voices and Two Pianos: Letters from Paris* (New York: Boosey & Hawkes, 1966).

W916.   **Roussel, Albert:** Symphony No. 4 (Paris: Durand, 1935).

Satie, Erik: B175, B183, B245, B329, B343, B412, B464, B520, B538, B539, B557, B624, B690, B728, B820.

W917.   *Trois mélodies.*
W918.   *Trois poèmes d'amour.*
Chansons (Paris: Salabert, 1988).
W919.   *La belle eccentrique* (Paris: Eschig, 1950).
W920.   *Genevièvr de Brabant* (Paris: Eschig, 1950).
W921.   *Relâche.* Version for four-hands, piano by Milhaud (Paris: Rouart, 1926).

W922.   *Parade* (Paris: Salabert, 1917).

Piano works: B322.
W923.   *Chapitres tournés.*
W924.   *Croquis et agaceries.*
W925.   *Descriptions automatiques.*
W926.   *Embryons deséchés.*
W927.   *Gnossiennes.*
W928.   *Gymnopédies.*
W929.   *Morceaux en forme de poire.*
W930.   *Préludes flasques.*
W931.   *Sonatine bureaucratique.*
W932.   *Sports et divertissements.*
W933.   *Vexations* SS 67.
W934.   *Vieux sequins et vieilles cuirasses.*
Piano Works (Paris: Salabert, 1989).

Schickele, Peter (P.D.Q. Bach): B318, Dd19–39.

W935.   *Erotica Variations* (Bryn Mawr, Penn.: Presser, 1979).
W936.   *Last Tango in Bayreuth* (Bryn Mawr, Penn.: Elkan-Vogel, 1992).
W937.   *The Little Pickle Book* (*Pöckelbüchlein*) (Bryn Mawr, Penn.: Presser, 996). D19.
W938.   *The Seasonings* (Bryn Mawr, Penn.: Presser, 1973).

W939.   **Schnittke, Alfred:** B245. *Quasi una sonata; MozART à la Haydn* (Vienna: Universal, 1988).

Schoenberg, Arnold: B760.

W940.   *Von heute auf morgen.* B598, B760.
W941.   *Drei Satiren* (Los Angeles: Belmont, 1926). The two choruses "Der deutche Michel" and "Ei, Du Lütte" are also humorous. (Los Angeles: Belmont, 1980).
W942.   *Pierrot Lunaire* (Los Angeles: Belmont, n.d.).
W943.   String Quartet No. 2 (Vienna: Universal, n.d.).
W944.   Serenade (Copenhagen: Wilhelm Hansen, 1924).
Sämtliche Werke (Vienna: Universal, 1966–85).

W945.   **Schuller, Gunther:** *Seven Studies on Paul Klee* (London: Universal, 1962).

Shostakovich, Dmitry: B124, B341.

W946.   *The Age of Gold* (New York: Edwin F. Kalmus, n.d.).
W947.   *The Nose* (Vienna: Universal, 1962).
W948.   Symphony No. 1.

W949.   Symphony No. 9.

(New York: Kalmus, n.d.).

W950.   Symphony No. 13 *Babiy Yar* (New York: Kalmus, n.d.).
W951.   Symphony No. 15 (Hamburg: Sikorski, 1972). B686.
W952.   *Festive Overture* (New York: Kalmus, n.d.).
W953.   Piano Concerto No. 2 (New York: Leeds, 1962).
Sobranie sochinenii (Moscow: Muzyka, 1979–).

W954.   **Slonimsky, Nicolas:** *Five Advertising Songs* (Lomita, Ca.: Cambria, 1988).

Sondheim, Stephen: B262.

W955.   *Company* (New York: Herald Square, 1980).
W956.   *A Little Night Music* (New York: Revelation, 1980).
W957.   *Sunday in the Park with George* (New York: Revelation, 1984).
W958.   *Sweeney Todd* (New York: Revelation, 1981).

Strauss, Richard: B264, B487, B755.

W959.   *Arabella* (Mainz: Schott, 1960). B20, B418.
W960.   *Ariadne auf Naxos* (New York: Boosey & Hawkes, 1944). B106.
W961.   *Der Rosenkavalier* (London: Boosey & Hawkes, 1943). B211, B570, B702, B718, B756, B790.
W962.   *Die schweigsame Frau* (Berlin: Fürstner, 1935). B353.
W963.   *Don Quixote* (New York: Eulenberg, n.d.). B286.
W964.   *Sinfonia domestica* (New York: Eulenberg, 1932).
W965.   *Till Eulenspiegel lustige Streiche* (London: Eulenburg, n.d.). B429. See B312 for all the symphonic poems.
W966.   *Burleske* for piano and orchestra (Offenbach: Steingräber, 1962).

Stravinsky, Igor: B245, B462, B469.

W967.   "The Owl and the Pussycat" (New York: Boosey & Hawkes, 1967).
W968.   *Le baiser de la fée* (New York: Boosey & Hawkes, 1952).
W969.   *Circus Polka* (New York: Schott, 1972).
W970.   *L'histoire du Soldat* (New York: International, n.d.). B245.
W971.   *Jeu de cartes* (New York: Schott, 1965).
W972.   *Mavra* (New York: Boosey & Hawkes, 1947).
W973.   *Petroushka* (Melville: Belwin Mills, n.d.).
W974.   *Pulcinella* (New York: Boosey & Hawkes, 1949).
W975.   *The Rake's Progress* (London: Boosey & Hawkes, 1951). B470, B512, B665, B687, B819.
W976.   *Renard* (London: Chester, 1917).
W977.   Symphony in C (Mainz: Schott, 1948).

W978.   Suite for Orchestra No. 1.

W979.   Suite for Orchestra No. 2. (London: Chester, 1926).

W980.   Capriccio for piano and orchestra (New York: Boosey & Hawkes, 1952).

W981.   Concerto for piano and winds (New York: Boosey & Hawkes, 1960).

W982.   *Dumbarton Oaks Concerto* (New York: Schott, 1966).

W983.   *Greeting Prelude for the 80th Birthday of Pierre Monteux* or *Happy Birthday Variations* (London: Boosey & Hawkes, 1956).

W984.   Octet (New York: Boosey & Hawkes, 1952).

W985.   Sonata (New York: Boosey & Hawkes, 1950).

W986.   *Five Fingers.* These also have been orchestrated by Stravinsky and are known as *Eight Instrumental Miniatures for Eighteen Players.* (New York: Omega, 1949).

W987.   *The Piano Rag Music* (London: Chester, 1920).

W988.   **Taylor, Deems:** *Through the Looking Glass* (New York: Fischer, 1923).

Tcherepnin, Alexander:

W989.   *Four Russian Folksongs* (New York: Peters, 1967).

W990.   Serenade for Strings (London: Eulenburg, 1964).

W991.   *Le Monde en vitrine* (London: Boosey & Hawkes, 1948).

Tcherepnin, Ivan:

W992.   *5 Songs.* Manuscript at Cambridge, Mass.; recorded on *Flores Musicales* CD 684 CRI (1995).

W993.   "Noel, Noel."

Thomson, Virgil:

W994.   *Four Saints in Three Acts* (New York: G. Schirmer, 1948). B572.

W995.   *Capitals Capitals* (New York: Boosey & Hawkes, 1968).

W996.   "Preciosilla" in *Romantic American Art Songs* (New York: G. Schirmer, 1990).

W997.   *Portraits* for Piano (New York: G. Schirmer, 1987).

W998.   ***Three Worlds of Gulliver*** (1960, British).

Toch, Ernst:

W999.   *Geographical Fugue* (Melville: Belwyn Mills, 1957). B363.

W1000. *Circus Overture* (Los Angeles: Affiliated, 1954).

W1001. ***Tom Jones*** (1963, British). The score by John Addison includes period pieces.

W1002. **Tommasini, Vincenzo:** *The Good Humored Ladies* (London: Chester, 1919).

W1003. *Tommy* (1975, U.S.A.).

W1004. ***Tous les Matins du Monde*** (1991, France). This film is based on the music of Marin Marais, a leading composer of the French Baroque. The English title is *All the Mornings of the World*.

Vaughan Williams, Ralph:

W1005. *Hugh the Drover; or, Love in the Stocks* (London: Curwen, 1952).
W1006. *Sir John in Love* (London: Oxford, 1971).
W1007. *Three Shakespeare Songs* in *English Pastoral Partsongs* (London: Oxford, 1994).

W1008. ***Victor/Victoria*** (1982, U.S.A.). The Henry Mancini score for this film won an Oscar.

Villa-Lobos, Heitor:

W1009. *Assobio a jato* (New York: Southern, 1953).
W1010. *Prole do Bebe* No. 1 (Paris: Eschig, 1918).

Volkman, Joachim:

W1011. *Komponisten auf Abwegen* (Wiesbaden: Breitkopf und Härtel, 1975).

Walton, William:

W1012. *Façade* (London: Oxford University Press, n.d.).
W1013. *Scapino Overture* (London: Oxford University Press 1950).

Webber, Andrew Lloyd:

W1014. *Cats* (Milwaukee: Leonard, 1981).
W1015. *The Phantom of the Opera* (Milwaukee: Leonard, 1987).

W1016. **Weill, Kurt:** *Die Dreigroschenoper* (Vienna: Universal, 1956).

W1017. ***The Wizard of Oz*** (1939, U.S.A.). The score is famous for its many humorous songs. Judy Garland sings "Somewhere over the Rainbow." The score is by Harold Arlen and E.Y. Harburg.

W1018. **Wolf-Ferrari, Ermanno:** *Il segreto di Susanna* (Leipzig: Josef Weinberger, 1910).

W1019. **Wolff, Christian:** *Looking North* SS 140.

W1020. **Youmans, Vincent:** "Tea for Two" from *No, No, Nanette* (New York: Warner, 1972). Shostakovich made an instrumental arrangement, also known as *The Tahiti Trot* (1928). (Japan: Zen-On Music, 1997).

W1021. **Zemlinsky, Alexander:** *Kleider machen Leute* (Vienna: Universal, 1922). B613.

For further reference:

R36.   *The Erroll Garner Songbook*, ed. S. Johnson (Greenwich, Conn.: Cherry Lane, 1977).

R37.   *Fifty Years of Movie Music 1940–90* (Miami: Belwin, 1990). This contains some major themes and songs from the era indicated by the title. Songs from *Tootsie* (1982) and *Beverly Hills Cops* (1984) are included.

R38.   *Pieces: A Second Anthology* (Naples, Fla.: Byron, 1976). This is an anthology of avant-garde compositions, often using unconventional notations.

HUMOROUS RECORDINGS

(Those in long-playing record [LP] form are so indicated):

D1.   *Amorous Dialogues of the Renaissance*, Nonesuch H-71272 (LP).
D2.   *Anna Russell Again*, Sony SFK 60316.
D3.   *The Anna Russell Album*, Columbia MG 31199 (LP); Sony MDK 47252.
D4.   *Anna Russell, Encore?* Sony SFK 60316.
D5.   *Battle Music*, Nonesuch (7)1146 (LP).
D6.   *A Celebration of Sellers* [Peter], Angel EMI 7243 8 27881 27.
D7.   *Flanders and Swann* (Complete), Angel EMI 974-64.
D8.   Florence Foster Jenkins. *The Glory (???) of the Human Voice*, RCA Gold Seal 09026-61175-2.
D9.   *Fun House*, Harmony ML 7224 (LP).
D10.   *The Hoffnung Astronautical Music Festival*, EMI: CDM7 633032 and CDM 7 63304 2 (LP).
D11.   *Eine Kleine Biermusik*, Angel DS-38070 (LP).
D12.   *Laugh-in*, Harmony KH 30976 (LP).
D13.   *Laughter from the Hip*, Joss J-CD-20 (LP).
D14.   Mozart, *Sacred and Profane Canons and Songs*, Philips 6500 917 (LP).
D15.   *Music from Classic Woody Allen Films*, Sony Classical SK 53549.
D16.   *Musical Fun & Games*, ASV 257.

D17.   *Opera's Greatest Drinking Songs & Other Intoxicating Melodies*, RCA Red Seal 09026-68095-2.
D18.   Phyllis Diller, *Born to Sing*, Columbia CS 95 23 (LP).

Peter Schickele:
D19.   *Little Pickle Book for Theater Organ & Dill Piccolos*, Telarc CD 80390.
D20.   *Music of P.D.Q. Bach:* Telarc CD 80210.
D21.   *Music of P.D.Q. Bach:* Telarc CD 80376.
D22.   *Music of P.D.Q. Bach:* Telarc CD 80307.
D23.   *Music of P.D.Q. Bach:* Telarc CD 80239.

P.D.Q. Bach:
D24.   *Black Forest Bluegrass*, Vanguard VMD 79427.
D25.   *Classical WTWP Talkity-Talk Radio*, Telarc CD-80295.
D26.   *The Dreaded P.D.Q.Bach Collection*, Vanguard 159/62-2
D27.   *An Evening with P.D.Q.Bach*, Vanguard VBD 79195.
D28.   *An Hysteric Return*, Vanguard VMD 79438.
D29.   *Liebeslieder Polkas*, Vanguard VMD 79438.
D30.   *A Little Nightmare Music*, Vanguard 79448-2.
D31.   *Music for an Awful Lot of Winds & Percussion*, Telarc CD-80307.
D32.   *Music You Can't Get out of Your Head*, Vanguard VMD 79443.
D33.   *Oedipus Tex*, Telarc CD-80239.
D34.   *On the Air*, Vanguard VMT 79262.
D35.   *Portrait of P.D.Q. Bach*, Vanguard 79322-2.
D36.   *1712 Overture*, Telarc CD-80210.
D37.   *The Short-Tempered Clavier*, Telarc CD-80390.
D38.   *The Stoned Guest*, Vanguard Vanguard 15707-6536-2.
D39.   *The Wurst of P.D.Q. Bach*, Vanguard VCD 2719/20.
D40.   *Tavern Songs, Catches, and Glees*, Bach Guild HM 62 (LP).
D41.   *Tout le charme de l'opérette française*, ARB 291812.

D42.   **Victor Borge**, *Caught in the Act*, Reissue of Columbia CCL 646 (LP); Sony WK 75008.
D43.   **Victor Borge**, *Comedy in Music*, Columbia CL 554 (LP).
D44.   **Victor Borge**, *The Two Sides of Victor Borge*, Gurtman & Murtha Associates.
D45.   **Victor Borge**, *Victor Borge Presents His Own Enchanting Version of Hans Christian Andersen*, Decca DL 734406 (LP).
D46.   *Victor Borge Live*, Sony MDK 48482.
D47.   *Villon to Rabelais* (The Newberry Consort), The Newberry Library CD.

Index

About the Author

ENRIQUE ALBERTO ARIAS is Assistant Professor at the School for New Learning, DePaul University, and the President of Ars Musica Chicago. He is the author of *Alexander Tcherepnin: A Bio-Bibliography* (Greenwood, 1989).